A CULTURE
OF
HAPPINESS

HOW TO SCALE UP
HAPPINESS
FROM PEOPLE
TO ORGANIZATIONS

THO HA VINH, PhD
FOREWORD BY THAKUR S. POWDYEL

LIFE LESSONS FROM BHUTAN,
THE ORIGINAL COUNTRY OF
GROSS NATIONAL HAPPINESS

 PARALLAX PRESS
BERKELEY, CALIFOR....

T0037846

2236B Sixth Street
Berkeley, CA 94710
parallax.org

Parallax Press
is the publishing division of
Plum Village Community of
Engaged Buddhism, Inc.

Printed in the United States of America

Cover design by Katie Eberle
Text design by Maureen Forys, Happenstance Type-O-Rama

The poem "Call Me by My True Names"
by Zen Master Thich Nhat Hanh
is reprinted courtesy of Parallax Press

Printed on recycled paper
ISBN 978-1-952692-31-4
E-book ISBN 978-1-952692-32-1

Library of Congress Cataloging-in-Publication Data
is available on request from the publisher

1 2 3 4 5 / 26 25 24 23 22

To my teacher,
Ven. Thich Nhat Hanh,
who taught me to live happily in the
present moment

To HRH Kezang Choden
Wangchuck, who leads the
Gross National Happiness Center of
Bhutan with wisdom and grace

To my family,
who has been my
greatest source of happiness

CONTENTS

FOREWORD

by Thakur S. Powdyel

*Minister of Education in the
First Democratic Government of Bhutan,
2008–2013*

I t could sound like a fairy tale to ears long tuned to the drumbeats of a visionless world—a world torn between the insatiable craving of the senses and the deepest yearnings of the spirit. The inner voice of humanity, however distant, is yet audible to guide the seeker looking for a vision that "stills the tooth that nibbles at the soul."* It took the rare wisdom of a young king to acknowledge that the most passionate desire of all human beings—at all times, in all places—is to be happy.

When His Majesty Jigme Singye Wangchuck, the fourth king of Bhutan, stated that "Gross National Happiness [GNH] is more important than Gross Domestic Product [GDP]," he ushered in a new development vision that seeks to harmonize the material and nonmaterial human needs along a more sustainable and fulfilling pathway that duly honors the ethical and planetary boundaries that support all life forms.

Over the four decades since the articulation of this profound, holistic development framework, some of the finest minds around the world have been engaged in understanding and advancing this refreshing call as a means of moderating the mindless, consumeristic impulses that

---

*Emily Dickinson, "This World Is Not Conclusion."

have done untold harm to life and planet Earth. One such enlightened soul is Dr. Tho Ha Vinh, who has dedicated his entire life to making a positive difference in the way things are—in whatever place he was called upon to serve.

Arriving in Bhutan at a time when Bhutan's sublime message of Gross National Happiness was gaining wide acclaim at home and abroad, Dr. Tho immediately set out to work as the program director of the newly established GNH Center Bhutan, which aims to honor the legacy of the enlightened king through action. Over the seven years that followed, Tho used his extensive and deep involvement with humanitarian situations around the globe in the implementation of GNH, deepening the scope and significance of the new development path among both Bhutanese citizens and citizens of the world.

A Culture of Happiness owes its birth to the awakenings of an amazing being who has seen life and received the myriad stimuli of our Mother Earth and responded to them with loving kindness and deep care. The book surveys the major wisdom traditions from around the world that have sought to answer some of the most fundamental questions of life and humanity's search for meaning and purpose. Tho has placed insights from iconic figures from East and West and results of scientific research side by side with spiritual realizations to demonstrate parallels with the core of GNH principles.

The book derives its energy from the moving accounts of a life lived in war zones and troubled regions—inhaling the stench of urine in prison cells and listening to soul-breaking stories of people in circumstances beyond their control—as well as heart-warming stories of walks though meadows and over the snowy Alps, throaty laughter around a family gathering, and much else. And then there are refreshing accounts of work helping the needy, transforming lives, and changing corporate and institutional culture to enhance well-being.

This book presents a practical, step-by-step approach to cultivating and sustaining happiness at individual, institutional, societal, and national levels—an excellent incentive for purposeful engagement for children and grown-ups alike. The nine domains of GNH and the survey tools spell it out clearly, as do the insights of well-known names.

Since the launch of the nationwide educational reform initiative in Bhutan in 2009—called Educating for Gross National Happiness through the Green Schools—I have searched relentlessly for a comprehensive, purposeful, and pragmatic approach to implement the country's national vision. I have found it in *A Culture of Happiness*. It presents a profound message in language that is intelligible and compelling, in a style that is endearing and evocative—the soul calling the world unto itself.

This book shows that pursuit of Gross National Happiness is not only desirable but also possible, as evidenced through the many powerful ways it has been implemented in real-life situations. As a firm believer that every nation ought to have its own north star—as every individual must have a dream—I am most grateful to Tho Ha Vinh for giving to us this powerful window to our national vision of holistic development. This book is also a journey to the core of the noble sector that, for me, education still remains.

Though the pain and pathos of the human predicament are never far away, the abiding spirit of this book is one of hope and possibility, of faith and good cheer. It is about Gross National Happiness. It is about happiness. It *is* happiness.

Read on. . . .

Currently the president of the Royal Thimphu College, Royal University of Bhutan, Thakur S. Powdyel is an educator by choice, conviction, and passion. He served as Bhutan's minister of education from 2008 through 2013. As a committed advocate of Gross National Happiness and Green Schools, he meditates on themes of holistic development, institutional integrity, national self-respect, and ethical literacy.

PREFACE

Since I first wrote the first version of this book, many things have happened: the COVID-19 pandemic broke out (and is still present) and a war broke out in Europe that came as a shock to many. We are learning to live with uncertainty. This crisis has highlighted many existing challenges.

In February 2022, Venerable Zen Master Thich Nhat Hanh passed away. He was a pioneer of socially engaged Buddhism during the Vietnam War, and he was also one of the first Buddhist teachers to promote mindfulness in the West beyond religious or spiritual circles. Many of the practices that are presented here are inspired by what I learned from him over several decades, and it is my hope that this book contributes to spreading his legacy into new sectors of society.

Contemporary society has lived under the illusion that we can control all risks with the sophisticated technology and systems we have put in place, and suddenly, a tiny virus—much smaller than the proverbial grain of sand that stops the gears of the machine—reminded us overnight of how little real control we have over life, nature, and our own lives.

When environmentalists proposed reducing excessive economic activities and unnecessary intercontinental travel to ease the pressures on the ecosystem and slow down global warming, it seemed impossible, absurd, even utopian, but overnight, that is exactly what happened when COVID hit.

The economic and industrial systems we have created seem to have a life of their own, with requirements to which we must submit—but in fact, all these structures are products of the human mind, of the way we think, feel, act, and interact with each other, with other species, and with nature. Therefore, we have the power to change them, but for this to be possible, it is essential to start from inside, with a transformation of our own consciousness, and this is demanding.

Gandhi is often quoted as saying, "Be the change you want to see in the world." Actually, it's unclear if he ever said those exact words, though he did say something similar—and more complete and profound:

> *We but mirror the world. All the tendencies present in the outer world are to be found in the world of our body. If we could change ourselves, the tendencies in the world would also change. As a man changes his own nature, so does the attitude of the world change towards him. This is the divine mystery supreme. A wonderful thing it is and the source of our happiness. We need not wait to see what others do.* *

If we take this seriously, it is both a great responsibility to bear and a deep source of hope, because we become aware of the fact that we can, at any time, become actors of change, without having to wait for the "powerful"—whether political, economic, or other leaders—to initiate change. It also invites us to stop looking for culprits to blame and to hold others responsible for the problems of the world, because we realize that in each moment, we cocreate the reality in which we live.

A good place to start is to decide what we want to focus our attention on, because energy follows attention. Too often, our attention is determined extrinsically by the media and the incessant solicitations of advertising and our digital tools. As long as we are not master of our own consciousness, as long as we do not decide for ourselves where we want to focus our attention, freedom remains an illusion. This is why

---

* Mohandas K. Gandhi, *The Collected Works of Mahatma Gandhi*, vol. 12, April 1913–December 1914 (Delhi: Ministry of Information and Broadcasting, Government of India), 158, *https://gandhiheritageportal.org/cwmg_volume_thumbview /MTI=#page/194/mode/2up*.

learning to direct our attention freely, according to our deep intentions, is an eminently political and even revolutionary act. To meditate is an act of resistance, even of civil disobedience. This is why determining what we want to measure as a society, as an organization, is an important form of activism. What we measure is what we pay attention to. If we measure only economic data, that is what guides our choices and our actions. Expanding the scope of indicators expands our awareness and redirects collective attention to areas more important to our well-being.

The German philosopher Jürgen Habermas talks about the colonization of the "lifeworld" by the system. The lifeworld represents the reality of our experience as a subject; becoming an actor and not accepting the role of victim implies affirming the primacy of human experience over structural requirements. People are not at the service of the economy, and the interests of the economy do not take precedence over human needs. Putting happiness as the objective of development simply means putting people back at the heart of the social project, because, ultimately, talking about happiness is another way of talking about the primacy of the lifeworld.

But nowadays we cannot speak of human happiness without simultaneously taking into account the well-being of all other forms of life and of the earth herself, because all are interdependent and participate in the one reality that cannot be divided.

I am firmly convinced that an old world is coming to an end, and that the crises we are experiencing are the harbingers of a new world that wants to be born. We can foresee aspects of it: simpler, calmer, and more inclusive; ecological, united, tolerant, compassionate, patient, and organic. On the other hand, we can already ask ourselves what we need to let go of, what are we ready to give up, so that the new can manifest itself, both individually and collectively.

In Plato, the concept of maieutics (from *maieutikos*, a Greek word meaning "skilled in midwifery") is associated with the character of Socrates, who argues that the soul of each person is pregnant and wishes to give birth. However, this birth can only take place in Beauty. It is precisely the role of the philosopher to guide the birth of souls in Beauty so a new, more beautiful narrative—and a beautiful world—can be born.

This is perhaps the most important mission of our time, to help the birth of a better world, because, deep down, we all know that such a world is not only possible but also necessary. It is the condition that ensures our survival as a species and as a planet.

Living in Bhutan and Working at the Gross National Happiness Centre

When I first landed in Bhutan, Dr. Saamdu Chetri, the executive director of the GNH Centre greeted me with a ceremonial scarf (*kada* or *katha*, a scarf given in a gesture of blessing or greeting) and took me to a nearby farmhouse for a welcome snack of butter tea (*suja*) and roasted puffed rice. It was my first impression of a Bhutanese household, and I remember the warmhearted and simple hospitality of my host, who made me right away feel at home.

Dr. Saamdu had been instrumental in hiring me as program director, and this first meeting set the foundation of a lasting friendship and spiritual brotherhood, which played a central role during my time in Bhutan. From the onset, he gave me his full confidence and allowed me great freedom to develop the GNH curriculum. He was also my guide and my mentor in all things Bhutanese, explaining me the intricate local code of etiquette, the *driglam namzha*, which guides every aspect of social interactions in Bhutan, especially in formal settings. Local tradition often traces the origins of Bhutanese etiquette to the Buddhist *vinaya*, monastic codes of discipline. Thus, in Bhutan, good manners are to a great extent defined by Buddhist ethics of wholesome physical, verbal, and mental conduct. In this respect, the concept of the *driglam* refers in a broad sense to the good manners adopted by individuals that are heavily influenced by the concept of Buddhist good conduct. In modern times, the Bhutanese state has further promoted *driglam namzha* as a marker of Bhutanese identity. He taught me how to put on my first *gho* (the Bhutanese national costume worn by men) and how to properly fold my *kabney* (the ceremonial scarf worn in official settings).

Soon after my arrival, I had my first audience with the prime minister Jigme Yoser Thinley in his office. It was a remarkable experience in an impressive setting in the government building. HE Jigme Thinley is a charismatic and eloquent person, and I felt deeply honored to be contributing in whatever small way to implementing the vision of Gross National Happiness, especially by developing transformative learning programs that would enable participants of all ages and all walks of life in Bhutan and internationally to integrate and implement this new development paradigm in their life and work.

I then started my work by conducting extensive stakeholders interviews to understand what the mission of the GNH Centre should entail. Looking back at these inspiring meetings, a few characteristics of the people I met stand out as being quite unique to Bhutan. Most of my interlocutors—all people who had important roles in the government—grew up in remote villages, often walking barefoot for hours every day to and from school. During their childhood they lived a traditional lifestyle that had hardly changed in many generations, and within their own lifespan, Bhutan had become a modern, twenty-first-century country. For example, Dr. Pema Gyamtsho then the minister of agriculture of the first democratically elected government of Bhutan, with a doctorate from the prestigious University for Science and Technology in Zurich, grew up in a remote village in Bumthang, in central Bhutan. I recall him telling me about the time when he was writing his doctoral dissertation on Himalayan yak breeding, spending half the year in Zurich and the other half living with nomadic yak herders at an altitude of 4,000 meters (over 13,000 feet), sleeping in black yak-hair tents at night. This unique mixture of having one foot in a traditional culture close to nature and one foot in modernity and science is a unique feature of Bhutanese society.

Having one-on-one conversations with many Bhutanese dignitaries gave me a unique opportunity to understand the cultural, social, and spiritual foundation on which GNH developed in Bhutan. For instance, when I first arrived in Bhutan, the prime minister invited me to join him and his whole cabinet on an outing. So, early Saturday morning, I found myself heading out of Thimphu in an official convoy of cars to the nearby Dochula Pass—3,150 meters (over 10,000 feet)—and from there, we walked for several hours on steep mountain paths to a sacred monastery to visit a hermit famous for his spiritual attainment. On the way, the prime minister pointed out various medicinal herbs that were growing along the path, explaining the healing properties of each one. I was impressed that the most prominent politicians in this country spent their weekend hiking in the mountains, collecting medicinal herbs, and visiting holy men. It was also remarkable to observe how fit they all were, and when I mentioned it, they laughed and explained that as elected officials, they spent quite a lot of time visiting their constituents, which often entailed hiking for hours to villages accessible only by foot. Very different from the way most Western politicians spend their free time or campaign for offices.

I cannot even begin to give a full report of all the interesting conversations I had, meeting with most of the ministers and other relevant dignitaries of the Bhutanese government, but I just want to highlight a few meetings that were defining for the development of the GNH Center.

One such meeting was with the minister of education HE Thakur S. Powdyel. I remember our conversation vividly. He spoke eloquently about education as "the noble sector" and how he shared his worry that modern education had lost its soul. He said, "Love of life, all life, is the first principle of education," and he went on to describe his educational vision (which he later formulated in his book *My Green School*).[*]

---

[*]Thakur S. Powdyel, *My Green School: An Outline* (2018).

Having worked in the field of education all my life, I was impressed to meet a minister of education whose concerns were not primarily administrative, financial, or political, but who was genuinely searching for the deeper meaning and mission of education. His contribution played a significant role in the way I later developed the programs at the GNH Center.

I would also like to mention one of our important partners in the field of GNH in education in Bhutan: Mrs. Deki Choden, a gifted and dedicated educator and the founder and principal of several schools, who was a pioneer in implementing GNH values and principles in her schools. She has been a source of inspiration for my work in this field.

During an international conference in Bhutan in 2009,* the prime minister had outlined the objectives of GNH in education:

> *What we want to see is nothing less than transformative: graduates who are genuine human beings, realizing their full and true potential, caring for others—including other species—ecologically literate, contemplative as well as analytical in their understanding of the world, free of greed and without excessive desires; knowing, understanding, and appreciating completely that they are not separate from the natural world and from others. In sum, manifesting their humanity fully.... In the end, a GNH-educated graduate will have no doubt that his or her happiness derives only from contributing to the happiness of others.*

What a profound description of the goals of education! One could only wish that this vision would be shared on a global scale.†

This overarching vision was also the guideline that enabled us at the GNH Center to develop programs both for Bhutanese and for

---

* Educating for Gross National Happiness in Bhutan, November, 2009.

† In Vietnam, I and others have developed a program called Happy Schools, which is directly inspired by Prime Minister Jigme Yoser Thinley's vision.

international participants to implement the objectives that we had thus formulated:

* Enabling participants to engage in a transformative learning process through dialogue, introspection, and self-reflection, leading to a deepening of their understanding of GNH philosophy, principles, and values.

* Enabling participants to have a living experience of GNH by living in and cocreating a conducive environment fully aligned with GNH principles and values.

* Enabling participants to implement GNH-inspired projects in their families, communities, villages, businesses, organizations, societies, and countries.

The highlight of my first year in Bhutan was a private audience with His Majesty, King Jigme Khesar Namgyel Wangchuck, the fifth Druk Gyalpo (Dragon King) of Bhutan. The audience took place in his office, which is in the Dzong, the monastery and fortress where the secular and spiritual powers of Bhutan are jointly located. The king's aide-de-camp led me to the royal audience room, where I waited for a few minutes, looking around at the beautiful traditional architecture of the room. After a short while, I heard footsteps—it sounded like someone running lightly down a staircase—and a few seconds later the king appeared. It was a striking sight—a handsome and charismatic young man (he was then thirty-two), wearing the yellow scarf that is worn only by the king and the head of the Bhutanese Buddhist community, the Je Khempo. The king greeted me warmly, and we had a friendly and informal conversation. His majesty shared his idea about GNH, telling me that it should be the common unifying vision for Bhutanese people from all ages and from all walks of life. He advised me to put emphasis on programs for young people, because they are the future of the country and thus the ones who most need to adhere to the GNH vision. This reminded me

of a speech that his majesty had given sometime earlier, in which he
had outlined his vision of GNH:

> *Gross National Happiness acts as our national conscience guiding us
> toward making wise decisions for a better future. It ensures that no
> matter what our nation may seek to achieve, the human dimension,
> the individual's place in the nation, is never forgotten. It is a constant
> reminder that we must strive for a caring leadership so that as the
> world and country changes, as our nation's goals change, our fore-
> most priority will always remain the happiness and well-being of our
> people—including the generations to come after us.*

In my meeting with the king, he spoke with an unusual mixture
of natural authority and humility. Both qualities emanated from him.
He asked for some advice, telling me that although he was the king, he
was also a young man who still needed to learn. I was deeply impressed
both by his wisdom and his direct and natural way of relating. As we
parted, he looked at me with a big smile and asked me if it was all right
to give me a hug—so I received my first and only royal hug, not knowing exactly how to behave in such a situation.

Finally, another significant personality that I had a chance to
speak with on many occasions during my time in Bhutan is Her Royal
Highness Ashi Kesang Choden Wangchuck, who is the president of
the GNH Center and one of the king's younger sisters. Before I first
met her, I wondered what she would be like, and I smiled to think of
how, as a child, I had imagined that a real princess would look like
the princesses in fairy tales. And when I did meet the princess, I felt
that my childhood ideas had been completely fulfilled. She not only
has the appearance of a fairy tale princess, but she is also an extremely
kind, caring, and personable human being. When I first met her,
she was just thirty years old, but throughout my time in Bhutan, she
consistently supported and led the GNH Center with a maturity far
beyond her age.

PART 1

WHY DO WE NEED GROSS NATIONAL HAPPINESS?

1

INTRODUCTION

MY WAY TO BHUTAN

In May 2012, I landed at Paro International Airport for the first time. Visiting a different country is always an adventure, but merely *landing* at Paro is an adventure in itself. Having flown by the highest Himalayan summits—including Mount Everest—the airplane slaloms between peaks, and when you look out the window next to you, the mountains seem so close that you could almost touch them. You begin to wonder why the pilot flies so near them, but when you look out the windows on the other side, you realize that it is that close on both sides! Then the plane flies straight toward another peak and, in the last moment, does a 180-degree turn to land. This is not an experience for those with a fear of flying—or maybe it's a good way to cure it, as so far there has never been an accident there.

Landing in Bhutan for the first time, I did not know anyone in the country. I felt a mixture of excitement and expectation, as I was coming to take up the role of program director at the Gross National Happiness Center, based in Thimphu, the capital city. Only a few weeks earlier, I had had the job interview over Skype with a panel of Bhutanese and international experts, and soon afterward I had flown to New York to join a high-level meeting convened by the royal government of Bhutan at the headquarters of the United Nations .

Since then I have conducted many workshops on Gross National Happiness in Bhutan and in many other countries. I have held dozens of presentations on GNH in universities, businesses, and NGOs, and in other contexts, for both large and intimate audiences. Very often I'm asked, "How did you get to Bhutan in the first place?" and "What was the path that led you there?"

Before going to Bhutan, I was working for the International Committee of the Red Cross (ICRC), and although I was based at the headquarters in Geneva, I regularly spent time in the field in war zones and conflict areas, including Darfur, Afghanistan, Palestine, and Ivory Coast. Although I was very engaged in this humanitarian work, I also felt some frustration—in this work we were working only with the consequences of the crisis and conflicts, and we were never really looking at the root causes, the structural and systemic issues underlying the conflicts.

These were some of the reasons why I became interested in the new development paradigm of Gross National Happiness, hoping that a different understanding of progress and development—an alternative way of looking at the economy—would offer solutions to the problems that I had been confronting in my humanitarian work. At that time, however, I never dreamed that I would ultimately live and work in Bhutan. That was until one morning when, going through my email (I must have had some spare time that day, because I didn't rapidly delete the emails coming from unknown senders, as I usually did) and reading through an academic network newsletter, I found a job opening for the position of program director of the Gross National Happiness Center in Bhutan. Upon reading the job description, I felt that this job was perfectly aligned with everything I'd experienced and done until then, the competencies that I'd developed, and my deepest aspirations. But it's one thing to sense that a job is perfect for you and something quite different to convince those who are doing the hiring. Nevertheless, I immediately sent in my CV and a letter of application explaining how my experience and competencies fully aligned with the needs of this job.

Several weeks later, I hadn't heard anything back from Bhutan and had almost forgotten about it, being fully engaged in my daily work at the ICRC. Then, one morning, I received an email telling me that I'd been shortlisted from over one hundred and fifty applicants and that I should send a short essay describing what I planned to do if I became the program director. I wrote one and sent it—and again, I didn't hear anything for several weeks. I was starting to lose hope when I received an email telling me that I was one of six finalists and that in the coming week I would have a job interview over Skype with a panel from Bhutan who would then decide who would get the job.

This message had been sent to all six finalists in such a way that I could see the names of my competitors, so I searched online to see who they were. When I read their CVs and biographies, I became worried, because most of them were—unlike me—known scholars, experts who had visited Bhutan several times and who had good connections in the country. I felt that my chances of getting the job were slim. Nevertheless, on the day of the interview, for some unknown reason, I felt quite assured, and when the conversation started, I felt even more confident. There was a very constructive atmosphere, friendly and warmhearted. It was not at all like usual job interviews, but more like a deep and honest conversation. At the end, I felt that I had a chance to get the job, because the panel had seemed to appreciate my answers to their questions, and I had had a chance to explain how the position felt so well aligned with my experience, competencies, and highest aspirations.

At the end of the week, once all the interviews had been conducted, I received a message from Thimphu telling me that I been chosen and that, if I wanted it, I could have the position. It's hard to convey the joy and excitement I felt. I called my wife immediately to tell her this incredible news: we were moving to Bhutan.

The first thing I had to do in my new position was to go to the head-quarters of the United Nations in New York, where the royal government of Bhutan was hosting a high-level international meeting, titled Happiness and Well-Being: Defining a New Economic Paradigm.* As I've mentioned, I had never been to Bhutan, and I didn't know anyone there, so when I arrived at the conference in New York I tried to find my way around, not really knowing whom I should address.

During a break I managed to meet with the prime minister of Bhutan, Jigme Yoser Thinley, and I said, "Your excellency, you don't know me, but I'm now working for you."

He looked at me, smiled, and said: "Of course I know you. I was involved in the decision to give you this position, and I hope that you will do a good job, because a friend of mine was also applying for this position, and he didn't get it, obviously because of you."

This is how my journey to Bhutan and to Gross National Happiness began.

But before looking at Gross National Happiness, let us first try to understand why such a new development paradigm is important in our time.

---

*Ban Ki-Moon, "Remarks at High Level Meeting on 'Happiness and Well-Being: Defining a New Economic Paradigm,'" United Nations, https://www .un.org/sg/en/content/sg/speeches/2012-04-02/remarks-high-level-meeting-happiness -and-well-being-defining-new.

2

THE EVOLUTION OF HUMANKIND AND THE NEED FOR A NEW DEVELOPMENT PARADIGM

THE ANTHROPOCENE EPOCH

For tens of thousands of years, the place of humankind on the planet was a relatively insignificant one. Natural forces of all sorts—weather, disease, food sources, predatory animals—were so much more powerful than the limited abilities of our ancestors. All ancient cultures felt this domination of these forces, visible or invisible, and initially submitted to them. But later, humans began working to control them—cultivating food sources rather than hunting and gathering, forging increasingly lethal weapons and building increasingly strong shelters and then cities.

The effort to gain the upper hand over these natural forces took millennia to bear fruit, but in recent centuries, this situation has begun changing rapidly. Today, it is the planet and all its species that are dependent on humans for their survival and well-being. Despite this, we humans are still behaving as our ancestors did, not realizing that the responsibility has shifted and that we are now accountable for the well-being—and possibly even the survival—of life on earth. In past eras our main concern was the well-being of our species, which was constantly threatened by natural forces far greater than us. Today, it is the reverse: our planet and all living beings are dependent on us, but we have not yet been able to fully grasp the responsibility that has been bestowed upon us, or which we have bestowed upon ourselves. Our human-centric world view has become destructive for the environment and all living beings. Furthermore, it will ultimately threaten our own future, if we do not wake up to our sacred duty: the need to care for the well-being of all life forms.

By and large, all our social systems and structures are remnants of a time when we were focused on our own needs, disregarding those of other species and nature. But if we don't take into consideration the reality of the Anthropocene—that we have assumed steward-ship over our planet—these structures and systems will become self-destroying. By devastating the natural world, our own survival will also be endangered.

This is a reason why any new development paradigm, such as Gross National Happiness, cannot focus only on the well-being of all people; the well-being of *all* life forms must be considered.

Most cultural traditions understood the sacredness of nature and the interconnectedness and interdependence of all life forms—they didn't see other life forms as mere resources to satisfy our own needs, but as living beings with their own right to exist and flourish. That kind of connection with nature and with the planet urgently needs to be rekindled in order to bring about happy individuals and a happy society. We can no longer afford to narrow our attention to our own needs; we need to view these needs as part of the larger picture of the needs of all living beings.

As I mentioned in the introduction, one thing that led me from working with the International Committee of the Red Cross to going to Bhutan was the realization that my humanitarian work was never addressing the deeper causes of the problems that I was witnessing in conflict zones and war-torn regions. Those crises were just the tip of the iceberg; they were the symptoms of deep-seated collective or social ills that are usually not addressed when trying to solve conflicts. These deeper causes can be seen, first of all, at a systemic or structural level, in the way we have organized in past decades our societies, economic system, and international organizations. After the end of the Second World War, Europe and most of the world had been devastated. Infrastructures were largely destroyed, economies were in a shambles, and political systems were trying to find a new basis in the world that was now divided into two competing systems: the communist world of the Soviet Union and China on one side, and the so-called free world in the US and Western Europe on the other. The material needs were tremendous on both sides of the Iron Curtain and the necessity to rebuild the economy naturally led to a strong focus on economic growth.

In 1989, the world entered in the new era. With the fall of the Berlin Wall and the disintegration of the Soviet empire, new possibilities were emerging. But it seems that we were not able to find sustainable and innovative solutions that could have emerged at that crucial moment in history. Too many economists and politicians interpreted the fall of the Soviet empire as the victory of the capitalistic system, without realizing that this consumerist, capitalistic system, when spreading throughout the world, would become self-destructive—because of the fundamental contradiction between the idea of endless economic growth and the reality of a finite planet. So the crisis that we are witnessing today in many different fields—economics, ecology, politics, wars, and famines, just to name a few—are, in my view, the symptoms of a system that has outlived its usefulness and has come to a dead-end.

Before analyzing the systemic challenges in a deeper way, I would like to look at an even deeper cause of the current challenges, namely, the mindset that has created these systems. All the social systems in which we live have been produced by us humans and are a manifestation of our own consciousness—of the way we think, feel, act, relate to one another, interpret the world around us, and tell ourselves and each other stories that explain the reality in which we live. Social systems are not God-given; they are not natural laws. They were made by humans, and therefore, they can be changed and transformed. But in order to transform any system in a sustainable way, we need to transform our mindsets and our consciousness. As Einstein is often quoted as saying, "We cannot solve problems with the same thinking that we used when we created them."

So, the two first questions I would like to address are the following: What was the mindset that we used and that created these problems? And, most importantly, how can we change our thinking?

Many thinkers whose philosophy has a spiritual dimension describe the history of humankind as an evolution of consciousness. Although coming from different traditions and developing different systems, Rudolf Steiner, Carl Gustav Jung, Sri Aurobindo, Pierre Teilhard de Chardin, Jean Gebser, and Ken Wilber all agree on one common idea: that human history and institutions are manifestations of this evolution.

It is not my intention to discuss this evolution in depth, but I would like to point to one specific dimension that plays a central role in the understanding of the situation we, as human beings, are facing today. All traditional cultures and religions created a certain understanding of what it means to be human, a narrative that we tell ourselves and others—and tell to future generations, through education—about who we are and what our life on earth is all about. Different traditions used different words, images, and symbols, but all had in common the awareness that human beings are of a twofold nature: we have a physical body that is grounded in the material world and a spiritual dimension that connects us to a higher world.

These traditions also knew that for human beings to acquire wisdom and knowledge, they had to go through an inner transformative process. Knowledge was never considered something that is only rational and intellectual; there was always also an ethical dimension that included qualities of the heart, such as empathy, compassion, altruism, generosity, and care. Originally, knowledge and wisdom were not separated, but this began gradually changing after the Enlightenment. The separation of knowledge and wisdom became more striking in the nineteenth century, with the predominance of natural sciences. From then on, the focus of learning shifted from a transformation of the subject—the individual human learner—to an understanding of the object. Furthermore, the subject had to be excluded from the process of knowing—subjectivity was considered contradictory to authentic knowledge, which had to be objective. Modern science was able to make tremendous progress through this new methodology of knowing, but it came at a price. Because ethics and human values were excluded from scientific knowledge, the outcome of science could potentially bring about destruction.

A purely rational apprehension of reality showed its limits and its dangers in two events that can be seen as archetypal, but from which we—mankind—don't seem to have really learned the lesson.

At the beginning of the twentieth century, Germany was probably the most educated and advanced country in the world. Its universities, scholars, philosophers, musicians, artists, and writers were some of the best that Western culture had ever produced. And yet this was not enough to prevent Hitler from taking power and bringing about some of the worst destruction the world has ever seen. Auschwitz and the Holocaust epitomize the horrors of the Nazi regime and are a frightening example of how modern bureaucracy, rational organization, and logistics can be used for the worst of purposes.

Hiroshima and Nagasaki were the first—and, so far, are the only—cities to be destroyed by the atomic bomb—another symbol of how modern technology and tremendous intelligence and knowledge can be used to kill and destroy in an unprecedented way.

I am reminded of the beautiful and profound poem by T. S. Eliot:*

> *The endless cycle of idea and action,*
> *Endless invention, endless experiment,*
> *Brings knowledge of motion, but not of stillness;*
> *Knowledge of speech, but not of silence;*
> *Knowledge of words, and ignorance of the Word.*
> *All our knowledge brings us nearer to our ignorance,*
> *All our ignorance brings US nearer to death,*
> *But nearness to death no nearer to GOD.*
> *Where is the Life we have lost in living?*
> *Where is the wisdom we have lost in knowledge?*
> *Where is the knowledge we have lost in information?*

These are indeed deep questions:

> *Where is the wisdom we have lost in knowledge?*
> *Where is the knowledge we have lost in information?*

The thinking that is behind this challenge can be described as "materialistic reductionism": the idea that human beings are merely material beings with solely material needs. For a long time, this materialistic understanding of the human being, of the earth, and of the universe was merely a theory. In the twentieth century, however, this theory was put into action, resulting in the inhuman way we have treated each other and our planet. And it was not only humans who were reduced to their material needs—the whole of society, economy, and politics only focused on the material dimension of human life. This idea of human behavior being explained and understood purely in terms of

---

*T. S. Eliot, "Choruses from the Rock." *The Rock* was actually one of Eliot's plays, first produced in 1934, but a part of it has been published in a collection of Eliot's poetry as "Choruses from the Rock."

material needs has led to the concept of the *Homo economicus*—the economic man. In economics, *Homo economicus* is the model used in most mainstream theories to predict behaviors and market variations. It portrays humans as consistently rational and narrowly self-interested agents who always pursue their subjectively defined ends. Generally, *Homo economicus* attempts to maximize utility as a consumer and profit as a producer, while minimizing the "disutility" that work is supposed to represent.

The evolution of consciousness is described by some thinkers, such as Steiner and Jung, as a process of emancipation and individualization. While our ancestors were completely dependent on forces of nature that they did not fully understand, through the development of agriculture they learned to domesticate animals and plants, gradually becoming masters of their natural environment. And while our ancestors had to follow behaviors, beliefs, and rules prescribed by accident of birth or (as some traditions put it) by destiny or karma—affecting their social status, profession, even food and clothing, this same process of the evolution of consciousness freed us from those constrictions as well. And while there is no doubt that, from the Renaissance to the Enlightenment, there was a tremendous process of liberation of the human individual that brought about human rights, democracy, freedom of speech, and greater tolerance, we seem to have overshot the goal. Individualism has become egotism, and emancipation has gradually become alienation.

As has been described, human evolution has been played out as an interaction between inner transformation (processes of the mind) and outer change (processes of our environment). Likewise, to understand Gross National Happiness, we need to focus both on the inner conditions of happiness—i.e., happiness skills—as well as on the structural and systemic changes that can bring about a conducive environment for the happiness of all people and the well-being of all life forms.

The first part of the book focuses on the inner dimensions of happiness and well-being, while also addressing the outer consequences connected to this inner transformation process. The second part of the book addresses the structural and systemic changes we need to bring about to ensure the conducive environment for all people and other living beings to flourish. Finally, the third part will share some practical examples of the steps that can be taken to transform educational organizations and businesses into GNH environments.

3

WHAT IS GENUINE HAPPINESS?

Connecting with Our Authentic Self

I f we want to understand the deeper meaning of happiness, we need to make a distinction between two experiences that are usually both called "happiness." In ancient Greek philosophy, two different words were used to describe it: *hēdonē*, from which the modern psychiatric term "hedonia" is derived, and *eudaimoniā*.

Hedonia describes pleasant experiences, such as sensory pleasures and moods, which are, by nature, short-lived and impermanent, like enjoying good food. There is no doubt that a meal can be a source of pleasure. However, if we continued to eat even the most refined dish, the pleasant experience would rapidly turn into an unpleasant one—we could feel stuffed and uncomfortable. That kind of excess practiced too often could even cause suffering or illness. Likewise, all sensual pleasures, if pushed beyond a certain limit, turn into their opposite. They become a source of suffering, the most obvious example being addiction in all its various forms, where the quest for pleasure turns into dependence and pain.

There is nothing wrong with seeking enjoyable experiences within reasonable limits, but there is little doubt that these experiences are necessarily short-lived. Modern consumerist society is based on an endless quest for pleasure, and we have all experienced how unsatisfactory this quest ultimately turns out to be. No matter how much we possess, how pleasant our experiences might be, we are never fulfilled by it. This experience has been called the "hedonic treadmill." As someone makes more money, their expectations and desires rise in tandem, resulting in no permanent gain in happiness. And the expected satisfaction is so short-lived that we tend to search for more and more at an increasing pace, ending up exhausted without any significant happiness.

Eudaimonia, on the other hand, comes from the Greek *eu-*, meaning "well" or "beautiful," and *daimōn*, a word could be translated "deity" but was also the word Plato used to describe our higher being, our true self. Eudaimonia basically means to live in harmony with one's higher calling or highest potential. The happiness we speak about in the context of Gross National Happiness does not focus on hedonic satisfaction but on creating the inner and outer conditions for a meaningful life, one that enables us to live in harmony with our deepest aspirations and highest potential. In order to understand the deeper causes of true happiness in the eudaimonic sense of the word, we need to look into the sources of suffering that disconnect us from our potential for true happiness.

Modern Western society has focused its attention and efforts on creating the outer, material conditions for physical well-being, and we have to recognize the tremendous progress that was made through the development of science and technology in the past hundred years. Life expectancy has increased significantly, many diseases that used to be deadly can be easily cured, overall living standards have dramatically increased—even though the distribution of wealth is still unequal—and the daily lives of hundreds of millions of people are certainly much more comfortable than the lives of their ancestors. Technological and scientific progress, paired with economic development, made technical advancements available to many. However, although tremendous development has been achieved, we must also admit that this is not yet true for everyone, and that the life of a contemporary Syrian or Afghani refugee is probably worse than the life of their ancestors. It is striking to observe that many of today's problems have arisen *because* of our material progress, even in the most "advanced" societies.

A question we might ask is whether focusing all our attention on material development has led us to forget the inner dimensions of happiness and well-being. In other words, has the result of one-sided development been an increasing disconnection from very important aspects of human life?

To quote T. S. Eliot again:

Endless invention, endless experiment,
Brings knowledge of motion, but not of stillness;
Knowledge of speech, but not of silence;
Knowledge of words, and ignorance of the Word.

We know from research that in early stages of a country's development, there is a strong correlation between an increase in living standards and happiness and well-being, but this correlation tends to end once basic human needs are covered.* Beyond a certain living standard, significant increases in material resources do not correlate with increased happiness. For example, while the GDP of the US has tripled in recent decades, self-reported well-being has remained stagnant. In addition, many unforeseen problems have arisen from material development. The development of personal mobility in the form of cars held the promise of greater freedom and independence for all, and at the beginning, this was obviously the case. However, at a certain point—once the number of private cars increased beyond the limits of infrastructure in a given area—mobility was reduced as people spent hours stuck in traffic jams, as we can see in big cities all over the world. Furthermore, the increase in the number of individual cars alienates people from each other. Look at the traffic in any big city—most cars

---

*Richard A. Easterlin, Laura Angelescu McVey, Malgorzata Switek, and Jacqueline Smith Zweig, "The Happiness-Income Paradox Revisited," *PNAS* 107, no. 52 (2010): 22463–68. *https://doi.org/10.1073/pnas.1015962107*.

are used by only one person. Lonely individuals encased in heavy metal boxes, separated from their fellow human beings, and all perceiving each other as a nuisance because of the congestion created by this situation.

I was recently in Bangkok, a city famous for its unending traffic jams. I went to see a movie and was struck by the commercials promoting flashy, expensive cars that were shown before the featured film. They all showed beautiful young people driving through scenic countryside and elegant cities on roads that were mostly devoid of other vehicles. I had to smile to myself: no matter how fast and advanced their brand-new car would be, the reality was that buyers in Bangkok would only be driving at an average of twenty miles per hour, bumper against bumper, day in, day out, on their way to and from work. In order to afford the car of their dreams, they would have to work longer hours to pay for it.

This is just one image of the paradoxical situation that has become prevalent in urban life. Statistics show that in major European cities, a growing number of apartments are used by only one person,[*] another example of the growing isolation that modern life has brought about.

Given that, as human beings, we develop our personalities through social interactions, we have to ask ourselves what the impact of this growing isolation is on each person. As we examine ways in which we create meaning for ourselves, we realize that it is mainly through social interactions that we become aware of the way we can make a contribution to society—by understanding the needs of others. Therefore, a life in isolation, in most cases, tends to become a meaningless one.

In developed societies, psychosomatic illnesses—stress, depression, sleeping disorders, eating disorders, chronic exhaustion—have become the number one factor of morbidity. Rich and peaceful societies have

---

[*] Esteban Ortiz-Ospina, "The Rise of Living Alone: How One-Person Households Are Becoming Increasingly Common Around the World," *Our World in Data* (December 10, 2019). https://ourworldindata.org/living-alone.

reached an unprecedented level of comfort, material facilities, and living standards, and yet, at the individual level, we see a great deal of personal suffering.

How can we understand this paradox? Coming back to the notion of eudaimonia, or living in harmony with one's highest potential or highest aspiration, we realize that the first cause of suffering is a feeling of disconnection from oneself. In all ancient cultures, from Greece to the Orient, the notion of self-knowledge was central to a meaningful life. This includes the perspective of Buddhist psychology, for which the first cause of suffering is *avidya*, "ignorance"—literally "absence of light." In this context, ignorance is not a lack of education or of scientific knowledge, but a disconnection from one's true being.

Modern materialistic culture, however, by focusing on the outer world and forgetting the inner, has greatly contributed to a lack of self-knowledge. When we look around, we see that the emphasis on the outer world at the expense of the inner is everywhere. In the pursuit of information, for example, scientific enquiry sets aside the subject in favor of the object in order to avoid so-called subjective bias. Most people—and families, schools, and employers—mostly focus on outer achievements, rarely valuing the richness of the inner world. Equating happiness and success with material wealth and social position reinforces this feeling of disconnection from ourselves, and this is not so much an individual problem as a social and cultural difficulty faced by many. Sadly, it is only when life takes an unexpected turn—sudden illness, the loss of a job or a loved one—that many people realize that outer achievements are of little value when it comes to facing deeper challenges.

Another unintended effect of modernization is our disconnection from the flow of natural rhythms. The natural rhythms of our planet—night and day, the seasons, the cycles of the moon and sun—as well as our own inner rhythms of sleeping and waking, have not changed significantly in thousands of years. Yet the way we live our daily life has undergone tremendous a transformation, the first dramatic one being the Industrial Revolution. Until then, most people lived with the cycles of nature, but then many moved from the countryside to cities to work in factories. The famous sequence in Charlie Chaplin's *Modern Times* is a telling metaphor of this transition: in this scene, we see Chaplin working on an assembly line, struggling to adapt to the ever-increasing speed of the machine until he is finally swallowed by the mechanism.

The cycles of nature are fundamentally in harmony with the cycles of our own body. Our heartbeat and breathing are living rhythms that determine the harmonious functioning of all our organs, constantly adapting to our physical and mental experiences. The pace of machines, however, is completely out of sync from our organic rhythms, imposing a mechanical tempo that does not respect the natural flow of life. This disconnect between our inner rhythms and the requirement of the workplace creates a tension that ultimately manifests as stress and burnout.

An even more radical transformation came about with the emergence of the computer technologies that have invaded not only our work life but also our personal time. Factory workers on the assembly lines of the twentieth century submitted to an inhuman work pace, but at least it ended when the workers left the building. Contemporary electronic devices, on the other hand, have invaded every moment of our waking lives.

I remember vividly when the first computers were introduced in my workplace. The argument was that we'd be able to do the same amount of work in much less time, and thus time would be saved. This promise was never fulfilled; on the contrary, as emails and social media entered our lives, our relationship with time has speeded up drastically. Gone are the days when I would write a letter on a fine sheet of paper with a beautiful fountain pen, taking time to craft graceful sentences and taking into consideration whom I was writing to, before folding the paper, putting it in an envelope, addressing it, sticking on a stamp, taking it to the post office, and waiting several days or weeks for the natural flow of time to elapse before I received an answer. Today, when I open my laptop in the morning, I might have dozens of emails in the inbox, and most of my correspondents will grow impatient if I have not replied within a few hours. While organic time is a flowing rhythm, electronic time is instantaneous.

But even email is already something of the past, and most young people hardly use it anymore, preferring the even faster pace of instant messaging on their smartphones. I believe that nothing has so drastically changed human behavior as the spread of smartphones around the world, and the paradox is that constant connectedness has created tremendous disconnectedness. There was a time when a few dozen friends was considered a good social network. When I recently looked at my Facebook page, I noticed that I have about five thousand friends. But how many of these people do I really know? And how much of my time is consumed by interacting with these virtual "friends," when I could be interacting with my real-life ones?

We all know the usual situation on public transport—bus or train— where almost every passenger is focused on their phone or tablet, and actual conversation with other people has become the exception rather than the rule. Likewise, it has become a common sight to see couples or families eating out in a restaurant, with everyone gazing at their own screen rather than interacting with each other and those around them.

One of the most widespread experiences related to stress is the feeling of not having enough time, of being under constant pressure, and one of the reasons for this is the discrepancy between our organic experience of time based on our breathing and on our heartbeat (which are the same as they were for our ancestors), while our daily activities are spiraling out of control in terms of speed. The first and most fundamental way to reconnect with ourselves, therefore, is to create intentional moments of slowing down and stopping—and mindfulness is an excellent way of doing that. The mindfulness movement has become widespread in what may at first seem the most unlikely of contexts— from the World Economic Forum in Davos and the British Parliament to the offices of Google in California. But as we shall see, this popularity is not so surprising after all.

What Is Mindfulness?

Mindfulness is the energy of being aware and awake to the
present moment. It is the continuous practice of touching life
deeply in every moment of daily life. To be mindful is to be
truly alive, present and at one with those around you
and with what you are doing.

—THICH NHAT HANH

Mindfulness means paying attention in a particular way: on purpose, in the present moment, and nonjudgmentally. It means maintaining a moment-by-moment awareness of our thoughts, feelings, bodily sensations, and surrounding environment.

Mindfulness also involves acceptance, meaning that we pay attention to our thoughts and feelings without judging them—without believing, for instance, that there's a "right" or "wrong" way to think or feel in a given moment. When we practice mindfulness, our thoughts tune in to what we're sensing in the present moment, rather than rehashing the past or imagining the future.

Though it has its roots in Buddhist meditation, a secular practice of mindfulness has entered the mainstream in recent years, in part through the work of Jon Kabat- Zinn and his mindfulness-based stress reduction (MBSR) program, which he launched at the University of Massachusetts Medical School in 1979. Since that time, thousands of studies have documented the physical and mental health benefits of mindfulness in general, inspiring countless programs to adapt mindfulness practices for schools, prisons, hospitals, veterans' centers, and beyond.

Perhaps the individual who has done the most to bring mindfulness to the Western world was my teacher, the Venerable Thich Nhat Hanh, whom *Time* magazine called "the monk who taught the world mindfulness." Exiled from his native Vietnam in 1966 for his peace work during the war there, he settled in France, where he founded five monasteries, and regularly gave teaching tours in the United States.

Mindfulness and Gross National Happiness

Soon after the end of the Vietnam War (called in Vietnam the American War), I had a chance to go to Vietnam with my father, and I met several members of my family, including an uncle who was a well-known Buddhist sculptor and his son, who was a painter. In the 1960s, both father and son had been students of Zen master Thich Nhat Hanh (whom they, like many, simply called "Thây," which means "teacher"), and they asked me if I had had the chance to meet with their teacher, who was then living in France. I was embarrassed to admit that I had never heard of him—in 1981, Thây was not yet well known in Europe.

When I returned to Europe, I wrote a letter to Thây asking if I could come and visit. His close disciple Sister Chân Không wrote back a very friendly letter inviting us to come and visit the newly opened mindfulness practice center Plum Village in southwest France. She also sent a copy of Thay's book *The Miracle of Mindfulness*. I read the book with great interest, but for some reason, it took several years before Lisi, my wife, and I actually went to Plum Village for the first time.

When we arrived, we were right away invited to have tea with Thây and Sister Chân Không, and at the time, we thought that this was usual for newcomers to be invited to Thây's hermitage. In fact, Thây knew many of my relatives, because my family was from Hue, which was also his hometown. My uncle and my cousin had been close students of his and had illustrated some of his books. Furthermore, Lisi has a Swiss cousin whom Thây had met in the 1960s in the US, because he was one of the first Westerners to be ordained as a Zen monk in Tassajara Zen Mountain Temple, founded by Suzuki Roshi in California. So for both of us, arriving in Plum Village for the first time almost felt like coming to a family reunion.

Beyond the personal level, the first time I heard Thây give a talk, I was deeply moved. In fact, it happened more than once that I found myself crying while listening to the teachings. Not because I was sad, but because it touched my heart so deeply. I knew that until then, my understanding of compassion had been very shallow, very theoretical, but when I was in Thây's presence, I had a direct experience of lived compassion, united with a wisdom so deep that he could express it in simple words without losing its profundity. I knew I had met my teacher. From then on, we went to Plum Village regularly for retreats, bringing our children with us in the summers, and we had the chance to develop a deep connection with Thây.

We were some of Thây's first students to have a chance to go back to Vietnam at a time when almost no foreigners or Vietnamese from abroad were allowed back, and we could reconnect with many of his students who had not seen him for many years.

In 2001, my wife and I both received the Transmission of the Lamp from Thây, a traditional ordination allowing us to teach as lay Dharma teachers (Dharmacharya) in the Plum Village tradition.

Looking back at the many years we had the chance to be in Thây's presence and to receive his teachings, I am filled with a deep sense of gratitude; he never asked anything from us, never expected anything, and left us completely free, but he was always there for us.

When I told Thây that I was moving to Bhutan to work at the Gross National Happiness Center, he was very supportive and told me that he would be happy to come and visit me there to give talks and retreats.

I discussed this possibility with the then prime minister, Jigmi Y. Thinley, who was delighted at the prospect and wanted it to be an official state visit. I also had a chance to offer an autographed copy of Thây's book *The Art of Power* to his majesty, the fourth king of Bhutan, who told me that he had read Thây's book *Old Path White Clouds: Walking in the Footsteps of the Buddha* several times and that he held Thây in great esteem.

The first youth retreats we organized at the GNH Center in Thimphu were cofacilitated by delegations of monks and nuns from Plum Village, and the hundreds of young Bhutanese who attended loved the whole experience of practicing mindfulness with them.

Unfortunately, the official state visit of Thây to Bhutan never happened. First we had to postpone it because of the national elections, and then, when it would have been possible from the Bhutanese side, Thây's health did not allow it. Yet Thây's teachings and practices have had a major influence in the way we conduct the GNH programs, and mindfulness is a core part of all our programs. Therefore, in a way, although Thây did not come to Bhutan in his physical body, his Dharma body has been there and is still there, because much of the way we impart GNH is deeply connected with his teachings.

Why Practice Mindfulness?

Studies have shown that practicing mindfulness, even for just a few weeks, can bring a variety of physical, psychological, and social benefits.[*] Here are some of these benefits, which extend across many different settings.

Mindfulness is good for our bodies: A seminal study found that, after just eight weeks of training, practicing mindfulness meditation boosts our immune system's ability to fight off illness.

Mindfulness is good for our minds: Several studies have found that mindfulness increases positive emotions, while reducing negative emotions and stress. Indeed, at least one study suggests it may be as good as antidepressants in fighting depression and preventing relapse.

---

[*] *https://scholar.google.ch/scholar?q=mindfulness+meta+analysis+2018&hl=en&as_sdt =0&as_vis=1&oi=scholar*

Mindfulness changes our brains: Research has found that it increases the density of grey matter in brain regions linked to learning, memory, emotion regulation, and empathy.

Mindfulness helps us focus: Studies suggest that mindfulness helps us tune out distractions and improves our memory and attention skills.

Mindfulness fosters compassion and altruism: Research suggests mindfulness training makes us more likely to help someone in need and increases activity in neural networks involved in understanding the suffering of others and regulating emotions. Evidence suggests it might boost self-compassion as well.

Mindfulness enhances relationships: Research suggests mindfulness training makes couples more satisfied with their relationship, makes each partner feel more optimistic and relaxed, and makes them feel more accepting of and closer to one another.

Mindfulness is good for parents and parents-to-be: Studies suggest it may reduce pregnancy-related anxiety, stress, and depression in expectant parents. Parents who practice mindfulness report being happier with their parenting skills and their relationship with their kids, and their kids were found to have better social skills.

Mindfulness helps schools: There's scientific evidence that teaching mindfulness in the classroom reduces behavior problems and aggression among students and improves their happiness levels and ability to pay attention. Teachers trained in mindfulness also show lower blood pressure, less negative emotion and symptoms of depression, and greater compassion and empathy.

Mindfulness helps health care professionals cope with stress: It assists them in connecting with their patients and improving their general quality of life. It also helps mental health professionals by reducing negative emotions and anxiety and increasing their positive emotions and feelings of self-compassion.

Mindfulness fights obesity: Practicing "mindful eating" encourages healthier eating habits, helps people lose weight, and helps them savor their food.

Reconnecting to Our Body

Another paradox of our time is the fact that although we have focused our attention on the material world, we have, by and large, lost connection with our physical body.

The first benefit of slowing down and stopping is to reconnect with our bodily experience, noticing how we feel in our body—whether we are tense or relaxed, at ease or exhausted—and an efficient way to reconnect with our bodily experience is to learn to reconnect with our breathing.

To breathe is the most fundamental experience of being alive; our earthly existence begins with our first breath and will end one day with our last breath. Between these two moments we will have been breathing without any interruption day and night, but mostly without being aware of it. Taking a few moments to simply notice that we are breathing means that we, at the same time, remind ourselves that we are alive.

The breath, together with the heartbeat, play a central role in our experience of well-being or of discomfort. They are the interface between body and mind, and any physical change will be reflected in our breathing and heart rate. For instance, if we are engaging in intense physical activity, like running, our breathing and our heart will increase in order to bring back harmony in our body. If we ingest coffee, alcohol, or similar substances that have an effect on our organs, then again, our heart rate and breathing will react accordingly. On the other hand, every emotion that we have also has an impact on our inner rhythm. If we observe what happens when we laugh or cry, we see that basically these are changes in our breathing and that every emotion—whether sadness, joy, anger, pain, or surprise—affects our breathing and our heart rate.

Therefore, training our awareness of our breathing helps us to become more aware of both our physical and emotional well-being. The following is a simple set of exercises that we can train ourselves to do regularly to enhance the awareness of our breathing.

Practice

Exercise 1: Mindful Sitting

Mindful sitting is like returning home to give full attention to and care for ourselves. We sit upright, with dignity, and return to our breathing, bringing our full attention to what is within and around us. We let our mind become spacious and our heart soft and kind.

Sitting meditation is very healing. We realize we can just be with whatever is within us—our pain, anger, and irritation or our joy, love, and peace. We are with whatever is there without being carried away by it. Let it come, let it stay, then let it go. No need to push emotions away or pretend our thoughts are not there. We can observe the thoughts and images of our mind with an accepting and loving eye. We are free to be still and calm despite the storms that might arise within us.

If our legs or feet fall asleep or begin to hurt during the sitting, we are free to adjust our position quietly. We can maintain our concentration by following our breathing and, slowly and attentively, changing our posture.

Exercise 2: Getting in Touch with the Breath

Why practice getting in touch with the breath?

* To experience the breath as a friend that is always there to help us return to ourselves in the present moment, creating moments of peace throughout the day.

* To increase our ability to focus and pay attention to what is happening here and now.

* To calm and anchor body and mind, in order to help manage difficult emotions and impulses.

* To relax and help relieve stress and tension.

* To increase the ability to recognize how we are feeling.

* To help unite body and mind.

* To help us be more present and therefore to enable us to listen to others more deeply and communicate more empathically.

Mindful breathing can help us focus. By bringing awareness to our breathing we can gently bring our wandering mind back to the present moment. Whenever we get carried away, overwhelmed by strong emotions, or caught up in worries or plans, we can come back and experience our breath in order to steady our mind, returning it to the here and now.

1. Prepare

Find a comfortable, relaxed, and stable sitting position. This can be on a chair, a cushion, or anywhere you feel comfortable. Sense the contact with the floor, the ground, the chair, or the cushion.

Close your eyes or keep them open with their gaze resting gently on the floor in front of you.

2. Notice that you are breathing

Take a few moments to gradually become aware that you are breathing. There is no need to change anything. Just be aware of, notice, and recognize the breath, just as it is.

3. Follow the breath

As you breathe in, follow with all your attention the whole length of your in-breath, as it comes through your mouth or nose, passes down through your throat, and fills your lungs. As you breathe out, follow with all your attention the whole length of your out-breath, the feeling of the air leaving your lungs, passing through your throat, and coming out through your mouth or nose. If you become distracted and lost in thought, just notice this and gently bring your attention back to the breath.

4. Feel the breath in the belly

Put your hands on your belly and try to become aware of it expanding with the in-breath and falling with the out-breath. No need to change anything; just stay with noticing the sense of the in-breath and the out-breath, feeling your hands and belly move, even if only slightly.

Notice the length of the breath, and the gentle transition between the in- and out-breath.

5. End

These are some of the questions you might use to reflect on your practice:

＊ How do I feel right now? What is happening right now in my mind or body? Do I feel calm, clear, relaxed, tense, anxious?

* How is my breath? Slow, deep, light, fast?

* What happened for me during this practice, in my mind, body, and breath? Did anything change? For instance, do I feel calmer and more present? Is my mind clear, or do I feel agitated?

* How easy was it to keep my mind on my breath?

* How did the practice feel (strange, good, enjoyable, difficult, boring)?

Exercise 3: Walking Meditation

Wherever we walk, we can practice meditation. In a walking meditation, we simply know that we are walking, and we walk just for walking. We walk with freedom and solidity, no longer in a hurry; we are present with each step. And when we wish to talk with someone else, we stop our movement and give our full attention to the other person, to our words, and to listening.

We should be able to do it in every moment. Look around and see how vast life is—the trees, the white clouds, the limitless sky. Listen to the birds. Feel the fresh breeze. Life is all around, and we are alive and healthy and capable of walking in peace.

Let us walk as a free person and feel our steps get lighter. Let us enjoy every step we make. Each step is nourishing and healing. As we walk, we imprint our gratitude and our love on the earth.

We may like to use some words to complement the meditation as we walk. Try taking two or three steps for each in-breath and each out-breath:

Breathing in, say, "I have arrived"; breathing out, "I am home." Breathing in again, "In the here"; breathing out, "In the now." Breathing in, "I am solid"; breathing out, "I am free."

A Formative Experience
of Reconnecting to Self

At this point I would like to share an experience that happened when I was just eighteen years old and that played a central role in my life.

In 1968, when I was seventeen, I was in a boarding school in Rambouillet, outside of Paris. It was the middle of the Vietnam War. In January 1968 the Viet Cong and the North Vietnamese Army had tried to make a decisive breakthrough in South Vietnam to overthrow the American-backed government during the Tết Offensive. Being of Vietnamese origin through my father, I was deeply touched by what was happening in Vietnam, wavering between a commitment to pacifism and nonviolence inspired by figures like Gandhi or Martin Luther King Jr. and a more revolutionary, even violent, stand, inspired by figures like Fidel Castro, Che Guevara, or Ho Chi Minh.

One day in May, I left school at dawn and hitchhiked to Paris in a truck bringing fruit and vegetables to the Les Halles vegetable market in the heart of the city. We arrived in the early morning, and the driver, who was sympathetic to the student movement, offered me a large crate of cherries. I can still see myself walking from Les Halles to the Sorbonne, which was the headquarters of the movement, handing out my cherries to passersby while humming "Le temps des cerises," which had been one of the resistance songs during the Second World War.

It is difficult to imagine the effervescence and the atmosphere that reigned in Paris at the time. On every street corner, groups discussed, exchanged, remade the world. Street musicians sang and played. Theater and dance were improvised in the streets, the walls of the capital served as an impromptu canvas where graffiti, slogans, and images sprang up every day: "Power to the Imagination!" "It is forbidden to forbid!" "Beneath the paving stones—the beach!" "I don't want to waste my life earning it!" "Be realistic, demand the impossible!"

More than a political revolution, it was a cultural revolution, the feeling that an old patriarchal, materialistic, hierarchical, and hypocritical order was falling apart, and that a new world still chaotic, still indistinct, but freer, spontaneous, and authentic was emerging. The days alternated between massive demonstrations; general assemblies in the amphitheaters of the Sorbonne University; intense activities of groups creating leaflets, newspapers, slogans—all in a joyful disorder. It was completely disorganized but filled with immense joy, hope, and idealism.

De Gaulle had left Paris and had consulted the chief of staff to ensure that the army would be ready, if necessary, to intervene to restore order. At the end of the spring, "order" was restored with police on every street corner, a ban on gathering in public spaces, and police checks at all times.

The old order, shaken for a moment, had regained power. It seems to me that the fundamental reason that did not allow a real transition was the absence of an alternative to which young people who aspired to a new world had access. For most of us who were aware of the limitations, systemic violence, and injustice of the capitalist system, the only alternative seemed to be socialism. But on the other side of the iron curtain, young people living under the communist, totalitarian regime had the same aspiration for a new world, and they hoped that the Western system would be the solution. I became aware of this in August 1968, when the tanks of the Warsaw Pact sent from Moscow crushed the Prague Spring with far more violence than the French government's police had used to put down the student revolt. For me, it was a terrible shock to realize that "real socialism" was in no way an alternative to the capitalist system I despised, but that, in fact, these two systems were two different manifestations of the same state of mind based on power, domination, materialism, contempt for nature, exploitation, and social injustice. It was a moment of great dismay for me, because I saw clearly what seemed unacceptable in the political, economic, and social systems around me, but I was unable to formulate a credible and constructive alternative. Looking back, I believe that my quest for a new development paradigm that I found when I met GNH, dates back to these experiences.

In 1969 I graduated from high school, and it was time to decide what I would study, but after my experiences during the student revolution in Paris, I felt little enthusiasm at the prospect of going to university.

My parents were going back to Vietnam, and I decided to join them. When we arrived in Bangkok, however, the war in Vietnam was raging, and my father, knowing that I was engaged in the peace movement, advised me not to go back to Vietnam, because as a Vietnamese citizen, I would have been drafted.

So instead of continuing my journey with my parents, I went from Bangkok to Nepal.

Nepal had only been open to foreigners since 1965, and the city of Kathmandu was still a medieval town—all the houses were made of wood, stone, and rammed earth. Arriving in this peaceful environment—so different from the big Western cities where I had spent most of my childhood—had a strong impact on me. Although the country was much less developed than the world I was used to, there was a quality in the way people lived that touched me. Religious rituals determined daily life, and each morning I woke up to the sound of bells, gongs, flutes, and drums and to the chanting of mantras coming from a little temple located near the small room that I had rented for a handful of rupees.

After a few weeks in Kathmandu, I decided to go with a group of new friends on a pilgrimage to a sacred lake called Gosaikunda, which is at an altitude of 4,380 meters (almost 14,400 feet) in the Himalayas. After taking a local bus to a small town at the base of the mountain, we started our trek. Back then, there were hardly any foreigners and no trekking offices or tourist guides, so we organized the journey ourselves, asking local people on the way for guidance.

My equipment was quite inadequate. I had Tibetan boots with slippery leather soles, a shoulder bag made of yak hair, and a locally made woolen blanket to keep me warm night. At the end of the first day, I slipped on wet stones while crossing a stream and fell in the water. I could not possibly continue my journey; everything I had was soaked. My friends and I agreed that they would continue on and that I would meet up with them in a monastery that was on the way to the lake. After spending the night in a farmhouse and drying as well as I could by an open fire, I walked back to the nearest town to get better equipment for the trek.

On the following day, I started again on my own, asking in villages and monasteries on the way for directions. It was not always easy; the villagers knew, at best, only a few words of English, and my knowledge of Nepali was limited to the few words that I had picked up in Kathmandu. Nevertheless, the first day went well, and as evening fell, I came across some villagers who kindly offered me shelter in their home. On the second day, however, I lost my way and could not recognize any of the landmarks my hosts had pointed out to me as I left their farm. By that point, it was late afternoon, and although it was still summer, at that altitude, the temperature was dropping rapidly. I was totally clueless as to what I should be doing next.

I had a book with me, Hermann Hesse's *Siddhartha*, which I was enjoying very much. As I got colder and colder, I decided I would try to light a fire; but summer in the Himalayas is the monsoon season, and all the wood that I could find was quite wet. In order to light a fire, I decided to use some of the pages from my book, starting with the first chapters that I had already read. Despite all my efforts, though, the fire would not really burn, and so gradually I had to sacrifice parts of the book that had not yet read. I still recall the dilemma I felt when I had to decide whether it was more important to light a fire or to keep the unread parts of my book. I ended up burning the whole book—still not being able to light a proper fire. Moreover, quite a few leeches had crept inside my shoes and underwear, so I had to burn them with a *beedi*—a local cigarette—so that they would drop from my body.

It really felt like a desperate situation. I went through many different emotions: despair, self-pity, anger, helplessness. It felt so unfair that my life would end in these mountains, only seventeen years old. I could picture the despair of my parents when they realized that I had disappeared, and I wondered how long it would take before people found my body, realized who I was, and informed my family. I cannot remember how long I dwelled in these negative emotions, but it certainly felt then like a very long time.

I struggled to find solutions. It would have probably been wiser to start walking in the hope of meeting someone or finding an isolated village or monastery, but night was falling, and I had no idea what direction I should go in. I felt as if I was paralyzed so I just sat there, leaning against a rock. As the despair became more and more powerful, I felt totally overwhelmed and had no idea what to do.

Then something utterly unexpected happened. It was as if, in the complete inner darkness, a light had started shining. Delicate at first, it became stronger and stronger until it fully transformed my state of mind. Although nothing outward had changed, a feeling of peace, stillness, confidence, and trust emerged. It was as if I had gone through layers and layers of negative emotions—fear, despair, and darkness—and then, as I reached the bottom of the pit, the darkest place of all, there was a breakthrough into a new dimension that had always been there, but that I had never been aware of. Until then, there was an intense antagonism and duality between me and my surroundings, but now, there was a sense of unity, of belonging. Just moments before, the mountain had felt like an enemy that was threatening me, that would probably destroy me, but now the whole of nature felt welcoming and safe. I felt embraced by the mountain, as if it was a motherly or fatherly presence—protecting me. And I knew that whatever happened, all would be well, there was nothing to fear. What happened would be the right thing, and I could welcome it, whatever it was.

I stayed for quite a while in this state of peace, stillness, and unity, not expecting anything. I felt complete confidence in my destiny, even if it meant that I was going to die.

I have no idea how long I stayed in in this peaceful state, but sometime later, an old man walked by. He was a wandering monk that was going from village to village to perform ceremonies and rites. When he saw me, he started laughing; he thought it was so funny and so strange to see this young foreigner in the middle of nowhere, sitting by a rock in the cold next to the remains of a fire that had never really started burning, and who, nevertheless, seemed so happy and content.

He came up to me and started chatting in Tibetan. Although I didn't understand a word, there was a deep communication between us, and we just kept laughing and smiling at one another. I showed him that I had leeches clinging to some parts of my body. He picked some plants that were growing nearby and showed me how to squeeze and rub the leaves around the leeches, which fell away as soon as they came in contact with the green juice. Then, he motioned me to follow him and, after about a two-hour walk, we arrived in a small village.

After this encounter, I continued my pilgrimage and reached the sacred lake where, together with hundreds of pilgrims, my friends and I purified ourselves by bathing the ice-cold lake of Gosaikunda.

When the pilgrimage was over, I returned to Kathmandu and rented a small room on the outskirts of the city, near the Monkey Temple in Swayambhunath. I still was perplexed by my experience on the mountain, and I wanted to understand what had happened. I spent quite a lot of time reflecting on it and had one insight that felt important: the fact that it was possible to experience a profound happiness that was not dependent on anything external and that came from facing some of the darkest aspects of one's heart and being able to transform it. I started reading Buddhist books and asking around to find out if other people had experienced similar things. My main question was, "Is it possible to reach the state of consciousness that I had experienced on the mountain through deliberate, intentional practice? Or is this kind of experience something that only happens naturally—or accidentally—when one is facing death?"

This experience of reconnecting with a deeper dimension of consciousness became the starting point of a lifelong quest.

Emotions as Seeds in Consciousness: The Baobab and the Rose

A significant breakthrough in Western psychology and psychoanalysis came about through Sigmund Freud's topographic schema mapping out the mind as conscious, unconscious, and preconscious. Later, researchers such as Carl Jung explored in greater depth the so-called collective unconscious, reconnecting ancient spiritual traditions with the emerging knowledge of the mind.

Through introspection and meditation over the past twenty-five hundred years, Buddhist psychology has explored the human psyche in great depth and has gained an understanding that goes far beyond the current psychological knowledge. A central notion is the idea of "seeds" (in Sanskrit, *bija*). According to this, all our potential experiences and emotions lay dormant in deeper layers of our consciousness (store consciousness, or *ālayavijñāna*) in the form of seeds, just as seeds can lay dormant in soil for a long time until the right conditions come together to allow plants to grow. In a similar way, all kinds of emotions remain hidden until certain stimuli from inside or outside awaken them, and they manifest in our consciousness. In his book *The Little Prince*, Antoine de Saint-Exupéry shared a beautiful metaphor describing precisely this phenomena:

> Indeed, as I learned, there were on the planet where the little prince lived—as on all planets—good plants and bad plants. In consequence, there were good seeds from good plants, and bad seeds from bad plants. But seeds are invisible. They sleep deep in the heart of the earth's darkness, until someone among them is seized with

the desire to awaken. Then this little seed will stretch itself and begin—timidly at first—to push a charming little sprig, inoffensively upwards towards the sun. If it is only the sprig of a rosebush, one would let it grow wherever it might wish, but when it is a bad plant, one must destroy it as soon as possible, the very first instant that one recognizes it. Now there were some terrible seeds on the planet that was the home of the little prince, and these were the seeds of the baobab . . . A baobab is something you will never, never be able to get rid of if you attend to it too late. It spreads over the entire planet . . . and if the planet is too small and the baobabs are too many, they split it in pieces . . . "It is a question of discipline," the little prince said to me later on. "When you finish your own toilet in the morning, then it is time to attend to the toilet of your planet, just so, with the greatest care. You must see to it that you pull up regularly all the baobabs, at the very first moment when they can be distinguished from the rose bushes, which they resemble so closely in their earliest youth. It is very tedious work," the little prince added. "But very easy."

This poetic metaphor shows how we can use introspection and meditation to deal with emotions. More often than not, we notice painful or destructive emotions only once they've become so powerful that we're unable to control them, and as in the story, our whole world might be destroyed if the baobabs—jealousy, anger, and depression—take over. How many families and communities have been split apart by hurtful emotions that have destroyed the love, trust, and care between its members? As the little prince rightly points out, if we learn to observe difficult emotions when they first emerge, it is easy to transform them.

The breathing exercise described above (exercise 2) is a good way to learn to observe the emergence of emotions. Emotions begin as a physical sensation, and we can learn to identify precisely in what part of the body various emotions manifest. Fear or sadness might be experienced as a tightening of the chest, anger as a surge in the belly, and all of these are accompanied by a change in our breathing and heart rate. In a second stage, these emotions manifest as thoughts or ideas, a narrative that justifies or rationalizes the emotion and usually blames it on something or someone. This narrative nourishes the emotion and strengthens the bodily sensation, which, in turn, fuels the narrative—a vicious cycle that can escalate to destructive or self-destructive behaviors.

When we learn to identify the emergence of an emotion—or, as the little prince puts it, a baobab, or a "bad seed of a bad plant— we can interrupt the process by shining the light of mindfulness on these otherwise unconscious sensations and thoughts. The energy of mindfulness has a healing and soothing quality that can transform any destructive emotion, if we become conscious of it at an early stage. Regularly slowing down, returning to our breathing and to the awareness of our body, allows us to regulate our emotions, transforming the negative ones and nurturing positive ones such as gratitude, compassion, kindness, and generosity.

But self-knowledge doesn't end with emotional regulation; it can be developed a step further to look deeply and understand the root causes of the emotions lying dormant in the deeper layers of our consciousness. These can stem from our childhood, our family history, our genes, society, culture, and even—for those of us who believe in rebirth—from our past lives. The more we are able to shine the light of mindfulness in the depth of our store consciousness, the more we can become free from unconscious impulses that can lead us to behaviors that might be destructive for ourselves and for others.

As the little prince wisely explained, self-knowledge is, in the first place, a matter of discipline, about creating a habit of regular moments of introspection, learning to observe in ever more subtle ways the sensations in the body, the movements of the mind, and the emergence of emotions. The following exercise will show you how to do this.

Practice

Recognizing and Taking Care of our Emotions

Using mindfulness to take care of strong emotions and painful feelings can be divided into five steps:

1. First, recognize that an emotion is present. When joy is there, we know that joy is present. When anger is there, we recognize the fact that anger is present. It helps to call the emotion by its name. If we don't recognize what emotion is present within us, it is difficult to take care of it.

2. Next, accept that the emotion is there. Don't try to suppress it or cover it up. It's okay to have anger—we're humans; it's completely normal to be angry at times. If we don't accept that the unpleasant emotion is there, we're likely to continue thinking in such a way that we feed that emotion. Mindfulness does the work of recognizing and accepting—not suppressing, not fighting. This is a nonviolent way of dealing with yourself, because the pain is you; it's not your enemy. And mindfulness is you—it helps you transform the pain. The same is true for pleasant feelings like happiness. We need to give ourselves permission to be happy and to continue to nourish our happiness so that it stays for a long time.

3. Next, embrace the emotion with mindfulness, like a parent embracing their crying baby. When a baby cries, a parent picks up and holds the baby tenderly. The parent doesn't yet know the cause of the baby's suffering, but the fact that they're holding the baby makes the baby suffer less. In the beginning, we may not know where our suffering has come from, but because we are able to recognize, accept, and embrace it tenderly, we already feel better.

4. Then look deeply into the emotion. The light of our mindfulness helps us to see the roots of our difficult emotions and how these roots have been nourished by our thinking and perceptions. Seeing the emotion clearly in this way is essential to transforming the compost of difficult emotions into the flowers of joy, peace, and happiness.

5. Finally, understand that we are more than just an emotion. Even in the grip of a strong emotion, we can see that that emotion is impermanent and ever changing. We see that the territory of our being is large and one emotion is just a tiny thing. With this insight, we know that transformation is possible.

Cultivating Gratitude

Besides learning to deal with painful emotions, the other important dimension of emotional regulation is to learn to intentionally cultivate positive attitudes and states of mind such as gratitude and kindness. In Bhutan, the Buddhist culture there might relate these prosocial emotions with the "four immeasurables"—or four sublime virtues—to actively cultivate happiness: loving kindness, compassion, empathetic joy, and equanimity. These can be expressed today in simple terms of gratitude and kindness toward ourselves and others.

Gratitude is a state of mind expressing appreciation for what one has—as opposed to, say, a consumer-oriented emphasis on what one wants or needs—and it's currently receiving a great deal of attention as a facet of positive psychology. Gratitude is what is poured into the glass to make it half full. Studies show that gratitude can be deliberately cultivated, and it can increase the sense of well-being and happiness among those who practice it. In addition, grateful thinking—and especially expressing gratitude to others—is associated with increased levels of energy, optimism, and empathy.

Studies have shown many benefits of practicing gratitude regularly:[*]

PHYSICAL

✳ Stronger immune system

✳ Fewer aches and pains

✳ Lower blood pressure

✳ Longer and better sleep

PSYCHOLOGICAL

✳ Higher levels of positive emotions

✳ Feeling more alert, alive, and awake

✳ More optimism and happiness

SOCIAL

✳ Feeling more helpful, generous, and compassionate

✳ Becoming more forgiving

✳ Being more outgoing

✳ Feeling less lonely and isolated

Gratitude has two components. The first is an affirmation of goodness. We affirm that there are good things in the world, the gifts and benefits we've received. This doesn't mean that life is perfect; it doesn't ignore complaints, burdens, and hassles. But when we look at life as a whole, gratitude encourages us to identify some amount of goodness in it.

The second part of gratitude is figuring out where that goodness comes from—specifically, the source that is outside of ourselves, not anything we've done ourselves, in which we might take pride. We can appreciate positive traits in ourselves, but the point is to acknowledge

---

[*]Joshua Brown and Joel Wong, "How Gratitude Changes You and Your Brain," Greater Good Magazine, June 6, 2017, *https://greatergood.berkeley.edu/article/item/how_gratitude_changes_you_and_your_brain*.

and be grateful for the people who gave us the many gifts, big and small, that help us achieve the goodness in our lives. For example, if someone compliments your cooking or gardening skills, remember who sparked your interest in those activities or taught you. Feel gratitude for your grandparents, who maintained a beautiful garden long into their old age, for the person who taught you how to cook the meal that received such high praise (your mother or father? An old college friend? A favorite cooking website?). Below are some formal ways of practicing gratitude, both by yourself and with others.

Practice

Gratitude Circle

The participants sit in a circle. You might put something like a vase of flowers in the middle of the circle. Have a nice piece of wood or bamboo available to serve as a "talking stick"—whoever has the stick can talk and will not be interrupted. When someone receives the talking stick, they describe their appreciation of or gratitude to the pupil on their left—perhaps gratitude for something they did or simply for their presence. Then they pass the stick to that person, who expresses gratitude for the next person. Continue until each person has expressed and received appreciation.

Gratitude Letter

Sit down and write a letter to someone who has exerted a positive influence in your life but whom you have not properly thanked. This can be a teacher or a mentor from your past, a grandparent, a friend, a loved one, or anyone else who helped you in some way. The letter doesn't have to be long, but make sure that you're specific about what the person did and how it affected you.

Gratitude Journal

At the end of the day, take a few minutes to write a list of five things about that day for which you are grateful. If you had a bad day and are struggling to think of anything (or even if you're not), remind yourself of the things you take for granted. Imagine losing some of the things that you take for granted, such as your home, your loved ones, your friends, your ability to see or hear or walk, or anything that currently gives you comfort. Imagine getting each of these things back, one by one, and consider how grateful you would be for each and every one.

Cultivating Kindness

Selfless acts of giving—a smile, a word of encouragement, or the offer of a helping hand—result in an emotional uplift not only for others but also for ourselves. Research has shown that kindness can be a major contributor to increased levels of happiness. Performing acts of kindness may well be a choice, but the ability and the tendency to be kind appear to be something innate, something that we have even in infancy.

Research conducted by Dr. Michael Tomasello of the Max Planck Institute demonstrated that children begin to help others at an early age.[*] A fourteen-month-old child seeing an adult experiencing difficulty, such as struggling to open a door because their hands are full, will automatically attempt to help.

Toddlers have a reputation for being stubborn, selfish, and incapable of sharing. But researchers from the Max Planck Institute for

---

[*] "Three-Year-Olds Help Victims of Injustice," Max Planck Gesellschaft (June 18, 2015), *https://www.mpg.de/9266847/three-year-olds-help-victims-of-injustice*.

Evolutionary Anthropology in Leipzig (Germany) and the Univer-
sity of Manchester (UK) have found that children as young as three
actually will show a surprising level of concern for others and an
intuitive sense of restorative justice. Young children prefer to return
lost items to their rightful owners, the studies show. If for some
reason that is not an option, young children will still prevent a third
party from taking what does not belong to them. What is more,
both three- and five-year-old children are just as likely to respond
to the needs of another individual—even when that individual is a
puppet—as they are to their own.

When we perform acts of kindness, we are being true to our own
nature, and this naturally makes us feel good. Furthermore, studies have
demonstrated that the psychological benefits of kindness are actually
reflected in the neural circuitry of the brain.* When we allow ourselves
to be kind, regularly engaging in random acts of kindness, we create
neural pathways that enhance feelings of well-being and the natural
flow of feel-good endorphins and mood-elevating neurotransmitters.

The warm feeling of well-being that washes over you when you've
done something kind isn't just in your head. It's in your brain chem-
icals, too. Acts of kindness can release hormones that contribute to
your mood and overall well-being. The practice is so effective it's
being formally incorporated into some types of psychotherapy.

Another fascinating feature of kindness is that it appears to be
contagious. When we perform an act of kindness, it often encourages
others to act in a similar way. When we are kind, we help make our
world a kinder place to live in. A study conducted by a University of
Pennsylvania research team headed by Dr. Martin Seligman looked at
the effects of writing a thank-you letter and personally delivering it to

---

* "The Science of Kindness," Cedars Sinai (February 13, 2019), *https://*
www.cedars-sinai.org/blog/science-of-kindness.html.

someone who had never been properly thanked for their kindness—an act of kindness and gratitude toward someone who had themselves been kind.* Participants who did this immediately experienced a massive increase in happiness, with benefits lasting up to a month after. Kindness is one of the most important habits that we should develop on our path to real and sustainable happiness. It is key to a good life: one in which we will remain healthy physically, mentally, and emotionally.

Practical Acts of Kindness

Here are some examples of simple acts of kindness that we can perform and that we can encourage our children to perform. You may wish to keep a kindness diary to keep track of the acts of kindness you've performed and how the recipient reacted and felt about it.

* ✳ Hold doors open for others.

* ✳ Let others enter a room or building before you.

* ✳ Say good morning with a smile to your colleagues, teacher, or classmates.

* ✳ Volunteer to be a tutor or mentor in a school, especially if there is an academic subject you are knowledgeable about.

* ✳ Give someone a compliment at least once every day.

* ✳ Color a picture, make a gift, or send a treat to a grandparent or another elderly person.

* ✳ Donate your unwanted toys and books to children who are in need.

---

* "In Praise of Gratitude," *Harvard Health* (blog), *Harvard Health Publishing*, November 21, 2012, *https://math.montana.edu/parker/courses/STAT401/project2_gratitude.pdf*.

* Write a thank-you note to your (or your child's) teacher, coach, mentor, or someone who has influenced you (or your child) in a positive way.

* Pick up the trash around your school or office or a local park.

* Call your grandparent(s) or other special family members who you do not see often.

* Write a note to your parent(s) or grandparent(s) and tell them why they are special to you.

* Smile! Smiling is easy, and happiness is contagious!

Cultivating positive attitudes such as kindness, gratitude, and altruism has a beneficial impact not only on the one practicing it but also on others: friends, colleagues, family, and the larger community.

Dear reader, please try these out for yourself. Observe how displaying kindness and gratitude brings happiness and joy to the one receiving it, but maybe even more to the one who offers it.

A few years ago, I travelled through Bhutan with Brother David Steindl-Rast,* whose message is centered around gratitude. Brother David was ninety years old at the time, and travelling on Bhutanese roads can be challenging, with many road blocks due to weather condition in the Himalayas. I was amazed by the positive attitude he would always display, no matter how difficult the situation was. When our bus had to stop for an unknown amount of time because a boulder had fallen on the road, and everyone else was getting impatient, he was grateful for the opportunity to have time to enjoy the scenery and to make friends with the people who were around. It was almost magical; whenever Brother David stepped out of the bus, he was immediately surrounded by children who were attracted by his kind smile

---

* https://gratefulness.org/brother-david/about-brother-david/.

and friendly manners. They did not ask anything from him, they just enjoyed being in the presence of this gentle old gentleman.

To conclude, a poem by Danusha Laméris:

SMALL KINDNESSES

I've been thinking about the way, when you walk
down a crowded aisle, people pull in their legs
to let you by. Or how strangers still say "bless you"
when someone sneezes, a leftover
from the Bubonic plague. "Don't die," we are saying.
And sometimes, when you spill lemons
from your grocery bag, someone else will help you
pick them up. Mostly, we don't want to harm each other.
We want to be handed our cup of coffee hot,
and to say thank you to the person handing it. To smile
at them and for them to smile back. For the waitress
to call us honey when she sets down the bowl of clam chowder,
and for the driver in the red pick-up truck to let us pass.
We have so little of each other, now. So far
from tribe and fire. Only these brief moments of exchange.
What if they are the true dwelling of the holy, these
fleeting temples we make together when we say, "Here,
have my seat," "Go ahead—you first," "I like your hat."

4

TRANSFORMING VIOLENCE AND HATRED WITH COMPASSION AND LOVING KINDNESS

A SIGNIFICANT ENCOUNTER IN A MILITARY PRISON IN THE MIDDLE EAST

I begin this chapter with an experience that played a central role in my understanding of the impact of connecting with and caring for others beyond our prejudices and superficial perceptions.

During the time I worked with the International Committee of the Red Cross, one of my jobs was to train field delegates whose task it was to visit prisoners of war. This meant that I had to understand the situation in the war zones, so I worked as a field delegate myself in many different countries.

The first time I visited a detention center, it was in a military prison in the Middle East. I spent most of the day privately (without a prison guard present) interviewing the dozens of detainees, the youngest of whom was fifteen, the oldest over eighteen. I listened to one story after another, tales of violence, fear, injustice, hatred, and despair. Taking all these stories into my heart, it was easy to feel compassion for the detainees and to feel anger arising for the soldiers guarding the prison, who had all the power, weapons, and authority.

At one point, as I was taking a short break in the courtyard, resting from the intensity of the encounters and the stench and the claustrophobic atmosphere in the prison cells, a young soldier came to sit next to me. I felt he wanted to talk to me. He was very young—most soldiers are very young, as war is always about old men sending young men to do things that they would not do themselves.

I asked his age and found that he was several years younger than my own son. He began to tell me about his life before the military, about journeys he had taken and countries he had visited, and about how he had been active in his community, helping teenagers who had problems with their families. He told me that when he left the army, he wanted to study education and do something useful for young people. I sensed that he wanted to show me another side of himself— he needed me to see beyond the uniform he wore and the machine gun he carried. I must admit, however, that I was not inclined to listen to him or to engage in a real conversation. After we had talked for a while, he looked at me directly and asked, "Do you think I am a bad person?"

The question touched me deeply. I realized how easy it is to perceive only the soldier, the one with power, and assume he was oppressing prisoners. In a flash, I realized that in a different situation, I could have been the one with the machine gun, and he could have been the humanitarian worker wearing the Red Cross insignia. And I could not be absolutely sure that if I had been the one with the weapon, I would have not been more cruel and harsher on the prisoners than he might have been. So I told him sincerely: "No, I don't think you are a bad person. I understand that you are in a difficult situation that is not your choice, but you have the possibility to be as humane as you can, given the circumstances."

This experience was an eye-opener for me, and it reminded me of a much-loved poem by Thich Nhat Hanh that I knew almost by heart but had never been able to put into practice in real life:

PLEASE CALL ME BY MY TRUE NAMES
Thich Nhat Hanh

Do not say that I'll depart tomorrow, because even today I still arrive.

Look deeply: I arrive in every second to be a bud on a spring branch,
to be a tiny bird, with wings still fragile, learning to sing in my new nest,
to be a caterpillar in the heart of a flower, to be a jewel hiding itself in
a stone.

I still arrive, in order to laugh and to cry, in order to fear and to hope.
The rhythm of my heart is the birth and death of all that are alive.

I am the mayfly metamorphosing on the surface of the river, and I am the
bird which, when spring comes, arrives in time to eat the mayfly.

I am the frog swimming happily in the clear pond,
and I am also the grass-snake who, approaching in silence, feeds itself on
the frog.

I am the child in Uganda, all skin and bones, my legs as thin as bamboo sticks,
and I am the arms merchant, selling deadly weapons to Uganda.

I am the twelve-year-old girl, refugee on a small boat,
who throws herself into the ocean after being raped by a sea pirate,
and I am the pirate, my heart not yet capable of seeing and loving.

I am a member of the politburo, with plenty of power in my hands, and
I am the man who has to pay his "debt of blood" to my people dying
slowly in a forced labor camp.

My joy is like spring, so warm it makes flowers bloom in all walks of life.
My pain is like a river of tears, so full it fills the four oceans.

Please call me by my true names,
so I can hear all my cries and laughs at once, so I can see that my joy and
pain are one.

Please call me by my true names, so I can wake up,
and so the door of my heart can be left open, the door of compassion.

A central question is to understand how—beyond the psychological and inner transformation of suffering in compassion and kindness—we can also contribute to creating social and economic systems that are conducive environments for the development of these central social skills.

Care for Others

Harvard's longest study of adult life showed that the strongest predictor of happiness, well-being, health, and success is the quality of our relationships: "Our study has shown that the people who fare the best were the people who leaned in to relationships with family, with friends, with community."[*]

Although we intuitively know that the quality of our relationships determine, to a large extent, our happiness as well as our unhappiness, the social skills that are the foundation of good relationships are hardly taught or practiced in schools, universities, or workplaces. Let us look at some of the ingredients of good, nourishing, healthy relationships.

As already discussed, compared to many other animals on the planet, human beings are small, slow, and weak. And yet we have unequivocally won the competition for global domination. What allowed us, as physical underdogs, to claim this unlikely victory? There are many ways of answering this question, but psychologists increasingly believe that it is our interpersonal faculties, especially our ability to cooperate with and understand others, that led to our species' success. These social skills, in turn, are supported by the multifaceted psychological construct of empathy.

Empathy is the ability to feel the emotions of someone else. It is the very foundation of social awareness. Research has shown that empathy

---

[*] Liz Mineo, "Good Genes Are Nice, but Joy Is Better," *The Harvard Gazette* (April 11, 2017), *https://news.harvard.edu/gazette/story/2017/04/over-nearly-80-years -harvard-study-has-been-showing-how-to-live-a-healthy-and-happy-life.*

is a natural ability and manifests at an early age, because it is linked to a function of the brain related to the mirror neurons.* Even babies perceive and react to the emotions of their parents or caregivers. It is easy to see how this ability to perceive the inner state of another person must have played a central role in our evolutionary success.

While empathy has many benefits, it also has a downside when it comes to the suffering of others. When we witness too much suffering—which is common among professionals working in the "helping" professions like health care, education, and humanitarian work—it can cause "empathic distress," which can lead to burnout. Finding a solution to this problem is critical, and a key to that is the distinction between empathy and compassion. These two feelings are closely linked—compassion builds empathy, and vice versa—but they are also different.

When we empathize, we share another's feelings, but when we show compassion, we do not necessarily share those feelings. Compassion arises from our commitment to help others, when we see that someone is in need of help. Linking compassion to empathy can help to lessen the pain that empathy alone can cause, as compassion can transform the suffering in something positive.

To summarize, we could say that living in harmony with others depends on three processes that are closely interrelated but depend on three different neuronal pathways:

Experience sharing is based on affective empathy, our inborn ability to experience other people's emotions. It is related to emotional contagion and can lead to empathic distress if we are confronted with too much suffering.

Mentalizing is related to cognitive empathy. It is not simply feeling other people's emotions but also understanding what someone else is experiencing and why. In addition, it is the ability that allows us

---

*Larry Charles Stevens and Christopher Chad Woodruff, eds., *The Neuroscience of Empathy, Compassion, and Self-Compassion* (London: Academic Press, 2018).

to understand other people's ideas, opinions, and points of view, even though they might differ from our own. It is related to what is usually called "perspective taking" or "theory of mind." These processes have been extensively researched in the field of cognitive psychology when studying the development of the child.

Compassion or empathic concern is related to empathy, because it is based on our ability to share and understand other people's experience. However, it goes beyond empathy because it motivates us to help others, to alleviate their suffering, and to behave in a prosocial manner.

Training Deep Listening Skills

Learning to listen is the foundation of empathy and compassion training, and a good starting point is to observe the way we listen to others.

More often than not in everyday life, when we're listening to someone else, we also have our own thoughts going through our mind. In our heads, we are agreeing or disagreeing, reacting to, and judging what we're listening to. These opinions of ours are based on our past experiences and what we know about the subject, and it also depends on our opinion of the person who is speaking—whether we respect them, whether we consider them to be important. Furthermore, while the other person is speaking, we are usually already preparing a response to them—so we're not really listening to what they have to say.

If we observe ourselves honestly, we might realize that this is the manner in which we are listening—or, rather, *not truly* listening to others—most of the time. Becoming aware of our tendency not to really listen is the first step leading to deep listening.

This first level of listening could be described as "distracted listening." When, through mindfulness practice, we become able to direct our awareness intentionally, we can master the art of keeping our mind still while the other person is speaking. This inner silence allows us to practice what could be called "factual listening," meaning that we can take in the information that we receive without reacting or judging right away, agreeing or disagreeing, or preparing our answer to what is being said.

This does not mean that we will not, at some point, evaluate what has been said and decide whether we agree or disagree with it. But before that, we must be able to really listen. Without truly listening to what is being said, we cannot pass a valid judgment.

Factual listening is the foundation of any scientific approach, because it allows us to take in information that may contradicts our previous knowledge base and therefore, potentially, allows us to broaden our understanding.

The next level of listening is "empathic listening." This goes beyond simply taking in the information we receive from others. It implies that we also perceive the emotional dimension what is being said: the state of mind, emotions, and body language of our interlocutor. We are aware of not only what is being said but also what is *not* being said. The ability to practice empathic listening is the foundation of social awareness and of care for others.

To summarize the levels of listening:

Distracted listening: While listening, we're busy with our own thoughts and inner chatter. We tend to agree with ideas that reinforce our previous opinions and disagree with contradicting views, without seriously assessing their validity. We constantly react and judge, and often do so on the basis of our opinion of the person who is speaking. In addition, we get distracted by other inputs—how often have you seen someone (even yourself) checking their phone or texting while having a conversation?

Factual listening: We are able to listen from a place of inner stillness and attention, fully focused on what is being said, holding back judgment and reaction, so that we can completely absorb all the data and information.

Empathic listening: Not only are we able to focus our cognitive attention on our interlocutor, but we also open our heart to perceive the feelings and emotions that are conveyed. We observe the body language and the tone of the voice, we sense what motivates the speaker, and we perceive their inner state of mind. Thus we are also attentive to what is not being said, to the silence between the words and to the deeper intentions.

Learning to observe the way we listen to others, simply noticing when we are moving from one level of listening to the other, is an important foundation of developing care for others.

The Healing Power of Compassionate Listening

A few years ago, my mother passed away in the south of France. At the time, I was in Vietnam in the community of the Peaceful Bamboo Family (Tinh Truc Gia, or TTG). My sister called to tell me the news. Our mother was elderly and had been severely ill for the previous few years, so her death was not entirely unexpected. Nevertheless, the news filled me with sadness and also with a feeling of guilt that I had not been by her side during her last moments on earth.

In the Peaceful Bamboo community, we have a weekly practice called Sharing from the Heart. Every Thursday evening all the members of the community take a shower after their day's work, dress in fresh clothes, and gather for dinner. Special care is given to the setting of the table and the presentation of the food to create a festive atmosphere. After we recite some verses expressing our gratitude to nature and to the many people who contributed to filling our plates with healthy and delicious food, we take our meal in silence and eat as mindfully as we can to appreciate the taste of the natural ingredients, feeling gratitude for our daily sustainment.

After the meal, the whole community gathers in a circle around a fountain where we have placed floating candles, and in this magical atmosphere, after a moment of mindfulness meditation, each member of the community is invited to share whatever experiences, feelings, joys, or pain they're currently having. The circle is comprised both of educators and young people living with various kinds of disabilities, and it's always moving to experience how in these moments of deep sharing and compassionate listening, the distinction between the "disabled" and "normal" people completely disappears, replaced by a profound sense of our shared humanity. Despite differences of age, gender, nationality, cultural background, or ability, we fundamentally share human joys and suffering that create a common ground for a meeting at a deeper level of the heart.

On that evening, I shared with the community about my mother's passing away, about my sadness, and also about guilt I felt that I had not been with her in this important moment of transition. Everyone listened intently with great empathy, and after a long moment of silence, Duc, one of the young men in the community living with Down syndrome, indicated that he wanted to share something. He said that he really felt with me, because he had lost his own mother a few years earlier and that he missed her every single day. He then turned to all the others and said, "If you're so lucky that your mother is still alive, please don't take it for granted. Take the opportunity to be with her and to tell her that you love her, otherwise you might regret it later on, once she is gone." Although it was not easy for this young man to express himself verbally in a fluent way, his message was clear, and I could feel that everyone in the circle felt deeply moved and took it to heart. For me, this testimony of empathy and compassion was deeply soothing. It reminded me of the universality of loss and grieving and that I wasn't alone in this moment but part of our human community.

I flew back to Europe as soon as I could to join the ceremonies around my mother's death. My whole family gathered to commemorate her life and to honor her departure. It was my task to give the eulogy and to share with all the family and our friends some aspects of her life story and some memories that we held dear. Again, it was quite an emotional moment, saying goodbye to a loved one. After I spoke, I went back to sit on a bench together with other family members. My little grandson Alexis, who was six years old at the time, sat next to me.

Softly, Alexis took my hand, caressed it gently, and, looking up at me, said in a sweet tone, "Are you okay, Grandpa? Are you not too sad?"

It was deeply moving to experience how a little six-year-old child could not only experience but also share his compassion. At that moment I looked deeply into my own emotions and tried to have a clearer understanding of what my grief and sadness were about. I realized that it was, of course, knowing that I would never again see my mother in her physical body, but this, in a way, was not the deepest source of the pain. I had been travelling frequently and, although I visited her regularly, being in her presence wasn't the central and most important part of our relationship. I realized that my grief arose more from the sense of loss of the care and love that I had received from her ever since I was born.

For most of us, our mother is the first human being that we completely depend on, and that dependence and bond endure for years. Although our social circle gradually widens, and we might have many other deep relationships in our lives, the motherly love that we received as infants and young children creates a basis for all the relationships that we create later in life.

Since Sigmund Freud and the psychoanalysis he helped develop, it has become common in Western societies to blame mothers for many of their children's psychological difficulties. Although I can understand the rationale behind this attitude, I find it a sad phenomenon, because it overlooks the amazing gift of life that mothers bestow upon us. Even though we might acknowledge that not all mothers have an equal ability to manifest their love in a skillful way, fundamentally, it is their love and care that has enabled us to grow and to develop.

There is a striking difference between the Western and Asian relationships between children and their parents. I have never met an Asian person who did not express the deepest gratitude, love, and affection for their parents, but I have met many Western people who express a lot of blame when speaking about theirs. I don't think that Asian parents are necessarily better than Western parents, but I do believe that, by and large, Asian culture nurtures the feeling of gratitude toward one's parents in a more healthy way than the critical relationship that has become so common in contemporary Western culture.

But to return to the story—when my grandson took my hand and I realized that the grief I was feeling was related to the feeling of loss of my mother's love, it dawned upon me that although her physical body was soon to be cremated, her love and care were still present, continuing to manifest through the heart and the hand of her great-grandson next to me. This insight helped me to transform my sadness, and I felt deeply that the stream of love and care that flowed from past generations through me to future generations did not end with the disappearance of one person. I knew that the best way for me to pay back the debt of gratitude I felt toward my mother was to perpetuate the love and care I had received and bestow it to my children, grandchildren, students, and friends. If I could do that, she would live on. Her disappearance would merely be an illusion, and, at a deeper level, I could continue to feel her presence.

In the years since her passing, I have thought of my mother every single day. The main feeling I experience is not of sadness but having been blessed.

Practicing Deep Listening, Social Awareness, and Relationship Management

Exercise 1: Dialogue Walk

A dialogue walk is intended to take participants to a more attentive level of listening and to raise awareness and understanding from another perspective. The role of the listener is to focus completely on the words of their partner, without interruption, and to observe their own listening: Am I paying attention? When do I notice thoughts coming? When do I feel the need to make a comment? When am I judging? As in every other form of mindfulness practice, such reactions are seen as a normal way of paying attention. Their role in this exercise is for you to notice them without judgment, to immediately allow them, and to redirect your full attention back to your partner.

The role of the speaker is to become completely immersed in their own thoughts and to verbalize those thoughts as they come up, so as to reach a deeper understanding.

A dialogue walk takes thirty to fifty minutes. This amount of time is needed to move together beyond just providing information and to reach a deeper point of reflection. Also consider including time for a group discussion after the exercise.

If you, as facilitator, are introducing a group of people to this activity for the first time, you should begin with a short description of the three levels of listening. Then you will introduce the purpose of the exercise and the roles of speaker and listener. The group divides into pairs, and the individuals in each pair should take turns as speaker and listener. This means that each person has about fifteen to twenty minutes to talk while their partner listens, and then vice versa. Before the partners change roles, advise them to walk together in silence for several minutes before the second person starts to talk. This period of stillness is a critical element and should not be left out. Another important element of the exercise is that the pairs do actually go for a walk. This helps create a safe space in which the speaker may offer their thoughts as unfiltered as possible, thus allowing for a more open form of communication, which can often lead to deeper insights.

When both partners have finished speaking, they should have a free dialogue about whatever comes up between them in that particular moment—thus really entering into a shared dialogue.

As a facilitator, you can frame the dialogue walk in order to fit the overall intention of your workshop or class. Encourage participants to share personal stories and be careful to stress that each participant is obliged not to share anything their partner says in the dialogue walk unless they have been granted permission to do so.

After the dialogue walk, it is helpful to debrief the whole group. Begin with a few minutes of silence in which the participants can write down any significant insights, experiences, or observations in their journals. During the group's debriefing, invite contributions openly and without pressure. For example, you may wish to ask how participants felt in the two different roles and what was the most important outcome for them.

Exercise 2: Paraphrasing or Reformulation

Paraphrasing is repeating in your own words what you have heard someone else say. Paraphrasing is powerful means of deepening the understanding of both you and your partner, and it can greatly increase the impact of a person's comments. Each person understands things in different ways, so paraphrasing is a practice that increases the likelihood that more people will understand what has been said.

When you are practicing this exercise, put the focus of the paraphrase on what your partner said, not on what you wanted them to say. That is, don't say, "I believe what you meant to say was . . ." Instead, say, "If I'm hearing you right, are you saying that . . .?"

Phrase the paraphrase as a question, so that you're not telling your partner what they said. And put the ownership of the paraphrase on yourself ("If I'm hearing you right . . .?" or "If I understand you correctly . . .?").

Put the ownership of the other person's words on them, so they have the responsibility and opportunity to refine their original comments in response to your question ("If I understand you right, you're saying that . . .?" or "You believe that . . .?" or "You feel that . . .?").

Don't judge or evaluate the other person's comments. Don't say, "I wonder if you really believe that?" or "Don't you feel out-on-a-limb making that comment?"

You can use a paraphrase to validate your impression of the other's comments. For instance, you could say, "So you were frustrated when . . .?"

The paraphrase should be shorter than your partner's original comments.

If the other person responds to your paraphrase by saying that you didn't understand them, give them another chance or two to restate their position and try with your own paraphrasing to understand them.

Looking back at the encounter I had with the young soldier, I realize that at first I had not been able to listen deeply; but gradually, I spontaneously started reformulating what he was telling me as a way to try and overcome my own bias, and after that a real meeting became possible, despite our differences.

5

THE INTERDEPENDENCE BETWEEN CARE FOR OTHERS AND CARE FOR THE PLANET

For one human being to love another human being:
that is perhaps the most difficult task that has been
given to us, the ultimate, the final problem and proof, the
work for which all other work is merely preparation.

—RAINER MARIA RILKE

In our effort to understand true happiness, we can identify two obstacles on our path: ignorance, or disconnection from self, and greed, which disconnects us from our natural environment and creates a situation where our fellow humans are perceived not as sisters and brothers but as competitors fighting over scarce resources. Insatiable desires lead each one of us to claim a much bigger share of the natural resources than our legitimate portion, and this leads to violence. The current economic system is built on the assumption of scarcity of resources and on the idea of the *Homo economicus*, a purely rational being that tries to maximize its own profit at any cost.

This vision of humanity and the system that has been built from it has become a self-fulfilling prophecy, replacing solidarity, generosity, and altruism with egoism, greed, and destructive competition.

I became more conscious of the situation during my missions in Darfur when I was working with the Red Cross. Although many ideological, political, religious, and ethnic reasons are put forward when explaining wars, when one looks at maps and compares the location of conflicts and areas involved in the production and transportation of oil, one cannot fail to notice that the two almost always overlap.

With Darfur, however, I realized that there is no oil in this region, which is located in West Sudan; in fact, there is hardly anything in this desert, yet it has been the theater of a violent conflict that has killed more than a million people and displaced many more. Most conflicts in our time are related to oil, but the conflict in Darfur is related to a resource that is far more precious: water.

Since time immemorial, two populations have lived in this barren land: Arab shepherds raising camels, horses, and sheep, and African farmers cultivating crops. Water has always been in short supply, and there have often been conflicts over it. Due to climate change, the situation has become worse, and the conflict—which used to be fought with sticks and stones, swords and spears—is now, because of the international arms industry, fought with modern weapons. The international strategic interests of other nations have only worsened the situation.

Violent wars have been fought over oil—in Afghanistan, Iraq, Libya, Syria, and elsewhere—but people can live without oil, even if, perhaps, not as comfortably. Without water, however, people cannot survive even a few days. This made me realize that the conflicts of the future, if we don't do anything to control climate change, could involve a kind of violence that we have not yet seen. I became aware of the fact that the current economic system, with its emphasis on profit at all costs, is one of the most important causes of conflicts. The more I reflected on development and progress, the more convinced I became that the way the concept of economic growth is promoted by most international organizations actually contributed to the suffering and destruction that I was seeing in so many regions of the world. So I asked myself if would it be possible to redefine development and progress in such a way that it would truly serve the well-being of all the people and the health of our planet.

We will continue this reflection when we describe Gross National Happiness as an alternative development paradigm. Before continuing, however, I would like to share a reflection on the sacredness of water.

Water Is Life

Some years ago, on a mission with the Red Cross, I crossed a desert in the Middle East. The landscape was barren and desolate—sand, stones, and dust. It started to rain one night, and the next morning, as we continued our journey, we witnessed a kind of miracle: little flowers and green shoots were covering the desert in an amazing display of color and life. Seeing this rare display reminded me of a fundamental but too often forgotten truth: water is the source of life.

All life forms originate in water—including humans, who originate in a water bubble growing inside our mother's womb. We are water beings, and we belong to the water cycle; we are part of it. As part of the water cycle, we can connect with the reality of our interdependence with all sentient beings and the earth herself.

When we ask ourselves why the earth is the only planet (that we know of) that supports such a variety of life—from single-celled bacteria to complex vertebrates—we discover it is because the earth possesses something unique that no other planet we know of in the same way: the gift of water.

Water is something the earth has in a significant quantity and which holds all life together. Without it, life as we know it would be impossible.

Water is in the soil, in the air we breathe. Water fills the oceans and the seas, rendering all life on this planet possible. Water is our body. As fetuses, we are 85 percent water; as adults, 70 percent. This is true not only of human beings but for all beings. The food we eat is also mainly made up of water—a tomato (95 percent), a potato (78 percent).

Yet the shocking reality is that today, more than a billion people worldwide do not have access to safe drinking water, with waterborne diseases causing nearly two million deaths each year—mostly children. At the same time, multinational companies want to privatize water and treat it as a mere commodity. This is in addition to climate change, a growing human population, and the spread of Western-style consumerism all over the world, threatening to make water the next resource-sparking conflict. And because humans and animals cannot survive without water for more than a few days, it's difficult to imagine the consequences severe water shortage could have and the ferocity it could trigger. Clearly our relationship with water must change.

I believe that we need to see this "water challenge" in a larger context. It is but a symptom of the disconnection of the dominant economic, social, political, and ideological systems with nature as a whole. This disconnection from nature manifests in so many ways: environmental destruction; soil, water, and air pollution; and animal exploitation and abuse.

Yet the disconnection between current social and economic systems and nature is merely indicative of a general tendency: the disconnection actually takes place in our own consciousness, and only in our own minds can the reconnection take place, through the intentional training of mindfulness and compassion.

Mindfulness strengthens our ability to perceive clearly what is going on inside us and around us, and compassion enables us to relate to the world in a less exploitative way. When we become aware of the fundamental interdependence of all life forms, we realize that water—as the very source of life—is sacred. And it has to be treated accordingly.

There is no doubt that modernity, science, and technology have brought about impressive progress and development that has contributed to a better life for many. But progress has also come with a price: by focusing almost entirely on satisfying the *material* needs of humans, we have lost sight of many other dimensions of value. These include the psychological, spiritual, relational, and artistic aspects of humanity, which are equally important. In addition, we have forgotten that if we do not take into consideration the well-being other life forms, and of the planet herself, even material human needs cannot be met in a sustainable way.

Unfortunately, by and large, the deeper reality of mutual interdependence is not acknowledged by the dominant systems. During my last stay in Vietnam, I witnessed a dramatic example of the consequences of this mindless disconnection: millions of dead fish had washed up along the coast of Vietnam's four central provinces. According to a figure given by an official at the time, the disaster had killed at least a hundred tons of fish.

At the same time, it is encouraging to see that there is an awakening, especially among young people, about the urgency of addressing the ecological challenge humanity faces. Many spiritual leaders from various traditions are speaking out, contributing to a new awareness of our interdependence with the environment. Thich Nhat Hanh demonstrated this sort of spiritual leadership when he wrote:

Dear Mother Earth,

I bow my head before you as I look deeply and recognize that you are present in me and that I'm a part of you. I was born from you and you are always present, offering me everything I need for my nourishment and growth. My mother, my father, and all my ancestors are also your children. We breathe your fresh air. We drink your clear water. We eat your nourishing food. Your herbs heal us when we're sick.

You are the Mother of all beings. I call you by the human name Mother and yet I know your mothering nature is more vast and ancient than humankind. We are just one young species of your many children. All the millions of other species who live—or have lived—on Earth are also your children. You aren't a person, but I know you are not less than a person either. You are a living breathing being in the form of a planet.*

---

*Thich Nhat Hanh, *Love Letter to Planet Earth* (Berkeley: Parallax Press, 2013).

It is time to rethink our overall concept of development from one motivated by economic growth at any cost to one focused on happiness for all people and well-being for all forms of life.

If we redefine our development strategy in this way, not only water but also the whole of the planet and all living beings on it will have a chance to flourish and thrive.

Care for the Environment and the Planet

At its essence, sustainability means ensuring prosperity and environmental protection without compromising the ability of future generations to meet their needs. A sustainable world is one where people can escape poverty and enjoy decent work without harming the earth's essential ecosystems and resources; where people can stay healthy and get the food and water they need; where everyone can access clean energy that doesn't contribute to climate change; where women and girls are afforded equal rights and equal opportunity.

—BAN KI-MOON

Contentment Versus Greed: From Self-Care to Care for the Planet

As we have seen, disconnection from ourselves leads to an experience of basic dissatisfaction that, in turn, creates an unceasing desire for fulfillment that cannot be achieved by outer means. Addiction—widespread in many forms—is an example of this process.

Let us see how, once more, *The Little Prince* illustrates this experience:

The next planet was inhabited by a tippler.... "What are you doing there?" he said to the tippler, whom he found settled down in silence before a collection of empty bottles and also a collection of full bottles.

"I am drinking," replied the tippler, with a lugubrious air. "Why are you drinking?" demanded the little prince.

"So that I may forget," replied the tippler.

"Forget what?" enquired the little prince, who already was sorry for him. "Forget that I am ashamed," the tippler confessed, hanging his head. "Ashamed of what?" insisted the little prince, who wanted to help him. "Ashamed of drinking!" The tippler brought his speech to an end and shut himself up in an impregnable silence.

All ancient cultures knew about the interconnectedness of all life forms, often called the web of life, and our forefathers were aware that they were just one species among the many that inhabit our planet. Furthermore, they knew of the sacredness of the earth—water, air, fire, rivers, mountains, oceans, and all living beings. Although scientific knowledge has enabled us to master natural laws and material processes, it has disconnected us from the awareness of the sacredness of nature, and we are beginning to pay a high price for this forgetfulness. The very survival of future generations might be at stake. However, it is important to realize that the root cause of this situation does not lie in governments or multinational companies, but in our own consciousness. By reconnecting truly with ourselves and realizing our interdependence with all other life forms, we become, once again, embedded in the web of life. Our endless greed can gradually be transformed into gratitude and contentment.

Moreover, in our quest for happiness, we need to understand the deep causes of suffering. We have seen that the root cause lies in a disconnection from ourselves and that the healing process begins by reconnecting to our deepest aspirations and highest potential. It has also been shown that a lack of connection with ourselves creates an underlying sense of dissatisfaction that generates insatiable greed that, in turn, has a destructive effect on our planet. Yet, while disconnection from nature might not be experienced as a cause of suffering as clearly as disconnection from self, there is ample scientific evidence to prove the negative consequences, especially on children, of a disconnection from the natural world.

Nature Deficit Disorder Needs Healing

"Nature deficit disorder" is a phrase coined by Richard Louv as a description of the human cost of alienation from nature. Reasons for this alienation include the proliferation of electronic communication, poor urban planning and disappearing open spaces, increased street traffic, a diminished importance of the natural world in public education, and parental fear magnified by news and entertainment media.

An expanding body of scientific evidence suggests that nature deficit disorder contributes to a diminished use of the senses, attention difficulties, obesity, and higher rates of emotional and physical illnesses. Research also suggests that the deficit weakens ecological literacy and stewardship of the natural world, problems that are linked, more broadly, to what health care experts call "the epidemic of inactivity," and to a devaluing of independent play.[*]

Society's nature deficit disorder can be reversed, however, and recent studies focus not so much on what is lost when nature experience fades, but on what is gained through more exposure to natural settings, including parks in urban settings. Care for the environment can only become a reality if the children get enough direct interaction with nature.

---

[*] Martha Driessnack, "Children and Nature-Deficit Disorder," *Journal for Specialists in Pediatric Nursing* 14, no. 1 (2009): 73–75.

The Benefits of More Time in Nature for Children*

Kids get along better. Research has found that children who play in nature have more positive feelings about each other. There is something about being in a natural environment together that stimulates social interaction. Another study showed how playing in a diverse natural environment can reduce or eliminate bullying. In several studies, researchers have found that some of the kids who benefit most are those with attention and learning challenges.

Imagination is enhanced. Early experiences with the natural world have been positively linked with a sense of wonder. Children are more likely to use their imagination outdoors.

Cognitive development is improved. Curiosity and wonder are strong motivators that make children more eager to learn. When children play in natural environments, their play is more diverse. Creative play, in turn, nurtures language and collaborative skills. Spending time in natural environments helps children improve their awareness, reasoning, and observational skills.

Physical health is improved. Children who play regularly in natural environments show more advanced motor fitness, including coordination, balance, and agility. They also get sick less often.

They are less stressed out. Nature buffers the impact of life stress on children and helps them deal with adversity. The greater the amount of nature exposure, the greater the benefits. Nature

---

*Danielle Cohen, "Why Kids Need to Spend Time in Nature," *Child Mind Institute*, https://childmind.org/article/why-kids-need-to-spend-time-in-nature.

helps children develop powers of observation and creativity and instills a sense of peace and connection to the planet.

They are more psychologically mature. A boost in maturity comes from the increased independence and autonomy that free play in nature encourages. Children with more contact with nature score higher on tests of concentration and self-discipline.

They are more environmentally conscious. Kids are more likely to love and protect the environment.

In order to teach children how to treasure nature, kids should be allowed to explore it in their own way and be given the time and opportunity to immerse themselves in its mysteries. Like a perfect mother, the earth welcomes us all with open arms.

In our community in Hué, the Peaceful Bamboo Family, we welcome hundreds of schoolchildren each month, who have an opportunity to reconnect with nature by learning organic gardening. Children are eager to put their hands in the soil, to plant vegetables, to tend to the garden, and to feed the animals. It is deeply moving to witness how happy children can become when working outdoors in nature. Although not every school can have its own vegetable garden, each class can at least have flowers, herbs, and some small vegetables growing in pots on the windowsills. And schools could partner with local gardeners and farmers to organize green camps at least once a year.

> *"Thousands of tired, nerve-shaken, over-civilized*
> *people are beginning to find out that going to the*
> *mountain is going home. Wilderness is a necessity."*
>
> —JOHN MUIR

What is true for children is true for adults, *shinrin-yoku* is a term that means "taking in the forest atmosphere" or "forest bathing." The idea was developed in Japan during the 1980s and has become a cornerstone of preventive health care and healing in Japanese medicine. Researchers, primarily in Japan, have established a robust body of scientific literature on the health benefits of spending time under the canopy of a living forest.[*] The idea is simple: a person is calmed, rejuvenated, and restored simply walking through a natural area in a relaxed way. We have always known this intuitively, but in the past decades, there have been many scientific studies that demonstrate the mechanism behind the healing effects of simply being in wild. Scientifically proven benefits of *shinrin-yoku* include:

* Stronger immune system
* Reduced blood pressure
* Reduced stress
* Improved mood
* Accelerated recovery from surgery or illness
* Increased energy level
* Improved sleep

The practice is simple: go to the forest, walk slowly, breathe deeply, open all your senses.

It is important to realize that reconnecting with nature has a triple effect. First, it helps us reconnect with ourselves. Then, by reconnecting with nature, we tend to be more respectful of our natural environment and learn to care for our precious planet. Finally, and most importantly, it enhances our care for others and thus has a positive effect on society at large.

---

[*] Qing Li, *Forest Bathing: How Trees Can Help You Find Health and Happiness* (New York: Viking, 2018).

From Inner Transformation
to Social Change

In our quest for happiness, we have seen that the first step is to identify the difference between superficial, short-lived pleasures and the sustainable, deep-seated conditions for a happy life: hedonia versus eudaimonia.

The French philosopher Paul Ricoeur describes the goal of human life as "a good life with and for others in fair institutions." It seems necessary to add "in harmony with nature."

In the first part of the book, we have focused our attention on the inner conditions of happiness. This has led us to also look at the main causes of suffering, because true happiness cannot be achieved by denying the reality of suffering, but by learning how to transform suffering in meaningful learning experiences. Thich Nhat Hanh often said, "No mud, no lotus." Without the experience of suffering, we wouldn't be able to develop compassion.

In the Buddhist tradition, it is said that each buddha has a Buddhaland, which is the projection of their pure mind creating a beautiful and harmonious environment. In many sutras, these pure lands are described in great detail, with beautiful nature, trees, flowers, pure streams, and all beings living together in harmony.

It is believed that the earth is the Buddhaland of the historical Buddha, Gautama Shakyamuni. According to a well-known story, at some point, people asked the Buddha, "Why is it that all the other buddhas have perfect Buddhalands, where there is only peace, harmony, and happiness, but your own Buddhaland, the planet earth, is so full of suffering and wars and diseases?" The Buddha answered, "My Buddhaland is the place to learn compassion. If there was no suffering, no one would be able to become compassionate and to develop loving kindness."

This anecdote highlights an important aspect of the quest for happiness. It is not about turning away from real life and from the challenges of our time. It is by facing the difficulties and learning how to transform them. This is how we can achieve a better future.

In our search, we have seen that the first cause of suffering is a disconnection from ourselves and that our modern lifestyle tends to aggravate this sense of alienation, so the first element that we need to cultivate on our path toward happiness is to reconnect deeply with our deepest aspiration, our highest potential, and to align our life and work with the values that we hold dear.

As we have seen, the first step in this direction is by learning to slow down, to stop, and to look within. As long as our awareness is constantly distracted by outer stimuli, our own inner world remains an unknown and foreign territory. As the German poet Rainer Maria Rilke wrote, "The only journey is the one within."

As we reconnect with ourselves, most of us realize that we already have more than enough and that the conditions to be content are more than fulfilled. There are so many aspects of our life that we take for granted and that can become a source of deep gratitude—we have eyes to see the beauty of nature and the lovely smiles of our loved ones, we have ears to hear birds singing at dawn or a majestic symphony, we have legs and feet to walk in the woods, and we have tongues to taste a ripe fruit we've just picked from a tree. Gratitude generates contentment, and contentment allows us to live a simpler—but a more fulfilled—life, and this, in turn, creates a lifestyle that does not need to plunder the resources of nature, but to live, as Satish Kumar, calls it "with elegant simplicity," in harmony with nature.

Reconnecting to self allows us also to reconnect with our environment and our planet, acknowledging the boundless generosity of the natural world, moving from a mindset of scarcity to a mindset of abundance.

Rediscovering the sacredness of all life forms is also the foundation to reconnect on a deeper level with our fellow human beings, as sisters and brothers embarked on our common journey on this beautiful yet fragile planet.

We have seen how deep listening is the very foundation of all other social skills and, in order to be able to listen deeply to others, we must also be able to listen deeply to ourselves.

Empathy, compassion, kindness, and generosity can become the foundation of a new social and economic order that will, at the same time, be fair to all those living on the earth today and sustainable for the well-being of future generations.

All social systems were created by the human mind, and they are neither god-given nor natural laws; because we have created them, we are also able to change them. But these changes need to be rooted in a transformation of our own mindset.

Having explored some aspects of inner transformation that are necessary to meet the challenges of our time, the next part of the book will focus on the structural framework that is necessary to create a conducive environment that will allow for the flourishing of humans and of all life forms.

Gross National Happiness is, among the various new development paradigms, probably the most holistic one, because it entails both the inner and the outer conditions leading towards societal happiness.

It is also the only alternative social system that has already been implemented in a whole country and even enshrined in a national constitution.

This is not to pretend that Bhutan has already reached the goals of Gross National Happiness or that its implementation is perfect in any way, but Bhutan can be seen as a kind of "lab" at the scale of a whole country from which we can learn from both the successes and the failures that it encounters. Foreigners who come to Bhutan for the first time tend to project on it a fantasy image of a paradise on earth—a Shangri-La hidden in the Himalayas—and this projection does not do justice to the reality of the country. Many of us dream that there could be a perfect place somewhere on earth, where all our aspirations and hopes could be fulfilled, but this is not what Bhutan is about.

Bhutan is a small country and is facing many challenges, but it is courageously trying to walk a different path of development.

When scientists conduct experiments in a lab, they don't learn only from their successes—on the contrary, a lot of the learning comes from the experiments that fail. Likewise, to be fair toward Bhutan, we should acknowledge both its successes and its difficulties, because there is much to learn from both when we try to implement a new development paradigm in different contexts.

Empathy, compassion, kindness, and generosity can become the foundation of a new social and economic order that will, at the same time, be fair to all those living on earth today and sustainable for the well-being of future generations.

Having explored some aspects of the inner transformation that are necessary to meet the challenges of our time, the next part of the book will explore the structural framework to create a conducive environment that will allow the flourishing of humans and of all life forms— Gross National Happiness—both as it is specific to Bhutan, as well as aspects that can be implemented in other contexts, from family to small communities, the educational system, the business world, and even to nations.

PART 2

UNDERSTANDING GROSS NATIONAL HAPPINESS AS A NEW DEVELOPMENT PARADIGM

6

FROM GROSS DOMESTIC PRODUCT TO GROSS NATIONAL HAPPINESS

At the end of the Second World War, European economies and infrastructures had been severely damaged. Economic recovery and development was at the center of all political efforts. And truly, the economic development of Europe during the thirty years following the war was spectacular. Already in the 1960s, however, a young generation started challenging a societal model that was narrowly focusing on economic growth and material progress, forgetting the many other needs and dimensions of human life—the psychological, emotional, social, and spiritual needs. The so-called student revolution in the 1960s was a clear message that true happiness cannot be attained by mere material gratification, but there was no credible alternative to the one-sided materialistic, capitalistic model of the Western world. Many turned toward socialism and communism without realizing that although those ideologies seemed different, their goal of achieving happiness through material fulfilment was the same. The deep-seated longing that led millions of young people all over the world to challenge the existing social order was, I believe, the intuition that a different life is possible: one that allows one's deepest values and aspirations to manifest in work and life.

It is worth noting that as long ago as 1968, Robert Kennedy—who at the time was campaigning for the US presidency—articulated the feeling that many were sharing:

> But even if we act to erase material poverty, there is another greater task, which is to confront the poverty of satisfaction—purpose and dignity—that afflicts us all. Too much and for too long, we seemed to have surrendered personal excellence and community values in the mere accumulation of material things. Our Gross National Product, now, is over eight hundred billion dollars a year, but that Gross National Product—if we judge the United States of America by that—that Gross National Product counts air pollution and cigarette advertising, and ambulances to clear our highways of carnage. It counts special locks for our doors and the jails for the people who break them. It counts the destruction of the redwood and the loss of our natural wonder in chaotic sprawl. It counts napalm and nuclear warheads and armored cars for the police to fight the riots in our cities. It counts the television programs that glorify violence in order to sell toys to our children. Yet the Gross National Product does not allow for the health of our children, the quality of their education or the joy of their play. It does not include the beauty of our poetry or the strength of our marriages, the intelligence of our public debate or the integrity of our public officials. It measures neither our wit nor our courage, neither our wisdom nor our learning, neither our compassion nor our devotion to our country. It measures everything, in short, except that which makes life worthwhile. *

In just one sentence, Robert Kennedy spells out the fundamental problem of GDP: "It measures everything, in short, except that which makes life worthwhile." In addition, he points out the two basic flaws of the GDP as a measure of the development of society. The first is that anything that increases economic growth is *per se* beneficial, despite

---

* Robert Kennedy, remarks at the University of Kansas, March 18, 1968.

even Simon Kuznets, who created the GDP measurement, clearly stating that, "The welfare of a nation can scarcely be inferred from the measurement of national income."*

The GDP simply measures a nation's raw economic activity in terms of production and consumption; it makes no attempt to factor in the depletion of natural resources or the degradation of the environment, and it cares not for income inequality and all the ills that come with it. It does not discriminate between beneficial economic activity (such as investment in education, health care, or infrastructure) and negative activity (such as the cost of crime, pollution, and ecological damages). As Kennedy points out, air pollution, cigarette advertising, napalm, and nuclear warheads are all counted as positive contributors to economic growth. To give a more recent example, a few years ago the European Union decided to count drug trafficking and human trafficking within their GDP measurement. From a purely economic standpoint, this makes sense, because these illegal activities generate important financial transactions—worldwide drug trafficking is estimated to generate over 500 billion dollars a year, and human trafficking is estimated to generate more than 150 billion dollars a year.[†] Therefore, including drug and human trafficking in the national accounts of EU members creates a significant increase of economic growth. At the same time, however, it's obvious that increased drug and human trafficking only causes more suffering. This is a grotesque example of the first fundamental flaw of GDP measurement—it counts economic transactions that have a negative impact on society as being positive, in the sense that it increases the economy.

The other problem related with using solely GDP as an indicator is that it leaves out any human activity that is not connected to a financial transaction. We all know the importance of friendship and love, or

---

*Simon Kuznets, in front of the US Senate, 1934.

[†] Global Financial Integrity, 2017, *https://gfintegrity.org*.

simply walking in nature, in terms of our well-being. But none of these activities is taken into consideration because they are not dependent on financial transactions. To give a practical example, let us imagine a family. The parents decide to prioritize the health and well-being of their children by reducing their working hours in order to spend more time at home. They might prefer to go camping or hiking with their children rather than giving them smartphones or tablets to play with, and they might forsake having a television and rather play games and read books as a family. In addition, they might buy fresh vegetables from a local farm stand—or plant their own vegetable garden—and take time to cook healthy meals at home, so that the children grow up physically and mentally healthy. All of this sounds wholesome and idyllic, but because these efforts and activities contribute little to the GDP of the country, they will never be accounted for.

Now let us take an opposite example: imagine a family that makes contrasting choices. Both parents work as much as possible to earn money, have so little time to spend with their children that they need to hire professional help, and are exhausted when they come home each evening, preferring to leave the children in front of the television or video games rather than spending time with them. To save time, they order fast food to be delivered at home. As a result, these children will likely face psychological and physical problems and will have to see therapists throughout their lives. And to alleviate their own stress, the parents may need to take medication or may even find themselves divorcing because of the lack of genuine communication and time spent together. Yet, although this picture sounds grim, from a GDP point of view, these parents are contributing a lot to their country's economic growth. They are earning more money and spending it by buying electronic gadgets, hiring a nanny, paying therapists, consuming antidepressants and sleeping pills, and paying large fees to the lawyers in charge of their divorce.

Although these two stories might seem a bit of a caricature, they nevertheless contain fundamental truths pertinent to the problematic reality of GDP measurement and its complete discrepancy from actually measuring what brings happiness and well-being to people and planet.

It is crucial to realize that the kind of measurement we use to assess the development of society plays an important role in directing the decisions that we make. What we count counts, because what we measure is what we are attentive to; it drives our decision-making process. Many of the political decisions that are made are driven by the one-sided fixation with economic growth; if it were not for economic growth, why would we have gone so far in the exploitation of the natural resources of our planet? But because our attention is completely caught by the factors enhancing economic growth, the negative side effects of these decisions are—more often than not—forgotten. Therefore, measuring the progress of society in a more holistic way is one of the fundamental conditions of transforming society. Since GDP is a measurement tool, we cannot simply replace it with a vision or values; we need to develop an alternative measurement tool. Gross National Happiness is not only a development paradigm, but it is also an indicator system that is able to provide a holistic understanding of the development of society.

How the Framework of Gross National Happiness Came to Be

The story of Gross National Happiness begins like a fairytale: "Once upon a time in a remote kingdom beyond seven oceans and seven mountains, there lived a young prince. . . ."

Jigme Dorji Wangchuck (1928–1972), the third king of Bhutan, is considered the father of the country in its modern state. He ruled for twenty years, and in that time, not only did he achieve the restructuring of society and government, but he also consolidated Bhutan's sovereignty and security, mobilizing resources from international donors and creating relationships with other countries. In addition, he reorganized the educational system and introduced Western science and technology, while at the same time preserving and promoting the traditional culture of Bhutan. After his abrupt passing in 1972, his son Jigme Singye Wangchuck (born 1955), became the fourth king of Bhutan. Ascending the throne at the age of seventeen, the young monarch realized that he didn't know how he should conduct his reign. According to ancient sages, the beginning of wisdom is knowing what one does not know, and from this point of view, the new king displayed wisdom and maturity beyond his young age. For the next two years he travelled extensively throughout the country, mostly by foot, as Bhutan contained very few drivable roads in the early 1970s. Going from village to village and monastery to monastery, he listened to what his subjects had to say, their hopes and expectations for the future.

While discussing happiness skills in the first part of the book, we saw the importance of deep listening as a fundamental social skill. Unfortunately, it seems that the ability to listen is not widespread among politicians and other leaders, who often feel that being a leader is about commanding rather than listening. If only our current leaders would follow the example of the young king who took the time to listen to what his people had to say before giving a clear direction to his reign.

Of course, different people want different things. The elderly don't have the same dreams, aspirations, and priorities as the young. The concerns of city dwellers are different from those of people in the countryside. But when the king considered everything that he'd heard, he realized that despite all the differences, what everyone has in common was a desire to be happy and to avoid suffering. The young king therefore decided that his reign would have the happiness of all people and the well-being of all life forms as its ultimate goal.

Of course, this insight about the universal desire for happiness was nothing new. From Buddha to Aristotle, the greatest thinkers have come to similar conclusions. His innovation lay in developing a political philosophy—a paradigm—based on this fundamental idea. The path from his initial vision to creating a functioning political and societal framework took several decades. Because his government was not focused solely on GDP, the economic development of the country was modest compared with other countries. Early in his reign, when a journalist in India asked him rather sarcastically about the slow development, but the young king gave an answer that defined GNH in just one sentence: "Gross National Happiness is more important than Gross National Product." Like a seed that includes all the later development of Gross National Happiness, this sentence points out a simple but deep truth: economic development is not a goal but merely a means to achieve what is genuinely important: happiness and well-being.

Going back to our reflection about GDP, we understand that this is precisely the fundamental problem: mistaking goals and means. To make it clearer, look at it from a personal level. If we ask ourselves why so many of us are striving to earn more money, the answer is easy: we are striving for a better life—more comfort and security and a better education for our children. Wealth is the means, and the goal is a better quality of life. Strangely enough, however, we often lose sight of the true goal, and accumulating wealth becomes a goal of its own, even at the expense of our well-being, our health, and the happiness of our family. On a national level too, economic growth obviously plays an important role in national well-being, especially if a country is not able to meet the fundamental material needs of its people. But in developed countries, it seems difficult to ask how much economic growth is enough. By not being able to find a sufficiency threshold, individuals, companies, and nations pursue endless growth, which, at a certain point, does not translate into more happiness and well-being but, on the contrary, becomes destructive for people and planet.

All ancient wisdoms knew about the importance of contentment and moderation. The temple of Apollo at Delphi—home of the famous Delphic oracle—for example, had two fundamental maxims inscribed above its entrance "know thyself" and "nothing in excess." Likewise, Buddhist wisdom speaks about the middle "noble" path between asceticism and indulging in sensory pleasures. Modern society seems to have forgotten this ancient wisdom, and our endless greed threatens both our planet and the very survival of our species. In a way, Gross National Happiness is a reformulation of ancient wisdom for the modern age.

From the young king's original intuition to a coherent social, political, and economic framework, there was a long path of research, trials, and errors. Then, in 2011, the then prime minister of Bhutan, Jigme Y. Thinley, eloquently formulated his understanding of GNH:

> *GNH, or Gross National Happiness, is the philosophy that has guided Bhutan's development process for about forty years. It is based on belief that development must serve a purpose, that development's role is not simply to promote continuous and endless economic growth, which is what GDP or conventional economic models tend to do. We live within a finite environment, within a finite world, so there are bounds within which growth can take place: natural and social resources and so forth. GNH, therefore, is based on the belief that development must be human-centered and that its objective must be to create those conditions that will enable the human individual to achieve what is most important to him, and that happens to be happiness.*
>
> *We believe that happiness is a condition that can be attained when one is able to balance the needs of the body with those of the mind, the physical and the mental needs being balanced. And likewise, the balance between the spiritual needs of the human individual and the material needs. And so, it is a human-centered, holistic, sustainable and inclusive development approach. Now more than ever, people are dissatisfied with the result of pursuing an economic development that is no longer sustainable, and they are seeing GNH as an alternative development paradigm.*[*]

---

[*] "Gross National Happiness—explained by the Hon. Prime Minister of Bhutan, 2012," an interview with Jigme Y. Thinley, GNHcentreMedia, April 1, 2012, video, 2:49, *https://www.youtube.com/watch?v=SPujYdcWCFU&t=41s*.

Gross National Happiness Beyond Bhutan

Until the beginning of the twenty-first century, GNH was confined to the small kingdom of Bhutan. Very few people had heard about it, and most who knew about it considered it to be the exotic, utopian ideal of a little Buddhist kingdom in the Himalayas that had little to do with the real world of international politics and economy.

There are several things that contributed to increased interest in Gross National Happiness around the world. The first is climate change and the ecological challenges that have gradually gained more attention from the public, due to the efforts of scientists and many others to raise awareness of the issue—for example, the 2006 film *An Inconvenient Truth*. Second, the economic crisis of 2008 manifested the unsustainable nature of the current economic system and led more and more people to reflect on the necessity to develop a new economic paradigm. Third, the field of happiness research gave a growing scientific legitimacy to the discourse on happiness, and in 2011, the UN General Assembly adopted a resolution on this question:*

The General Assembly,

Bearing in mind the purposes and principles of the United Nations, as set forth in the Charter of the United Nations, which include the promotion of the economic advancement and social progress of all peoples,

Conscious that the pursuit of happiness is a fundamental human goal,

Cognizant that happiness as a universal goal and aspiration embodies the spirit of the Millennium Development Goals,

Recognizing that the Gross Domestic Product Indicator by nature was not designed to and does not adequately reflect the happiness and well-being of people in a country,

---

*UN Resolution 65/309, July 19, 2011.

Conscious that unsustainable patterns of production and consumption can impede sustainable development, and recognizing the need for a more inclusive, equitable and balanced approach to economic growth that promotes sustainable development, poverty eradication, happiness and well-being of all peoples,

Acknowledging the need to promote sustainable development and achieve the Millennium Development Goals,

Invites Member States to pursue the elaboration of additional measures that better capture the importance of the pursuit of happiness and well-being in development with a view to guiding their public policies;

Invites those Member States that have taken initiatives to develop new indicators and other initiatives, to share information thereon with the Secretary-General as a contribution to the United Nations development agenda, including the Millennium Development Goals;

Welcomes the offer of Bhutan to convene during the sixty-sixth session of the General Assembly a panel discussion on the theme of happiness and well-being;

Invites the Secretary-General to seek the views of Member States and relevant regional and international organizations on the pursuit of happiness and well-being, and to communicate such views to the General Assembly at its sixty-seventh session for further consideration."

Suddenly, Gross National Happiness had transformed from a utopian idea to an international resolution of the United Nations. In May 2012, a high-level meeting was convened by the royal government of Bhutan at the UN's headquarters in New York, in accordance with that resolution. As I described in the introduction, it was then that I started my role as program director at the GNH Center and had my memorable first meeting with Jigme Y. Thinley.

The day before the UN meeting, the Earth Institute of Columbia University, led by Prof. Jeffrey Sachs, convened an international panel of more than eighty renowned experts in the field of happiness. The strongest impression I recall from this day-long panel, during which one expert after another shared the results of their academic research, was the realization that happiness could not be understood through the lens of one specific academic discipline; it needed an interdisciplinary, even transdisciplinary, approach. Neither psychology nor sociology, economics, or neuroscience could, on their own, provide a credible understanding of the inner and outer conditions of happiness and well-being. This, for me, was an important insight, because it strengthened my conviction that in order to advance Gross National Happiness, we needed to create open spaces for deep dialogues that would go beyond limited disciplinary knowledge and look at the human being in its totality, including the biosphere, which is essential for the life of all beings.

On the next day, May 2, 2012, the UN's meeting—titled Happiness and Well-Being: Towards a New Development Paradigm—took place in the main building of the UN. A distinctive feature of this meeting was the mix of participants: heads of states and Nobel Prize–winning scientists and economists along with philosophers and spiritual leaders. The secretary-general of the UN, Ban Ki-moon, hosted the meeting together with the prime minister of Bhutan and the president of Costa Rica. After many years of isolation, Gross National Happiness had conquered the world stage.

7

THE GROSS NATIONAL HAPPINESS FRAMEWORK

An important result of the UN meeting was the formation of a working group of international experts that had the task of writing the report for the UN on Bhutan's Gross National Happiness framework. For almost two years, this panel of experts worked together to distill the best of their understanding to create a coherent framework that could be understood and implemented beyond Bhutan. Their final report, *Happiness and Well-Being: Towards a New Development Paradigm,*[*] played a significant role in the UN's formulation of the Sustainable Development Goals (SDG) that replaced the Millennium Development Goals (MDG). One of the most important differences between the MDG and the SDG is that the former were meant to be implemented primarily by so-called developing countries, the assumption being that developed countries had already reached these goals. The SDG, on the other hand, apply to all countries, including the "developed" ones, because they are based on the insight that it is precisely the advanced economies that contribute the most to unsustainable development.

---

[*] *Happiness and Well-Being: Towards a New Development Paradigm*, Report of the Kingdom of Bhutan: *https://sustainabledevelopment.un.org/index.php?page=view&type=400&nr =617&menu=35.*

The universal goal to pursue happiness and the existence of planetary boundaries are the two fundamental premises of the development paradigm of Gross National Happiness. This differs from the GDP paradigm by making sustainability the top concern, reorienting development to ensure that life—of humans, other species, and the earth itself—is valued and prioritized. The principles of GNH are as follows:

1) Transformation of what we value: A shift from regarding economic production and consumption as the most important dimensions of society to integrating the psychological, emotional, and spiritual needs of human beings and the fundamental dignity of all life forms as the center of development.

2) Reconsideration of the purpose of development: It seems we have forgotten that economic growth, money, and material goods are only a means to an end and that the goal is to improve happiness, well-being, and quality of life. Instead, the current development trend tends to consider economic growth and the accumulation of material goods as an end by itself, regardless of whether this growth actually improves the well-being of all people and life forms.

3) Reorientation of humanity toward service: This has two meanings. First, we have focused production largely on the provision of material goods, rather than considering the services those goods provide. As a result, we are inundated with goods that often quickly become obsolete and need to be replaced. A new development paradigm will recognize, for example, that we do not necessarily need a car (the machine itself); we what need is to get from one place to another (the service a car provides). Second, orienting ourselves toward service also means seeing our work in terms of its purpose and benefit to society. In the current economic model, work is considered a disutility; the consequence of this is that people try to maximize their profits

while minimizing the work performed to make that money. This, in turn, leads to an attitude of selfishness and competition, rather than generosity, altruism, and kindness. Looking at our own life, we might realize that financial compensation is but one aspect of the reasons why we work. The actual purpose of work is to serve others, thereby giving meaning to our existence.

4) Recognition of our interconnectedness: Western society has developed with a dualistic worldview, separating spirit and matter, subject and object, and, most importantly, humans and nature. In reality, we, the human species, are completely interconnected with the natural world and with each other. The phenomenon of globalization and the devastating impacts of economic activity on the living biosphere (through climate change, resource depletion, species extinctions, and more) have made our mutual interdependence more obvious than in any prior generation. None of our actions occurs in a vacuum, so recognizing the causes and consequences of our actions and daily economic activity is essential if we are to coexist with our fellow beings. In a time when political nationalism seems to be on the rise again, we need to become aware of the fact that "we" are neither a nation nor a race nor a religious group. "We" are the 7.5 billion humans embarked on a common journey on a beautiful and fragile planet: our Mother Earth.

5) An ethos of cooperation: Based on the realization of our fundamental interconnectedness, a new basic attitude needs to guide all human activities: collaboration and cooperation. In the current economic and social system, competition is the name of the game, but this attitude necessarily leads to more destruction and more violence and ultimately threatens the very survival of our species and of other life forms.

The Four Pillars of GNH

What GNH has to offer is a new paradigm as a basis for exploring alternative approaches to development. In this model, the vision of societal happiness is taken as a wider lens to view human progress within planetary limits, thus fulfilling the needs of all humans rather than the wants of just a few. Looking in more detail at the overall Gross National Happiness framework, we see that four pillars form its core dimensions:

1) **Environmental conservation and resilience:** By now it should be clear that the foundation of any new developmental agenda can only be the health and resilience of the entire biosphere. A healthy environment is essential for the survival of humanity as well as all other life forms. Structures, principles, and policies are required to conserve and protect our planet, such as:

   * Application of the precautionary principle.

   * Investment mechanisms to repair damage already done and to support green spaces, appropriate technologies, renewable energy development, sustainable infrastructures, and organic agriculture.

   * Establishment of governance mechanisms for the global commons, including the atmosphere and oceans.

   * Incentives and penalties to reduce carbon emissions and nonrenewable resource use.

The core value and insight guiding our relationship with the natural world is the deep experience of interdependence, or as Thich Nhat Hanh formulates it, "interbeing."

2) **Sustainable and equitable social and economic development:** There is no doubt that socioeconomic development remains an important component of society. Human material needs have to be met to create a healthy foundation for other human activities. Nevertheless, let us remember once again

that the economy is there merely to serve the well-being of all people, and it can only develop within the natural boundaries of our ecosystem. Therefore, the value underlying the economic system should be brotherhood and sisterhood based on the awareness that all humans need to share the resources available to them fairly.

3) **Preservation and promotion of culture:** Looking back at ancient civilizations, we see that culture was the foundation of society. Churches and cathedrals were built at the center of cities all the way through to the European Middle Ages. In our time, however, banks, department stores, and business centers have become cities' most prominent features, and culture tends to be merely a subsystem of the economy. This has resulted in an impoverishment of cultural life, and yet culture—understood as science, philosophy, art, and spirituality—is the very heart of our humanity. It is in these fields that the creative human spirit manifests, and the value that underlies their creation is freedom.

4) **Good governance:** Surveys have shown that in most countries, politicians are the social category least trusted by the larger public. For understandable reasons, many perceive political activity as mostly serving vested interests rather than the common good. It is a sad reality of the twenty-first century that that which should be regarded as selfless service of the people is perceived as an egoistic striving for money and power. Good governance simply means striving to serve the well-being of all, and this noble task needs to be redefined so as to be able to truly serve the needs of society. With regards to the law, equality should be the guiding value ensuring the fair treatment of all citizens.

In summary, the four pillars of Gross National Happiness—environmental conservation and resilience, sustainable and equitable social and economic development, preservation and promotion of culture, and good governance—can be understood as the implementations of the three ideals of the French revolution—freedom, equality, and brotherhood and sisterhood (*liberté, égalité, fraternité*)—within the larger context of interdependence as the foundation of all human life on earth. To achieve these goals, we need to envision and implement policies for the responsible management of natural, human, social, and economic resources to ensure present and future sustainability.

8

THE NINE DOMAINS
OF GROSS NATIONAL
HAPPINESS

If Gross National Happiness is to replace GDP as an assessment tool of societal progress, it cannot remain a mere vision or ideal. GNH is also an index with domains and indicators to assess and pilot the development of a company, region, or country—or even a family or our own personal development—so the GNH survey was developed by the Center for Bhutan Studies for the purpose of assessing Bhutan's development. Every three years, pollsters visit each of the provinces of the country and interview a representative sample of more than seven thousand people to assess the happiness and well-being of the various segments of the Bhutanese population. The hundred and fifty questions in the survey are based on GNH's nine domains and thirty-three indicators.

Let us briefly describe each one of the nine domains of Gross National Happiness to understand the holistic approach used to measuring GNH in Bhutan.

THE NINE DOMAINS OF GROSS NATIONAL HAPPINESS

1. Psychological well-being

2. Health

3. Time use

4. Education

5. Cultural diversity and resilience

6. Community vitality

7. Good governance

8. Ecological diversity and resilience

9. Living standards

1. Psychological well-being: This domain attempts to understand how people experience the quality of their lives. It includes reflective cognitive evaluations, such as life satisfaction, and reaction to life events, such as positive and negative emotions, in addition to covering spiritual practices that can contribute to our overall well-being.

As we have seen when discussing the inner conditions of happiness, research has shown that certain inner attitudes contribute greatly to our own sense of happiness. In a well-known Ted Talk, Brother David Steindl-Rast proclaimed that it is not happy people who are grateful, but grateful people who are happy.* Steindl-Rast truly embodies the qualities of gratitude that he advocates. A few years ago, I had the opportunity to travel with him through Bhutan for several weeks. It was during the monsoon season, and the roads were difficult. We regularly had to stop the car because a boulder had fallen into the road. We often had to wait for hours before continuing. Most people would have become impatient in such a situation, but each time it happened, Steindl-Rast just got out of the car and looked around with a sense of wonder at the mountains and forests expressing his joy and gratitude for having the opportunity to have the time to enjoy the beauty of nature. After a short while, whenever he got out of the car, children

---

* "Want to be Happy? Be Grateful," Brother David Steindl-Rast, Ted Talk, TedGlobal, November 27, 2013.video, 14:30, *https://www.youtube.com/watch?v=UtBsl3joYRQ.*

gathered around him, seemingly coming out of nowhere, and he would happily chat away with them. It seemed as if he radiated an invisible energy that children felt drawn to.

Likewise, generosity is mindset that creates happiness for oneself and for others. Some years ago I had the opportunity to travel to Costa Rica with my friend Nipun Mehta, a well-known advocate of the gift economy. Nipun is the creator of Karma Kitchen restaurant chain. In these restaurants, at the end of your meal, you get a bill that says, "Your meal costs 0 dollars, because it has already been paid for by a previous customer. But if you wish to pay forward for a future guest, you can leave whatever you want." This practice of "paying forward" initially raised a lot of skepticism, but it turned out to work very well. Karma Kitchen has been flourishing; the first restaurant opened in Berkeley, California in 2007, and has since spread across the US and around the world. When we were in San Jose, the capital of Costa Rica, Nipun suggested that we go for a coffee, and when we left the cafe, he randomly selected some customers who were sitting at a table nearby. Without letting them know, he paid for their drinks while he paid for our own. When he did this, I noticed the joy we all felt at the pleasant surprise that the strangers would get when they were told that their beverages had already been paid for. Hopefully, it would inspire them to do the same at some point. These are just two examples of how psychological well-being can be improved through the conscious cultivation of a positive mindset.

2. Health: In addition to physical and mental health, this domain also analyses the quality of life that allows us to get through our daily activities without undue physiological or psychological stress.

Until recently, the field of psychology focused mainly on mental and emotional problems. Lately, however, a focus on the conditions that allow for a healthy and flourishing mental and emotional life has gained traction. Similarly, Western medicine has also traditionally focused on pathologies, but here again the field of *salutogenesis* has emerged as a new medical paradigm, concentrating on conditions that create and enhance good health.*

Traditional medicine in many cultures, on the other hand, has always paid much attention to the conditions of good health—diet, exercise, and a healthy lifestyle. So much so that in ancient China, families used to pay their doctor regularly, as long as everyone in the family was healthy. Once someone fell ill, however, the doctor stopped being paid until the good health of that family member was regained.

In Bhutan, the health sector balances traditional Himalayan Buddhist medicine with Western science. In every Bhutanese hospital, the patient has the choice between consulting with a traditional practitioner or a Western-trained medical doctor. It is a rare example of traditional medical knowledge and practices not being completely overshadowed by Western science, and the practitioners of both styles of medicine cooperate with each other. While living in Bhutan, I myself experienced how the traditional practitioner would sometimes recommend his Western-trained colleague, and vice versa, depending on the nature of the illness. To me this complementary collaboration between a spiritually based traditional knowledge and a scientifically based contemporary approach could serve as a model in many fields. Moreover, in Bhutan, all medical treatments—from consultations to complex surgeries—are entirely free of charge, for both Bhutanese citizens and anyone living in Bhutan. I believe it is the only developing country that has managed to guarantee full health coverage for all its citizens without any charge. If it is possible for a relatively poor country, how peculiar that in the richest country in the world, the US, tens of millions of people still go without insurance coverage and thus don't have proper access to medical care.

---

* "Salutogenesis" is a term coined by Aaron Antonovsky, a professor of medical sociology, to describe an approach focusing on factors that support human health and well-being, rather than on those that cause disease (pathogenesis).

3. Time use: To my knowledge, GNH is the only alternative measurement system that includes time use, and research has shown that our relationship with time plays a very important part in our overall well-being. Rhythm is one of the fundamental laws of the universe—the earth, sun, moon, and all planets follow their individual rhythms. The seasons and even life itself are structured by rhythms. At a micro level, our heartbeat and breathing create biological rhythm that determines, to a large extent, our physical and mental well-being, and all our other organs also follow patterns in their functioning.

Traditional civilizations understood the relationship between the micro rhythms of human beings and the macro rhythms of the universe. Ancient Daoist philosophy described through the hexagrams of the Yi King rhythmical patterns that define both the cycle of the year and the cycle of human life.

And in every culture, rural life was determined by natural cycles—sunrise and sunset, full moon and new moon, and the seasons of the year. One of the most disrupting transformations in human life was the development of industrial work, which replaced the natural rhythm of farm life with the mechanical beat of factories.

But the Industrial Revolution was only a first step in the loss of connection between the human and cosmic rhythms. In recent decades, because of computers and then smartphones and tablets, every minute of our waking life is filled with unceasing stimuli and information that disconnects us from natural rhythms much more deeply. This is one of the reasons why mindful breathing has become such an important part of our mental hygiene. Simply using mindfulness to reconnect with this most fundamental rhythm, our breath, allows us to take a break from the relentless demands and inhuman speed of modern life.

Stress-related illnesses and burnout have become the most prevalent cause of morbidity in the developed world, and these symptoms are becoming more and more widespread in the rest of the world as well. One of the causes of stress is the feeling of not having enough time, of constantly chasing after life, never being able to slow down.

Our relationship with time, which is part of our relationship with rhythms, is a powerful indicator of our well-being—or, in some cases, of our *ill-being.*

The so-called work-life balance is increasing discussed in workplaces, which, in many ways, is good, but this idea implies that work and life are a duality. And since we spend most of our waking hours in our workplace, it means we have little time for our actual life. The question, therefore, is whether—instead of being torn between work and life as an antagonistic duality—we can perceive our life as a whole, with work, family time, leisure, cultural activities, time in nature, and so on, creating a healthy rhythm in which we can thrive. Analyzing the way we spend our time and reflecting on our priorities is a good starting point to increasing our well-being.

4. Education: In addition to incorporating formal education, this domain also assesses many types of knowledge, values, and skills that are generally acquired informally, through life itself. A later chapter will describe in more detail how the field of education can play a central role in redefining a new development paradigm focused on happiness and well-being (see chapter 11).

The current education system focuses narrowly on academic skills and achievements, disregarding fundamental aspects of learning such as social and emotional competencies or, generally speaking, "happiness skills." In 2009, the royal government of Bhutan convened an international conference on the theme of GNH in education. Many of the world's experts in this field gathered to reflect on how best to include GNH values in the educational system of the country. Following this event, all the school principals in Bhutan were brought together—which is possible in a small country like Bhutan, where there are only about seven hundred schools—to develop an action plan on implementing GNH in education. Under the leadership of the then minister for education, Thakur S. Powdyel, a teacher-training curriculum based on GNH was developed, and within four years all the teachers of Bhutan had been able to implement this training in their classrooms. In collaboration with the Mind and Life Institute,* the GNH Center in Bhutan developed a follow-up program called "A Call 2 Care," deepening the promotion of happiness skills for children of all ages. Minister Powdyel wrote an inspiring book on his vision of the educational system, *Green Schools for Green Bhutan*, which explained in great detail how to create a conducive environment for both teachers and students.† It is important to note that there was almost no formal education system in Bhutan, except for monastic education, before the 1960s; since then, Bhutan has managed to bring every child in the country—even those living in the most remote mountain areas—into the school system, which is entirely free of charge from kindergarten all the way to university.

But even successes have their shadow side. An unintended consequence of the achievement of academic qualification among the younger generation was youth unemployment, something that did not exist when most young people worked on farms. The creation of job opportunities for school graduates in a country with a very small business sector has become a challenge for the current Bhutanese government.

5. Cultural diversity and resilience: We have already briefly discussed the importance of culture as the heart and soul of any society. Participation in cultural life is a strong indicator of the inner creativity that contributes a meaningful life.

Bhutan is one of the rare Asian countries that was never colonized. Wherever Europeans took power, the message that they spread was the superiority of Western culture and science over traditional knowledge and spirituality, which were scorned as ignorance and superstitions. In the same way that our extractive economy had depleted the biodiversity

---

* *https://www.mindandlife.org*

† Thakur S. Powdyel, *Green Schools for Green Bhutan* (2016).

of flora and fauna, colonization depleted the cultural diversity of the world. Indeed, the influence of colonization has been so strong that most people in colonized countries gradually became convinced of the supposed superiority of Western culture and were almost ashamed of their own traditional values, knowledge, and practices.

Not so in Bhutan. Because the country was never colonized—partly because of the rugged geographical terrain and partly because of the wisdom of its leaders—traditional culture and spirituality has remained intact and is still very much alive. The example that I gave of traditional medicine and scientific medicine working together in health care is a good example. When Padmasambhava—or Guru Rinpoche, as the Bhutanese call him—introduced the Vajrayana school of Buddhism to Bhutan in the eighth century CE, he did not try to destroy the shamanistic beliefs and practices that were prevalent; on the contrary, he managed to integrate previous cultural elements with the new spirituality.

Living in Bhutan, one gradually understands the several layers of the country's culture. The first is a form of nature religion, which recognizes the sacredness of all natural beings. To the Bhutanese, a lake is not a mere body of water, but the home of water spirits; a mountain is not only a heap of rocks, but also the abode of gods; a forest is not merely a potential natural resource for the economy, but also a kingdom where natural and supernatural beings reside, which therefore needs to be respected. This is the deeper reason why ecological consciousness is easy for Bhutanese society: it has not lost the sacred dimension of our planet as a living being.

The second dimension of Bhutanese culture arises from a strong Buddhist tradition. Monastic scholars spend over nine years studying Buddhist psychology, epistemology, and cosmology, and after graduation, most of them spend three years in solitary retreat to experience, through deep meditative states, the inner reality of what they have learned through their academic studies. Moving from their university in Tango Monastery outside Thimphu to the various caves and hermitages around Chagri Dorjeden Monastery, the young graduates give up worldly pleasures and several years of their youth in order to concentrate fully on their life of contemplation.

In every Bhutanese home the most important room in a house is the shrine room. Even the humblest farmhouse has a beautiful shrine richly decorated with statues, hand-painted *thangkas*, and other religious symbols. The family regularly gathers at the shrine to carry out rituals that are performed not only for the well-being of the family and their village but also for the well-being of all sentient beings.

In Bhutan, when a child is born, the parents will consult an astrologer, who will prepare a detailed astrological map of the child's strengths, weaknesses, talents, and life path. He will point out the challenging moments of the child's lifetime and give advice on how to conduct daily activities and spiritual practices. Bhutan is the only country in the world were astrology is an academic discipline taught in a university, and it takes nine years of study to fully master this complex art. All important decisions, both private and professional, as well as national decisions taken by the government, are always done after consulting a master astrologer. To the Western mind, these practices could be regarded as superstitions, but they are an expression of deep-seated cultural values and practices that express the feeling of connectedness between the individual, the society, and the whole of the cosmos. Indeed, astrology may be understood as a way of harmonizing human behavior with the laws of the universe.

The third layer of Bhutanese culture is influenced by contemporary science, as a growing number of young Bhutanese go through advanced academic training, in addition to studying abroad. A Bhutanese friend of mine once expressed how he experienced this shift in consciousness: "If you had asked my grandparents where they were from, they would have said, 'We come from the Land of the Thunder Dragon, which is located south of Mount Kailash and north of Bodhgaya' [Mount Kailash is identified with Mount Meru, the center of the world, according to Buddhist cosmology, and Bodhgaya is the holy place where Lord Buddha attained Enlightenment]. But if you ask young Bhutanese today, they'll say, 'I'm from Bhutan, a small country squeezed between two economic giants, China and India.' "

So far in Bhutanese society, a certain balance has been kept between these various culture identities, but it remains to be seen how traditional knowledge and culture will be able to survive the powerful influence of the scientific, rational, and materialistic thinking of the West. All the senior officials I met when I was in Bhutan had spent their childhood barefoot in remote mountain villages, often walking for several hours a day to go to school. Most of them too had only been exposed to Western culture through academic studies in Bhutan and abroad. Therefore, they could still find a balance between their traditional upbringing and Western culture. But as more and more young Bhutanese grow up in the city with smartphones, social media, and other contemporary stimuli, it is hard to tell whether traditional culture will be able to maintain its rightful place.

Living in Bhutan, my experience was that having these several cultural streams was incredibly enriching for society—not contradicting each other, but giving a fuller flavor to life. For example, when we were establishing the GNH Center in Bumthang, the foundation stone ceremony took place—in accordance with astrological advice—in July (during the monsoon season, when it rains almost daily). Since ceremony was held before any construction on the center started, it took place in an open field. We had invited Her Majesty the Queen and many high officials, as well as hundreds of local villagers. We had prepared a tent for the queen and her entourage. But there was no shelter for the hundreds of other people joining on that day and, knowing what monsoon season was like, I was worried how we would manage a day-long ceremony if it rained. My Bhutanese colleagues all seemed relaxed about it, as they had asked the local lama to perform a ritual so that the day would remain dry. I was not as confident as they were, and the day before the event, I went up to the little temple where the local lama was preparing the rain-prevention ceremony. I felt a bit embarrassed to challenge his expertise, but nevertheless, I asked him if he was quite sure that he could guarantee sunshine for our festival. He told me not to worry, that his grandfather and his father had also been lamas at this temple in this valley, and that he was very familiar with the local deities, who would certainly be willing to support our project as it was created with a pure intention.

Only half-reassured, I went back to meet with my colleagues. I still felt the need to ask them whether they had prepared a plan B, just in case of rain. But they just smiled and told me not to worry, that everything would go according to plan. The next morning, I woke up very early. It was still dark outside, and rain was pouring down. All my worries seemed to be justified. How we would get through the day? However, as the sun rose, the clouds disappeared, and a bright and sunny day began. By the time Her Majesty arrived, everything had dried, and we had a wonderful festival with hundreds of farmers sitting on the ground, which we had covered with pine needles, sharing meals, songs, games, and dances. I was invited by the queen for tea and a snack, and I shared with her the story of my visit to the lama and the rain. Amused, she smiled and told me that in Bhutan, it was always like that, that when any important and positive event was happening, the local lamas had the power to ask the local deities for auspicious weather. Even as highly educated and sophisticated a person as the queen of Bhutan, who had studied abroad—she has a degree in international relations at Regent's University London—found it quite natural to relate to traditional wisdom and practices. At the end of the day, the queen left the compound, as soon as she was gone, the rain resumed.

You might think that this was just a freak occurrence, but while living in Bhutan, I experienced this kind of situation many times. I have no rational explanation for it—I simply accept it as a fact of life in Bhutan.

6. Community vitality: This domain focuses on the strengths and weaknesses of relationships and interactions within communities. It gathers information on social cohesion among family members and neighbors and on practices like volunteering. One of the questions that is asked to assess this domain is the following: "If you are facing a serious challenge in your life, how many people do you think would be willing to go out of their way to help and support you? In turn, for how many people do you feel responsible and would you be willing to help if they faced a serious problem?"

In one of the surveys, an old Bhutanese farmer first seemed puzzled by this question. Then, as if it was self-evident, he answered, "If I have any problem, every single person in my village will be there to help me, and if anyone in my village faces a problem, I will of course be there to support them." This is in stark contrast with what most urban dwellers experience. In contemporary Western cities, many people live alone and don't even know the names of their neighbors. When facing life challenges, most rely on public services, insurance companies, or other bureaucratic institutions for help and support. Even most elderly people either live alone or in retirement homes cared for by paid professionals. This trend of replacing human interaction with anonymous institutions, which developed only during the last century, has played a significant part in the isolation and loneliness that is so prevalent in Western societies. I'm certainly not undercutting the importance of good state-run social services; I'm simply pointing out that bureaucratic institutions cannot fulfill the need for warmth, contact, friendship, and trust that is central to a fulfilled human life.

Now in my late sixties, when I look back at my life, it is not the jobs and positions I held, the money I earned, or the possessions I acquired that stand out. What really matters is the people I met, the relationships we built, and the friendship, love, and care that we developed for one another. A few years ago, my wife and I celebrated our fortieth wedding anniversary, and for this occasion we invited about eighty friends and family members to come together with us in a beautiful mountain village in the Swiss Alps. At one point, we gathered in a large circle, with everyone standing in chronological order according to when they had first met us. The first were our elder sisters, who had known us from the day we were born; then there were childhood friends, friends from university, former colleagues, and our children and grandchildren, all the way to people that we had only met recently, but with whom we had created strong bonds of friendship. Looking around the circle, I had the feeling of looking at our destiny, which was embodied in these many people.

Some say that at the moment of death, one sees one's life passing as a film before our mind's eye, and standing with my circle of friends and relatives, I felt that this will probably be the most important dimension of the vision I'll have at the end—all the people that I have met and loved and interacted with during my life. Compared to that, all the other external circumstances of social and professional life seem unimportant.

7. **Good governance**: The domain of good governance evaluates how people perceive various governmental functions in terms of their efficacy, honesty, and quality. Indicators have to evaluate the level of participation in government decisions at a local or national level, and the presence of various rights and freedoms. Democracy is certainly one of the great achievements of Western culture, but unfortunately, as we have seen in recent years, there has been an increasing erosion of democracy and loss of confidence in their elected officials. Reinventing a democratic system that allows more direct participation of ordinary citizens in governmental decisions is an important task for the future. The model of direct democracy, as implemented in Switzerland, is one possibility—although certainly not the only one—of a more participatory and responsible political system.

A major challenge that our current political system faces is the fact that many officials have short periods in office. The problems the world is facing today must be seen in a long-term perspective— not from the vantagepoint of only two to six years in office. An

encouraging example of how to assess the impact of political decisions on future generations is the Well-Being of Future Generations
(Wales) Act of 2015 in Wales.* Inspired by the Bhutanese concept of
Gross National Happiness, the Welsh government passed a law that
focuses on the long-term consequences of governmental action for
future generations:

> *The Well-Being of Future Generations Act is about improving the
> social, economic, environmental and cultural well-being of Wales.
> It will make public bodies think more about the long-term, work
> better with people, communities and each other, look to prevent
> problems, and take a more joined-up approach. This will help
> create a Wales that we all want to live in, now and in the future.
> This decision places at the centre of all public action the duty of
> well-being.*

Other examples of good governance include the Bolivian and
Ecuadoran notion of *Buen Vivir*, which describes a way of life that
is community-centric, ecologically balanced, and culturally sensitive.† Similarly, the expression *pura vida*, widely used in Costa Rica,
describes a way of life that emphasizes well-being and satisfaction
rather than the pursuit of material goals. Costa Rica goes beyond
this popular saying too, continuing to be a pioneer in many social
and political approaches. And let's not forget that Costa Rica was the
co-host, with Bhutan, of the UN's meeting on happiness and well-
being, was one of the first counties in the world to abolish the death
penalty, and remains one of the few countries without an army. Likewise, Jacinda Adern, the prime minister of New Zealand, pledged to
build "a kind and equitable nation where children thrive and success

---

* *http://futuregenerations.wales/about-us/future-generations-act/*

† *https://blog.pachamama.org/buen-vivir-new-era-great-social-change*

is measured not only by the nation's GDP but by better lives lived by its people."

In the case of Bhutan, a striking example of good governance is embodied by the behavior of the fourth king, His Majesty Jigme Singye Wangchuck, who was deeply loved and respected by his people as a wise king and a benevolent leader and who always pursued the well-being of his people as his highest goal. He was an absolute monarch, but used his power only to serve, not to dominate. And at the height of his popularity, in 2006, he decided that it was time for Bhutan to transition from an absolute monarchy to a constitutional monarchy with a democratic constitution. He helped to write the new constitution and traveled around the country to present it to the people and get their feedback. Once the constitution was in place in 2006, when he was fifty-one, he abdicated the throne, transferring it to his son Jigme Khesar Namgyel Wangchuck, who was crowned in December 2006 as the fifth king of Bhutan, and the first democratic elections were held in 2008. While we see so many examples of rulers who cling to power and are willing to using force and violence even against their own people, this example of a benevolent king who handed the power of government to his people—and later who stepped down of his own accord—is a shining example of good governance.

In Bhutan, I once helped organize a workshop on good governance and democracy for a group of young people. The whole day was spent talking about participation, transparency, lack of corruption, and all the elements that constitute political best practice. At the end of the day, we sat in a circle, and I asked the participants how they felt about democracy in Bhutan. Paradoxically, most of them answered that while they appreciated free elections and the transparency of open political life, they actually missed absolute monarchy under the fourth king—they looked back on it like a golden age, when a wise leader united the people and showed a clear direction to the country. This reminded me of Churchill's assessment of democracy: "Democracy is the worst political system, except for all the others."*

8. Ecological diversity and resilience: This domain encompasses indicators that measure people's own evaluation of the environmental conditions of their neighborhood. We also make assessments of eco-friendly activity, as well environmental and natural hazards like forest fires and earthquakes. A few years ago, Bhutan pledged not only to remain carbon-neutral for all time but also to be become negative.† The country renounced certain economic advantages that could have been gained through extensive logging or mining. In fact, the Bhutanese constitution stipulates that forest coverage of the country should always remain over 70 percent (currently it's well over 70 percent). Bhutan also formulated the goal of having 100 percent organic agriculture in the coming years, and it has the largest biodiversity of both fauna and flora in the Himalayas. Furthermore, all the unclimbed Himalayan summits over seven thousand meters (twenty-three thousand feet) are located in Bhutan. According to Bhutanese culture, these peaks are the abodes of the gods and should not be disturbed by unnecessary human activities.

These are just a few examples of how Gross National Happiness is not merely a theory but a practice that guides the development of the country. As has been described, one cannot really understand how Bhutan has been able to maintain such high ecological standards

---

*Winston S. Churchill, in a speech to the House of Commons, November 11, 1947: "Many forms of Government have been tried, and will be tried in this world of sin and woe. No one pretends that democracy is perfect or all-wise. Indeed, it has been said that democracy is the worst form of government, except for all those other forms that have been tried from time to time." https://winstonchurchill.org/resources/quotes/the-worst-form-of-government.

† "This country isn't just carbon neutral—it's carbon negative" Tshering Tobgay, Ted Talk, April 1, 2016, video, 18:54, https://www.youtube.com/watch?v=7Lc_dlVrg5M&t=29s.

without taking into account the spiritual connection between the people and nature. The challenge most developed countries face in questions regarding the environment is not just legal or economic matters but also the inner disconnection between humans and the natural world. It is that disconnection that is the true source of destruction. Legal frameworks are extremely important, but for true protection of the environment to occur, human hearts and minds need to reconnect with the reality of our planet as a living, spiritual being.

9. Living standards: This domain includes levels of material comfort as measured by income, financial security, housing, and asset ownership. There is little doubt that increases in living standards correlate to an increase of well-being. Beyond a certain point, however, further increases do not translate into more happiness. On the contrary, the time and effort required to earn more tends to cause a decrease in other vital areas of well-being, such as relationships with one's family and community, and one's cultural or spiritual engagement. A question that each one of us should seriously ask ourselves is, "How much is enough?" As Gandhi famously stated, "The earth has enough resources to meet everyone's needs, but not everyone's greed." Our ability to discriminate between our legitimate needs and our endless greed is an important part of contributing to collective well-being.

One of the fundamental tenets of the current economic system is the inseparable connection between work and salary. With the development of artificial intelligence in the coming decades, our relationship with work will completely change, and the connection between work and income will have to be radically revisited. We tend to forget that what seems to us to be a universal truth—the relationship between work and salary—is, in fact, a relatively recent social construct. Before the Industrial Revolution, the vast majority of people never worked for a salary; employment as we know it today was a marginal type of work contract. With industrialization and urbanization, the equation of work and income became a dogma that has remained unchallenged ever since.

Over the years, my family and I have spent long periods in communities that consciously disconnected work from money. Created during the Second World War, the Camphill communities were an attempt to provide a healing environment for people with special needs (intellectual, emotional, and behavioral disabilities).* They were also a social experiment to implement some of the ideas that had been formulated by Rudolf Steiner in his vision of the threefold social order.† In Camphill communities, work is seen as the contribution that individuals give in service of society. Through work, we fulfill our aspiration to serve others, thus giving meaning to our own life by employing our best abilities for the well-being of all. In return, the community takes care of our needs by providing whatever is necessary for our well-being.

Seen in this way, work ceases to be the "disutility" it is in mainstream economic thinking (i.e., working as little as possible while maximizing profit) and instead becomes a way of having a meaningful life by making a useful contribution to society. In a Camphill community, each one of us is assigned tasks according to our competencies and the needs of the whole, but these tasks have no relationship with our income. All the income flowed into a common fund and was then redistributed according to the actual needs of the individual or the family. A gardener with several children, therefore, might receive more than a medical doctor who was single.

When we share the story of our years living with our family in this way, many people think it must have been complicated to organize and arbitrate between the various needs of up to a hundred people, but actually it was quite easy. We met only twice a year to discuss expenses, such as changing a car, paying for studies, or leaving for a longer journey. For the rest of the year, each one of us simply took whatever we needed to meet the needs of our family. In all that time, we never spent more than

---

* *https://www.camphillfoundation.org/about-camphill*

† *https://en.wikipedia.org/wiki/Social_threefolding*

we had; on the contrary, at the end of each year, when we looked at our accounts, we would find money left over, which we would give away to a charity or other philanthropic cause, because we always wanted to start the year with a clean slate. The reason we were always able to spend within our means was simply that we were always aware that what we were taking was subtracted from what was available to all the others.

This is actually always the reality of the economic world: what is consumed is no longer available for others. In the current system, we have no awareness of it, because we have the illusion that whatever we earn and whatever we buy belongs to us and has nothing to do with anyone else. This is the root cause of the deeply unethical economic inequality that has worsened significantly in the recent decades. Moving toward a caring economy that takes into consideration the well-being of all people rather than just a few is also an ecological challenge. The two are intimately related and are the biggest tasks we face currently and will in the future.

Summary of the Domains of Gross National Happiness

The nine domains and thirty-three indicators that are used in the GNH survey in Bhutan:

DOMAIN	INDICATORS
Psychological well-being	Life satisfaction
	Positive emotions
	Negative emotions
	Spirituality
Health	Self-reported health status
	Number of healthy days
	Disability
	Mental health

DOMAIN	INDICATORS
Time use	Work
	Sleep
Education	Literacy
	Schooling
	Knowledge
	Value
Culture	Artisan skills
	Cultural participation
	Speaking of native language
	Traditional etiquette
Community vitality	Donation (time and money)
	Safety
	Community relationship
	Family
Good governance	Political participation
	Services
	Governance performance
	Fundamental rights
Ecological diversity and resilience	Wildlife damage
	Urban issues
	Responsibility to environment
	Ecological issues
Living standards	Income
	Assets
	Housing

Even in Bhutan, where there is a conscious focus on the happiness of its population, not everybody is overwhelmingly happy. But the survey helps the government learn the areas that need more care and where resources should be allocated. It is also interesting to observe that progress made in certain areas also comes with a cost in other fields. For instance, while modernization has led to an increase in living standards, education, and health, at the same time, community vitality and culture have decreased. These kinds of insights are crucial in political or economic decisions, because we become aware that any progress in a specific area can come at the cost of another. A holistic overview, keeping in mind the various domains of development, helps us make decisions and allows for balanced progress and a more responsible life.

This being said, when assessing the nine domains, we should not forget that we are focusing on the outer conditions that contribute to a happy life. No matter how conducive the environment might be, in the end, it is our inner attitude and state of mind that is the most important factor. Therefore, it is important to find the right balance between enhancing external conditions and simultaneously cultivating inner conditions. When we implement GNH in any context, the balance between the inner and outer conditions of happiness is of utmost importance.

Western culture in the past two hundred years has made tremendous progress in enhancing the outer, material conditions of well-being. Scientific progress and technology have allowed for unprecedented advancement, and yet it has become clear that the outer conditions alone are not sufficient to guarantee a good and meaningful life. In the context of developed countries, putting the emphasis on the inner conditions and the transformation of consciousness is the priority to meet the challenges we are currently facing. When confronted with social, economic, and ecological difficulties, we tend to blame systems, structures, or those who seem to be in a position of power within these systems. But we should never forget that systems are nothing but the result of the way each one of us thinks, feels, acts, and relates with others and the world. Only a change in mindset can bring about a lasting change in social and economic structures.

From this point of view, the nine domains and their scores are only symptoms that can help us identify the areas in which we need to make progress; they are not, in themselves, root causes, either of our happiness or of our suffering. Nevertheless, shifting our attention from the mere financial and economic dimensions of social life to a holistic and comprehensive perspective does play an important role in making the decisions that can lead us toward a better quality of society and greater well-being of all.

The GNH Screening Tool for Responsible Decision Making

While the GNH survey gives a picture of the existing situation of society, the GNH screening tool assists leaders and government in taking responsible decisions by predicting, as accurately as possible, the impact that any policy decision will have on all the nine domains. In addition to serving as evaluative tools to track developmental progress over time, GNH indicators also offer a common direction and purpose to programs and policies that are in line with the values of GNH. The screening tool is used to systematically assess the impact of any policy and project on Gross National Happiness, thereby simultaneously selecting GNH-enhancing policies and projects and rejecting those that adversely affect key determinants of GNH. In the Bhutanese government, the GNH Commission is tasked with screening all major government policies and decisions in the light of GNH indicators.

The process is as follows: when a ministry or another government agency proposes a new project or policy, it first has to be approved by the cabinet (the prime minister and all the ministers). It is then sent for review to the GNH Commission, which screens the project in the light of the nine domains, using twenty-two indicators that can be scored between one and four. What will the impact be of this project?

1. a negative impact on the given indicator

2. an uncertain impact on the given indicator

3. a neutral impact on the given indicator

4. a positive impact on the given indicator

VARIABLES	DOMAIN	VARIABLE SCORE (1-4)
Spiritual pursuits	Psychological well-being	
Stress		
Public health	Health	
Leisure	Time use	
Skills and learning	Education	
Culture	Cultural diversity and resilience	
Values		
Social support	Community vitality	
Family		
Decision-making opportunity	Good governance	
Anti-corruption		
Legal recourse		
Rights		
Gender		
Transparency		
Water and air pollution	Ecological diversity and resilience	
Land degradation		
Bio-diversity health		
Equity	Living standards	
Economic security		
Material well-being		
Engagement in productive activities		

To give a real-life example of the impact of the GNH screening tool on governmental decision making, I'd like to share a story that was told to me by a government official who was present when this event occurred.

At some point the Ministry of Economic Affairs of Bhutan proposed that Bhutan should join the World Trade Organization (WTO). The rationale behind this proposal was that by becoming a member of the WTO, Bhutan would benefit from better trade agreements, easier access to international capital and a stronger economic position in the world market. When this proposal was first discussed within the cabinet, nineteen of the ministers voted for the motion, and six were opposed to it. The proposal was then sent to the GNH Commission for further analysis of the impact such a decision would have on the overall development of the country. Using the screening tool just described, the GNH Commission looked at the effect this decision would have on the nine domains of GNH. The result was that it would definitely have positive effects on economic security, material well-being, and engagement in productive activities. However, for most of the other variables, such as equity, public health, water and air pollution, land degradation, biodiversity, health, family, leisure, and stress, it would have a negative impact. Once the result of this analysis was consolidated it was sent back to the cabinet and, after the full report had been read, the motion was once again put to a vote. This time the result was reversed: nineteen members voted against it, and six were for it. As a consequence, Bhutan is one of the few countries that has not joined the WTO.

This shows that if the government had focused its attention on GDP and economic growth alone, the decision would have certainly been the opposite one. But because the Bhutanese government took a holistic perspective and analyzed not only the economic and financial impacts but also the overall impact on the well-being of society, it decided not to join the WTO. This also demonstrates the importance of measuring the current situation and using a screening tool to take into consideration any consequences decisions will have on further development. This applies when implementing GNH at both organizational and national levels, and the two tools—the GNH survey and the screening tool—belong together as two pillars of GNH governance.

Having gained an overview of the GNH framework as it has been developed in Bhutan at a national level, we will now discover how it can be used at a personal, familial, organizational, and regional level, by looking at real-life examples in which I've had the opportunity to implement it in the past years.

PART 3

IMPLEMENTING GROSS NATIONAL HAPPINESS

Introduction

Between stimulus and response there is a space.
In that space is our power to choose our response.
*In our response lies our growth and our freedom.**

—VIKTOR E. FRANKL

We can implement GNH at a personal level, for our family, in education, in business, and also at political level. At all levels, there are always two core dimensions: assessing the structural or outer conditions with the help of the nine domains and cultivating happiness skills.

Many of the exercises presented in this book can be used in all context—from personal to business and political—although some are more appropriate to a specific setting. For the sake of avoiding too many repetitions, and also to make the reading hopefully simpler, I have distributed the practical exercises in different chapters. But the reader should be aware that most practices remain valid in all circumstances.

Fundamentally, happiness skills are based on two main pillars that are mutually interdependent: mindfulness and emotional intelligence. All the mindfulness practices can be adapted to be relevant to any context: mindful breathing, mindful sitting, mindful walking, mindful eating.

Emotional intelligence comprises five core competencies:

The first two are related to self—self-awareness and self-management. They include being aware of one's emotions, knowing how to deal with painful and difficult emotions, and knowing how to cultivate positive attitudes and states of mind such as compassion, gratefulness, kindness, and equanimity—states of mind that nurture positive emotions such as delight, peacefulness, or joy.

---

*Viktor E. Frankl. *Man's Search for Meaning*, trans. Ilse Lasch (Boston: Beacon Press, 1992).

The next two competencies—social awareness and the ability to create and sustain trustful, loving relationships—are the foundation of social skills. They are crucial in all social contexts: family, education, and workplace.

Finally, the fifth competency—responsible decision making—builds on the four previous ones and includes an ethical dimension that underlies any meaningful and happy life.

Mindfulness is the precondition to training all the other abilities, because as long as our attention is scattered and determined by extrinsic factors, we cannot access the introspective self-knowledge that is necessary to develop happiness skills.

Therefore, I suggest to read all the following chapters, even if one's own focus is more related to one field, such as business or education, because in each part there will be practices that can be relevant to any other dimension.

9

HOW TO ASSESS
YOUR PERSONAL
HAPPINESS WITH GNH

We have seen how the nine domains of Gross National Happiness are used as to assess the levels of happiness and well-being of the Bhutanese population. The same domains can be used as an assessment tool for companies, organizations, families, and even oneself. An important part of the process is to define the right indicators for each one of these domains. When we do it in an organizational context, the process of defining the right indicators is, in itself, a transformative learning experience, as it creates opportunities to share with and listen to one another and to build a consensus on what we consider important in each of the domains.

To give a taste of how the nine domains might help assess one's personal situation, I'll give an overly simplified version with just one question per domain.

Imagine a scale that goes from 0 to 10. The top of the scale represents the best possible life for you, and the bottom is the worst possible situation. For each of the domains you will answer one simple question and rate your answer simply from 0 to 10.

Psychological well-being: I regularly practice cultivating positive emotions and an optimistic mindset.

0   1   2   3   4   5   6   7   8   9   10

Health: My lifestyle contributes to preventing diseases and maintaining good physical and mental health.

0   1   2   3   4   5   6   7   8   9   10

Time use: There is a nice balance in my life between my various activities: family, work, leisure, spiritual life, time in nature, and so forth.

0   1   2   3   4   5   6   7   8   9   10

Education: I have plenty of opportunities to continue learning throughout my life, both in formal and informal ways.

0   1   2   3   4   5   6   7   8   9   10

Cultural diversity and resilience: I participate actively in cultural life—in the field of art, such as playing music, singing, acting, or dancing; in the field of science, such as studying and researching; or in the field of spirituality, such as regular spiritual practices.

0   1   2   3   4   5   6   7   8   9   10

Community vitality: I trust that there are enough people in my immediate surroundings who would be willing to help me in case of major challenges. And I am committed to supporting my friends and relatives when they are facing difficulties.

0   1   2   3   4   5   6   7   8   9   10

Good governance: I trust that the people in leadership positions, either in my organization or in my country, consider the well-being of all as their main objective.

0   1   2   3   4   5   6   7   8   9   10

Ecological diversity and resilience: I make conscious efforts to reduce my ecological footprint through concrete daily actions, such as reducing waste, saving energy, and consuming in a more conscious and responsible way.

0   1   2   3   4   5   6   7   8   9   10

Living standards: I feel that my financial situation allows me to meet my basic needs and those of my family.

0   1   2   3   4   5   6   7   8   9   10

Once you have filled out the scales of the nine domains, you can transcribe the results onto the Happiness Wheel and connect the dots. The lines connecting the dots form a star that gives you a glimpse of your self-assessed well-being as measured through the nine domains. Obviously, this first image is not a scientifically valid assessment of your life situation, but it gives you an impression of the areas where your life is well balanced and those that need more attention. You can also create your own questions that are more pertinent for your life situation.

After you have completed this exercise, take a few minutes to contemplate your well-being star and write down any reflections that arise: Where should I put more attention in the coming months and years? Where are my strengths and weaknesses? How could I find a better life balance between these various domains?

It is important to note that, from the perspective of GNH, the goal is not to score ten out of ten in each of domains—this would be unrealistic—rather to find a harmonious balance between the different areas so that we achieve harmony in our lives. GNH has an idea of a "sufficiency threshold." Even with happiness and well-being, we need to ask ourselves how much is enough. In the GNH survey, having high scores in six out of the nine domains is considered sufficient.

In our personal lives, we constantly have to make choices and arbitrate between competing goals. If we want to earn more and have a more comfortable material life, it might mean less time with friends and family. If we want to travel the world and discover new cultures, it will come with an increased ecological footprint. The nine domains help us make choices that are better informed and that align with our deeper intentions.

Journaling Practice

An additional practice that I often use in GNH workshops to help participants reflect on their life situations is the journaling practice inspired by Theory U methodology, which was developed by Dr. Otto Scharmer at the Presencing Institute.* Guided journaling leads through a process of self-reflection. This process allows you to step into a deeper level of reflection than an unguided journaling process, and it helps you to identify concrete action steps once a first diagnostic has been reached through the GNH Wheel assessment.

These are some of the questions you might want to think about in this context. In all of these questions, consider all aspects of your life (work, personal life, etc.).

Challenges: Look at yourself from outside, as if you were another person: What are the three or four most important challenges or tasks that your life currently presents?

Self: Write down three or four important facts about yourself. What accomplishments you have achieved? What skills or good qualities do you have? (Have you raised children? Finished your education? Are you a good listener?).

Emerging self: What three or four important aspirations, areas of interest, or undeveloped talents do you have that you would like to focus on more in the future? (Writing a novel or poems? Starting a social movement? Taking your current work to a new level?)

Frustration: What is it about your current life that frustrates you the most?

---

* Presencing Institute, "Field of the Future Journaling Practice," *https://www.presencing.org/files/tools/PI_Tool_UJournaling.pdf.*

Energy: What are your most vital sources of energy? What do you love?

Inner resistance: What is holding you back? Describe two or three recent situations in your life where you felt stuck.

Your community: Who makes up your community and what are their highest hopes in regard to your future journey?

Footprint: Imagine you could fast forward to the last moments of your life when it is time to pass on. Look back on your life's journey as a whole: What would you want to see at that moment? What footprint do you want to leave behind on the planet? What would you want to be remembered for by the people who live on after you?

Intention: Think about what you just wrote about the footprint you want to leave behind when you pass on. Crystalize what it is you want to create. What do you want to do to achieve that? In the next three to five years, what vision and intention do you have for yourself and for your work? What are the core elements of the future that you want to generate in your personal, professional, and social lives? Describe as concretely as possible the images and elements that occur to you.

Letting go: What would you have to let go of (behaviors, thought processes, etc.) in order to bring your vision into reality? What is the old skin that you need to shed?

Seeds: What in your current life provides the seeds for the future that you want to create? Where do you see your future beginning?

People: Who can help you make your highest possibilities a reality? Who might be your core partners?

Action: If you were to take on the project of bringing your intention into reality, what practical first steps would you take over the next three days, weeks, and months?

Journaling is a powerful practice that helps you reflect on your life journey. I have done it regularly in the past, and seeing how the answers change over time is an interesting barometer of your own development. While it can be done alone or in a group, practicing it in a group is a still richer experience; two or more partners can take turns sharing their journal entries and listening deeply to each other, which can lead to an in-depth dialogue. I have witnessed many times how this practice has helped people find solutions or new directions in their life journeys.

What Does Happiness Mean to You?

Another interesting practice to deepen your understanding of happiness is a contemplative practice that also brings together meditation and writing.

First, consider two fundamental inner techniques in meditation— mindfulness (or open awareness) and concentration. The former is about being fully present to whatever occurs, without judging or interfering, simply remaining a curious yet neutral observer. It involves opening and widening our sphere of attention, while remaining alert and wakeful. With the latter, concentration, we focus our attention carefully on one thing.

It is useful to master these two distinct techniques when practicing any kind of meditation. It can be compared with the process of breathing in and breathing out at the level of our consciousness. The practice that I would like to share is based on these two processes. It can be used to get deeper insights about any question we are grappling with, but in this case, I would like to apply it to a specific question: what does happiness mean for me? Use the steps below for this practice.

1. Ask yourself, "What does happiness mean for me?" Focus your whole attention on this question. Don't try to answer the question—just focus on the question itself. If it is helpful, you can repeat the question over and over in your mind, or you can simply

concentrate on the question inwardly without actually thinking of the words. Do this five to seven minutes.

2. Now move from focused attention to open awareness on this question. Generate a state of inner listening, without trying to answer the question intellectually. This step also takes five to seven minutes.

3. Now take a pen and a piece of paper and write down whatever comes to mind. Don't think too much about it. Just let your hand freely and intuitively write whatever comes up.

4. Carefully read what you've written and then try to summarize it in just one short sentence (or, if you're a more a visual person, in a symbol or picture).

5. Now go back to focused awareness, this time focusing on the short sentence or symbol from step 4. Once again, keep your attention carefully focused for five to seven minutes on this content.

6. Move again to open awareness, listening intuitively to what emerges in the silence about the sentence or symbol. Again, five to seven minutes.

7. Finally, take your pen and paper again and write whatever occurs in the moment.

This exercise moves us beyond our superficial intellectual knowledge and opinion that usually springs up when we answer a question. It can take a little time to get used to this practice, but it helps us access deeper layers of our consciousness and discover insights that were already present, but which we were not aware of. Very often, the result is quite surprising and different from what we would have expected.

I recently practiced this exercise during a GNH workshop with a group of master's degree students at the University of Vienna, and the outcome was extremely interesting and diverse. One participant shared that she had suddenly experienced the deep well of happiness that was already inside her, and that she now realized that she could access it at any time. Another participant shared that she had become conscious of the fact that she didn't allow herself to be happy. A third was surprised to observe that while she was asking herself the question about happiness, what emerged were the sources of suffering lying deep in her consciousness.

That last student's experience is especially valuable, because if we want to attain authentic happiness, we need to become aware of the sources of suffering that create obstacles. Only through learning how to transform suffering can we obtain deep and lasting happiness.

In summary, when starting a GNH investigation for oneself, one needs to look at the outer conditions of life and how they can be improved or transformed. We also need to investigate our inner dimension. This will help us discover not only the sources of our suffering and how they can be transformed or healed but also how to strengthen the positive qualities we have, as well as any additional competencies we can develop intentionally.

10

GNH IN FAMILIES

The family is the most important unit within society. Our family has an enormous impact on us; our relationships with our parents and siblings are the basis on which we form all later relationships. The family can be a place of warmth, love, trust, and security, but unfortunately it is also where a lot of suffering and trauma can originate. Bringing happiness to the family, therefore, creates the strongest possible foundation both for personal and societal happiness.

I recently had the opportunity of facilitating a GNH retreat for just one family. It was a deeply moving experience to see how, by focusing on the question of happiness, the family members were able to transform patterns of behavior that had created suffering and open up to each other in a much more authentic way. Too often we overlook those closest to us, because we wrongly think that we already know them. We rarely take the time to listen deeply to their feelings and experiences.

The most fundamental practice within a family is simply to take sufficient time to be together, without any agenda other than sharing and listening. In many families, this rarely happens, and with today's smartphones and tablets, this situation has worsened considerably. It always troubles me when I see a family sitting together in a restaurant, each member staring at their smartphone instead of speaking with each other.

Mindful Parenting

When our own children were young, my wife and I made the conscious choice not to have a television at home, so that we could spend evenings interacting with each other. Every evening, once homework was done, we would play music together (both our children played the violin, my wife played the harp, and I played the flute), or we'd play games or read books together. I remember vividly one summer holiday in Denmark when we read the whole of Tolkien's *Lord of the Rings* together as a family. Each evening we would sit around a campfire, taking turns reading aloud from the book. Often we were so thrilled that it was difficult to stop reading and go to bed. Then, the next day, in a nearby forest, we would act out the scenes we'd read the night before.

Now grown up, our children have their own children, but they enjoyed their childhood so much that they have continued the tradition of not having televisions at home, and they play games and music and read long books together as a family. It is often said that young people do not read anymore, but I have observed from my children and grandchildren that if the culture of reading is instilled from early on, children naturally become avid readers. Once a child discovers the magic of the imaginative world of books, it opens up a whole world of fantasy and freedom that can never be acquired in the classroom.

The quality of time we spend with our children is probably the most important preparation we can give them for their future life. Most parents want the best for their children, but in our consumerist society, many mistake "the best" with material toys or gadgets. Spending time together—sharing, listening, playing, reading, walking in nature—is the most precious thing we can give our children.

When we understand how children develop, we realize that for the first six or seven years, the most important educational dimension is the environment in which the child lives. In the first part of the book, we described the mirror neurons that enable human beings, even from birth, to perceive intuitively the inner world of the people around them.

Like a sponge, a young child soaks up whatever happens in their surroundings. Being a parent, therefore, is about nurturing children, and according to Buddhist psychology, there are four kinds of nutriments that nourish the human being. Being mindful of these nutriments is of utmost importance for the development of our children.

The Four Nutriments

Edible food*

Sense perception

Volition

Consciousness

Edible Food

The first nutriment is edible food. It is easy to understand how the quality of the food we eat has a strong impact not only on our body but also on our mind. In a time when the agri-food industry is more concerned with profits than with the health of consumers, it is crucial for parents to be mindful of the quality of their children's food. The ecological and social impacts of what we eat also need to be taken into account. Although we are not usually conscious of these dimensions of our food, all these elements are ingested with what we eat. For example, when animals that are raised for meat are poorly treated, experiencing a lot of stress and suffering, and then die in agony and fear, these elements too become part of the food we ingest. Therefore, a healthy and

---

* "Edible food" is the term used in Buddhism to denote material food for the physical body, to distinguish it from food for the senses, the mind, and consciousness.

balanced diet that takes care of not only human health but also the health of our society and planet is important for the healthy development of children.

Fortunately, it has become increasingly easy to buy organic or biodynamically raised food almost everywhere, and in developed countries, the percentage of income spent on food is relatively low for an average family. The additional cost of organic fruits and vegetables is relatively modest, and it will be compensated by lower medical expenses in the long term.

Sense Perception

The second nutriment is sense perception. With the process of urbanization, humanity moved from a natural environment, where the beauty of the forms and colors of nature was all around us, to an artificial one, one that often adversely affects the quality of all of our sense perceptions. It is one of the sad manifestations of a materialistic society like ours that a sense of beauty seems, by and large, to have vanished. Looking at ancient architecture or simply at the objects that were used in daily life, one can be moved by the care and attention to detail, the sense of harmony and the beauty that shines in all aspects of traditional cultures. In contrast, when walking through a modern city, one can be shocked by the carelessness that is evident everywhere: the garish colors of advertisements, harsh lights, soulless architecture, the smell of exhaust from cars, and noise pollution.

Even typical Western clothing is disappointing. After living for a number of years in Bhutan, where most people still wear traditional clothes made from beautifully colored hand-woven materials, I was shocked by the contrast with the image of the streets in European cities, the scarcity of fantasy and beauty in the way most people were dressed, as well as the lack of colors—grey, blue, and black being most common. The uniformity of shapes and design also makes for a boring sight. Looking at traditional costumes all over the world, one can't help but be impressed by the manifold colors, shapes, and structures of clothes that give them soul, an expression of a culture, and of the natural world in a given place on earth. The uniformity of contemporary Western garments is a symptom of the soullessness of contemporary society.

The quality of the materials—both clothing and other objects, like toys—that surround a child is of great importance, yet in the Western world, a young child is more likely to wear clothes made of synthetic fabrics and play with plastic toys in lurid colors than organic materials such as wood and natural fabrics. Being attentive to the quality of the sense perceptions that a child receives is a more important aspect of educating younger children than teaching them theoretical or abstract knowledge, which doesn't have a deep effect at that age.

Recently, I met a young Tibetan man, and I was deeply impressed by his shining smile and joyful nature. He gave the impression of being a very well-balanced and happy individual, and I wondered what had forged such a radiant personality. He told me about his early childhood, how he had grown up in a nomadic family of herders, living in a tent of black yak wool at an altitude of 4,000 meters (13,170 feet). He described waking up each morning, the tent cold from the fresh air of the high Tibetan plateau, but he would be cozy under the yak-wool blanket that his mother had lovingly wrapped around him to keep him warm—and the fire, which his parents had kindled back into life, was quickly warming the tent. His mother would already be up, milking the yaks nearby, and he would hear the sound of the milk hitting the copper bucket, as well as the sounds of wind blowing and the animals moving around. He remembered feeling safe, snug, and protected, being one with his natural environment.

As I heard this story of his early childhood, I understood clearly what had contributed to his shining joyfulness and friendliness. Of course, it is not possible for our children, most of whom grow up in cities, to have a similar experience of being one with nature in the same intimate way, but we can try our best to create an environment in which they feel safe, protected, and connected with the whole universe. The most precious experience we can provide for a young child is the feeling that the world is good and that life and people can be trusted. If we can instill the feeling that the universe is a benevolent place, all the rest is secondary.

Volition

The third kind of nutriment is volition. On the one hand, this means our intentions and, on the other, our actions. Whenever someone acts, it has an impact not only on the world but also on the doer. A central element of education is creating wholesome habits so that the will of the child is encouraged in a positive direction. One of the secrets of educating the will is repetition: the more there is rhythm, the less we need effort, and whatever habit is created becomes a natural flow. Choosing the right habits is a crucial aspect of guiding the child in the right direction. This is one of the reasons why learning a musical instrument is such a precious element in education. In addition to opening up a whole new world of sounds, harmony, and beauty for the child, it also, and most importantly, creates a habit of regular, steadfast daily practice. This, in itself, is a powerful pedagogical tool.

Another aspect of the education of the will is to help the child become aware of the consequences of their actions. True discipline is not so much about enforcing rules and forbidding certain things, but rather about helping the child understand that certain actions bring suffering to self and others, while others bring happiness to self and others. The more clearly we understand the inevitable consequences of every action we take, the more a natural sense of ethics will arise. Being mindful of the consequences of our actions is the best foundation for a sense of responsibility toward ourselves, others, and the planet.

In the Vietnamese Zen tradition of Plum Village, children have the opportunity to take part in a ceremony called The Two Promises. The promises are these:

> *I vow to develop my understanding in order to live peacefully with people, animals, plants, and minerals.*

*I vow to develop my compassion, in order to protect the lives of
people, animals, plants, and minerals.*

One might think that such promises sound a little abstract for young
children, but, actually, I have observed that most of them understand
quite easily what they might mean. Here are some testimonies from
children who decided to take The Two Promises:

*I want to take The Two Promises because I really want to under-
stand and help others. I want to be a veterinarian, so I want to
make sure there are no more poachers in the world. I want to plant
a lot of trees, and I want to help people who are suffering.*

Maeve, age seven.

*I want to receive The Two Promises because if I have understanding
then I can be respectful, nice, helpful, and giving. If I have compassion, then I can love my relatives more, and I can also listen to
people better.*

Ryah, age eleven.

*I want to take The Two Promises because I care about nature, ani-
mals, and people. I want to live peacefully and be happy.*

Laeticia, age eleven.

*I want to receive The Two Promises because it will help me under-
stand my brothers and sisters and know when I water their seeds
of anger or their seeds of joy and compassion. It will help me to live
peacefully with them.*

Hylan, age twelve.

*I want to take The Two Promises to help me to remember to be nice
to all living things.*

Julia, age six.

Consciousness

The fourth nutriment is consciousness. In the first part of the book, we described how every thought, emotion, and potential experience is present in the deeper layers of our consciousness in the form of a "seed" and how these seeds manifest in our daily consciousness depends on which seeds are watered and nurtured and which ones are rooted out, as the little prince did with the bad seeds of the baobab. Whatever lives in our consciousness—thoughts, emotions, or intentions—is a kind of nutriment that can be poisonous or nourishing in the same way that food can be. Therefore, being attentive to how we nourish the consciousness of our children is also a crucial aspect of their healthy development.

It is worrying—and a sign of a complete lack of common sense—that the question whether violent video games are detrimental to children is still a point of controversy. I would like to remind the reader how these games came about in the first place, so that we can understand what kind of seeds they nourish in our consciousness. During the Vietnam War, the American military was appalled to notice that hundreds, if not thousands, of bullets were being fired for each enemy soldier who was killed. In the process of examining the reasons for this low ratio they realized that, very often, soldiers tended not to shoot accurately when aiming at a person. The reason behind this was that, as human beings, we have an inborn reluctance of killing another human being, and most military training is aimed at suppressing this natural inhibition. Regular training, they realized, was not efficient at this, so one of the methods developed to overcome the inhibition was violent video games, where the player develops the reflex of shooting rapidly without letting any thought or ethical judgement disturb his accuracy. Since this is the origin of these games, it is obvious as to what kind of seeds are being watered in the consciousness of children who are exposed to them, sometimes for hours each day.

The choice of books, films, games, and other influences that children are exposed to determine the content of their consciousness, and this has significant consequences on their overall development.

Rites of Passage into Adolescence

Mindful parenting is about making skillful choices in these four nutriments that feed our children, so that the seeds of happiness and well-being will be watered, while the seeds of suffering, fear, violence, and despair are left dormant or are transformed when they arise. When we understand this, we realize that educating is not so much about telling children what to do—requiring some behaviors and forbidding others—but much more about creating a healthy harmonious and nourishing environment.

When our own children became preteens, my wife and I realized that they needed a strong experience to help them cross the threshold from childhood to adolescence. In traditional societies, there are rites of passage that help a young person move from one phase to the other, but these rites have almost completely disappeared in contemporary Western societies. As a family, we decided to create our own ritual to help our children in this moment of significant transformation. That ritual was to hike over the Alps from Lake Geneva to the Mediterranean Sea, a trek that takes three full weeks of hiking for at least eight hours per day. Most people who hike this trail stay the nights in the hotels or refuges (simple shelters much like youth hostels) that are available at regular intervals and eat in restaurants. But to make our ritual more interesting and challenging, we decided to carry our own tents and sleep each night in the wild, camping near rivers or lakes, and to carry our own food and cook our own meals. At the time, we lived a few kilometers away from the lake, so with our backpacks, we walked down to the lake, took a boat over to the French side, and started our ascent.

For the first few days, it was a great physical effort to be hiking eight hours a day on steep mountain paths with heavy backpacks. But with time, we gained strength, and it became easier. The main challenge was that we had four adolescents who had quite strong appetites, and there was only so much food we were able to carry. Every three days, we had to walk down to the nearest village to purchase new supplies, and usually we were running short on food the day before. I remember vividly one day ascending a high mountain and, when we arrived at the top, all we had left were three apples, which we divided between the six of us. After the first bites, the children exclaimed how amazed they were by the wonderful taste of these apples, asking what kind of apples they were, and how come they had never eaten such delicious fruit before. In fact, they were very common apples, and at home we had piles of them—and probably would have never paid attention to eating them—but in this situation, after a long hard climb, they suddenly fully tasted their wonderful flavor and fragrance! It was as though they were eating apples for the very first time.

Our children grew up in Switzerland, and obviously it would have been absurd to deprive them intentionally of food so they could realize the exquisite taste and preciousness of a simple apple. But in this situation it had occurred naturally, and it gave them the opportunity of a deep experience that they would have never had in their ordinary lives. This is just one of the many memorable experiences we had during this journey, and, looking back on it, it remains one of the highlights of our family life. Even today, when we speak with our children about their childhood, it is not holidays in a comfortable seaside resort or a cozy mountain chalet that stand out but this challenging adventure of hiking for hours on end, day after day, through the beauty of the mountains.

We will speak more about education in the next chapter, but here I wish to emphasize the importance of creating a supportive family environment as a foundation of happiness for both for the individual and society.

Beginning Anew*

One of the practices from Plum Village that I can recommend in a family or community is known as Beginning Anew, a four-part process in which, at each stage, each participant has the opportunity to speak and will not be interrupted by others during their turn. While one person in the family is speaking, the others practice deep listening.

Relationships are just like living beings; they need attention, care, and nutrition to thrive and develop. Once we take a relationship for granted, and we don't feel the need to invest time and attentiveness in it, it is bound to wither. More often than not, it is our nearest family circle that we tend to take for granted. With people less close to us, we know we have to make an effort and display our best behavior; but actually, it is with our loved ones that we should be our best, as it is with them that our conduct has the strongest impact. Simply talking and listening to one another can work miracles. It is not difficult to do, but it needs commitment and the willingness to offer each other the wonderful gift of our true presence and full awareness.

I have seen this practice enabling family members who had become estranged reconnecting and bonding in moving ways. In my own family, we have always made a conscious commitment to take enough time for deep conversations—and I must admit that my wife has been the leading force in this context.

1. **Flower watering:** This is a chance to share our appreciation for others. Too often we take our loved ones for granted, and while we might be aware of their qualities, we seldom make the effort to consciously perceive them and express

---

*The Beginning Anew practice, *https://plumvillage.org/books/beginning-anew*.

our appreciation. Flower watering is an opportunity to shine a light on the other person's strengths, to mention specific instances when the person said or did something that we admired, and to encourage the growth of their positive qualities.

One of my granddaughters was born with a health problem, and during the first years of her life, her development was quite challenging. She has two older brothers, and I have witnessed many times how they practiced the reinforcement of her good qualities by always pointing out what she succeeded to do, rather than mentioning what was difficult for her. When her oldest brother was about eight years old and she was only three, he drew a picture of his little sister dressed in a Superwoman outfit and wrote her name and the word "Superhero." I observed how this repeated flower watering allowed her to develop a strong self-esteem that also helped her to overcome her difficulties.

I have often witnessed people moved to tears when their good qualities were acknowledged. But it's not just the person who receives the appreciation who benefits. The giver is also nourished by putting into words their awareness on the beauty of their loved one. The self-confidence of both the giver and the receiver is strengthened, and both are given more courage to develop in a positive way. Sometimes doing just this first step of the process is enough to restore or strengthen the harmony and the warmth between the family members.

There is a proverb that says "Love makes you blind," but I would argue that the opposite is true: love allows you to see the wonderful qualities in someone that other people might have overlooked. When we fall in love, we can almost be blown away by the beauty of our beloved. But as time passes, the danger is that we gradually lose this clear sight, and we take the other one for granted, forgetting the wonder we experienced when we first met. A practice like flower watering helps both of us to rekindle the awareness that could be forgotten.

2. **Sharing regrets:** Often, we may hurt our loved ones—not intentionally, but simply through lack of attention and mindfulness. We let our own preoccupations consume us and don't really listen to others' needs, because own life or work seems more important. Even when we do notice that we have hurt someone, we often don't take time to acknowledge it, thinking that it's not very important and that the pain will heal by itself. But when these unspoken wounds accumulate, it can end up destroying a relationship.

   As a younger man, I had a certain fiery energy, and I could come across as too direct. Most of the time, I did not mean to hurt others, and I was often unaware that I had offended someone. Actually, it was usually my wife who noticed it and brought my attention to it. It took me a while to accept it and to able to express regrets to those had upset. I used to think that since I did not have any bad intentions, why should I apologize? But with experience, I realized that I had to acknowledge the painful emotions that I had caused, even unintentionally. Having the opportunity to express sincere regrets in a ceremony of Beginning Anew helped heal situations that could have disrupted a friendship or a relationship with some of my students.

As soon as we notice that we might have inadvertently hurt someone's feelings, it is important to acknowledge it and share our regrets. In daily life, however, we might not have the opportunity to do so right away, and this practice provides a moment when we intentionally take time to apologize for any careless action or speech that might have hurt others. Even though the actual hurt might have seemed not very deep, this practice has a strong healing effect.

3. **Expressing hurt:** In order for others to understand us, we must have the courage and honesty to share the hurt that others have inadvertently caused us, without accusing them of having done it intentionally. It is important to realize that our emotions belong to us and, although someone else might have triggered it, the root cause always lies within our own consciousness. The expression of hurt, therefore, is a process of self-knowledge, though at the same time, it might help those who are close to us to be more sensitive to our vulnerabilities and to learn to refrain from hurting us unintentionally. This part of the process is very sensitive and needs to be done with great care—after having practiced the flower-watering step, for example—so that it does not create more tension and suffering. Expressing hurt can only happen if there is a genuine feeling of warmth and trust between the participants.

It is often difficult to admit our own vulnerability. Even when we've been offended by something someone said or did, we often pretend it has not touched us, although this creates inner turmoil, especially when it is not expressed. For instance, one might say to one's partner: "Darling, yesterday evening, I had a worry that I wanted to share with you, but while I was talking, you kept being distracted by incoming messages on your phone. I had the feeling that my concern was not being taken seriously, and it was painful for me."

4. **Sharing a long-term difficulty and asking for support:** We all, at times, experience pain that arises from our past. If we have a circle of people we trust, sharing such issues can help those around us understand us better and offer the support we really need. Structures and hierarchies within families and organizations can often create obstacles to sharing vulnerabilities, and yet our vulnerability is an important part of our humanity. Sharing it allows us to create more authentic relationships and helps bring about transformation and healing within ourselves and the community.

    I have always had a very good relationship with my daughter, so I thought there were no problems between us. Once, when she was a teenager, she told me: "Daddy I know you love me very much, but I also feel that your expectations of me are too high, and it feels like a burden." I was a bit shocked by her statement, but I was also grateful, because by expressing her feelings so honestly, she helped me become aware of an unconscious pressure I was putting on her without wanting to do so. It helped us both to develop a deeper and more relaxed relationship.

While the Beginning Anew practice can be done in a formal setting where family members or friends have gathered intentionally, it can also help guide the way we interact with one another on a daily basis and in a much more informal way. In fact, sometimes an informal and discreet practice is more efficient than a formal, structured process. Keeping in mind these four steps can help guide the creation of healthy and fulfilling relationships within the family or community.

11

GNH IN EDUCATION

My Path toward Happy Schools in Vietnam

I have been an educator all my life. After completing my first studies at the age of twenty-four, I became a teacher in a Waldorf/Rudolf Steiner School in Germany. Waldorf education attracted me because it's focused on the phases of a child's development, with the aim of supporting the blossoming of the full human being, not just the intellect. The Swiss educator Johann Heinrich Pestalozzi (1746–1827), inspired by the pedagogical ideas of Jean-Jacques Rousseau (1712–1778), started a pilot school and famously proclaimed that education is about developing the head, heart, and hands, thus creating the foundation of a holistic pedagogical approach. Despite the fact that many agreed with this concept, it was never really applied on a large scale. Waldorf education, which follows the teachings of the Austrian philosopher Rudolf Steiner (1861–1925), is one of the few examples that systematically puts into practice these threefold dimensions of education. In these schools, children have a schedule balanced between academic, artistic, and practical disciplines. Moreover, Waldorf teachers seek to address the body, soul, and spirit of the child, taking into consideration not only material needs, but also psychological, emotional, and spiritual dimensions. This first teaching experience had a lasting impact on my understanding of education.

From there I moved to the field of special education, researching, for many years, the curative and healing impact of education on children with different needs. In 1982 I had the opportunity to return to Vietnam, seven years after the end of the Vietnam War. The country had been devastated. The American military had sprayed fifty million liters (over thirteen million gallons) of the highly toxic dioxin-based defoliant known as Agent Orange over the land. Many women who had been exposed to this poison during pregnancy gave birth to babies with severe physical and mental disabilities. Upon returning to Vietnam, I met many such children, and my desire to help led to the creation of the Eurasia Foundation. Together with my wife, I devised special education classes in primary schools and other initiatives, developing teacher-training courses and building a team of dedicated educators who contributed to this work over many years. Vietnam is a Communist country, and education is strictly controlled by the state, but because the needs in the field of special education were so urgent and the available resources so limited, the authorities were happy to support us in developing our programs.

When working in the field of special education, and especially with children with mental disabilities, one cannot focus the pedagogy on academic disciplines alone; it is necessary to take into consideration the whole human being, as well as the uniqueness of each child. This is in stark contrast to the pedagogical approach that is common in most schools. After several decades of working in this field, we were able to form strong and trusting relationships with the local and national authorities, and some years ago, when the Vietnamese Ministry of Education realized the challenges it was facing were similar to those of other Asian countries, the education department of the province invited us to discuss how we could offer programs for the overall education system. Thus the Happy Schools project was established. The fact that UNESCO had published their Happy Schools! report was also a helpful argument, because, as a consequence of this study, all member states were encouraged to incorporate into the educational system the happiness and well-being of students. This is how we embarked on the Happy Schools in Vietnam journey.

Why Do We Need Happy Schools?

With small variations, the current educational system is, by and large, the same all over the world. A product of nineteenth-century European social organization, it is modeled upon the needs of the Industrial Revolution: workers, managers, and executives. It is striking how similar the hierarchical organization of industrial production and the educational system are. In industrial production, quality control has to do with conformity—if a factory is producing parts for cars or machines, they have to be exactly the same to in order to work. This idea of equating quality to conformity has been transferred to the educational system, where exams and assessments test how well students have met specific standards, without taking their individual talents and aspirations into consideration.

And when we look at the spatial organization of schools and classrooms, it reminds us strongly of that of factories. The children are lined up in square rooms, facing the blackboard, with the teacher standing in front of them; similarly, in photographs of nineteenth-century factory workrooms, we see workers sitting or standing at machines, as the foreman supervises their work.

Furthermore, the division of labor in a factory meant that each category of workers needed a limited set of skills. Likewise, the educational system doesn't promote the development of the full human being, but only addresses those aspects of knowledge and training that fulfill the perceived needs of the job market or social expectation.

In summary, the goal of the current educational system is not, in the first place, to allow the development of the full potential of the human individual. Rather, it is to develop those competencies that are thought to be needed in the workplace. Paradoxically, work has changed tremendously in the past decades, but the goal of developing the skills needed for the workplace has not actually been reached. When comparing the competencies taught in schools and universities and the actual competencies needed in today's workplace, we see a great discrepancy.

Until the end of the twentieth century, information was more difficult to obtain than it is today, so it is understandable why a lot of education was traditionally about memorizing as much information as possible. Today, anyone with a smartphone has access to more information than was available in the largest university libraries fifty or one hundred years ago. But the educational system has not evolved accordingly, and a lot of the time spent in the classroom, from primary school to university, is still used transmitting and learning information.

In January 2018 Jack Ma, the founder of Alibaba, pointed out at the World Economic Forum in Davos the consequence of the rise of artificial intelligence for the field of education:[*]

> *Education is a big challenge now. If we do not change the way we teach, in thirty years' time we will be in big trouble. Because the way we teach is the way we have taught our kids for the past two hundred years. It is knowledge-based and we cannot teach our kids to compete with machines who [sic] are smarter; we have to teach something unique that machines can never catch up with, so that thirty years later our kids will have a chance. [So what do we need to teach our kids?] Values, independent thinking, teamwork, care for others. These are the soft parts that knowledge will not teach you. That's why I think we should teach our kids sports, music, painting, arts—everything we teach should be different from machines. If the machine can do better, think about it.*

So the first challenge the current educational system has to face up to is the fact that it has not evolved in sync with the needs of society.

---

[*] "Jack Ma on the future of education (teamwork included)," TEAM MUSIC, video, 1:59, *https://www.youtube.com/watch?v=rHt-5-RyrJk*.

A second and probably even more troubling challenge for this same educational system is to accept that it does not deliver a harmonious development of the whole human being. It generates a lot of suffering, frustration, and stress in children and young people. The Program for International Student Assessment (PISA), created by the Organization for Economic Cooperation and Development (OECD), is an international survey that aims to evaluate education systems worldwide by testing the skills and knowledge of fifteen-year-old students. The PISA test is available in eighty-two languages and is considered to document the quality and performance of educational systems worldwide—one could say that it represents, in the field of education, what GDP represents for the economic system. In 2015, over half a million students—representing twenty-eight million fifteen-year-olds in seventy-two countries—took the internationally agreed-upon two-hour test. Students were assessed in science, mathematics, reading, and financial literacy. When we look at the test results, the seven highest scores in the world were obtained by Singapore, Hong Kong, Macao, Taiwan, Japan, China, and South Korea (in that order). If we believe that the scores are a valid assessment of the educational systems, this would mean that the whole world should emulate these Asian countries. In 2016, however, the Asia-Pacific Bureau of UNESCO did a survey that indicated that although these countries did have the highest scores, the physical and mental health of adolescents in these countries, as well as their overall happiness and well-being, was very low. Stress, burnout, depression, and suicide rates clearly indicated that although their academic achievements were impressive, the well-being of the children did not correlate with their performances. Based on these findings, UNESCO conducted an in-depth study that was published as the "Happy Schools!" report. In the foreword to this report, Gwang Jo Kim, the director of the UNESCO Bangkok office wrote:*

---

* "Happy Schools! A Framework for Learner Well-Being in the Asia-Pacific," UNESCO Bankok (September 8, 2020), *https://bangkok.unesco.org/content /happy-schools-framework-learner-well-being-asia-pacific.*

I believe that all children are entitled to be happy and enjoy their lives in school, whether through a genuine love of learning, through building positive friendships and relationships, or through feeling a sense of belonging in the community and wider society. Moreover, we need all learners to be happy in order for future generations to contribute to a more peaceful and prosperous world. For me, this is what "Happy Schools!" is all about.

Four Pillars of Learning

The increased pressure about academic performance has resulted in alarming trends in schools: growing mistrust, competition, bullying, and violence among students, as well as increasing fears about expressing their personalities and about making mistakes. Today there is an increasing recognition of the need for learning assessments to look beyond strictly academic outcomes and to place importance on measuring the social and emotional domains of learning that are conducive to enhancing learner well-being. The UNESCO report *Learning: The Treasure Within* identified four pillars of learning:[*]

* Learning to know
* Learning to do
* Learning to live together
* Learning to be

The report placed a particular emphasis on learning to live together as an overarching goal. Arguably, equipping learners with the skills, attitudes, and values pertaining to learning to live together and learning to be—such as empathy, tolerance,

---

[*] *Learning: The Treasure Within*, UNESCO (1996), https://unesdoc.unesco.org/ark:/48223/pf0000109590.

communication, and creativity—requires holistic development within the school environment. The Happy Schools in Vietnam project focuses on the psychosocial and emotional dimensions of learning, in order to promote happiness within the school context.

Three Main Areas of Development Reflecting Three Areas of Care

1. **Self-care:** students develop their full potential through a holistic approach that fosters:

    * Learning to learn and learning to know (head, cognitive): how to master one's attention using mindfulness as a foundational skill that will support all other fields of learning and help students acquire true knowledge in an age of information overload.

    * Learning to be (heart, social, emotional): how to cultivate social and emotional competencies such as self-awareness, self-management, empathy, and social awareness.

    * Learning to do (hand, behavioral): how to develop practical skills and the ability to engage actively in society.

2. **Care for others and society:** creating harmonious and meaningful relationships between teachers, students, parents, administration and the larger society:

    * Learning to live together: social skills such as compassion, altruism, generosity, deep listening, nonviolent communication, and conflict management.

3. **Care for the environment and the planet:** living in harmony with the natural environment, and education for sustainable development, including:

   * Deep ecology: reconnecting to nature in a deeper way.

   * Creating projects around climate change and fostering biodiversity.

   * Practical student lead projects, such as gardening, planting trees, and cleaning campaigns.

When looking at the overall framework of the Happy Schools program, we can see that it has been directly inspired by the concept of happiness described as the foundation of Gross National Happiness—living in harmony with oneself, living in harmony with others, and living in harmony with nature. In my view, these three fundamental competencies should be at the very heart of all educational systems, because they determine personal well-being, the well-being of society, and the very survival of our planet.

For schools to be able to promote such a vision, the first requirement is to transform the way we train teachers, because these qualities are not a matter of mere knowledge; they need to be embodied by the educators in order to have an impact on their students. The Happy Schools in Vietnam project begins, therefore, by offering transformative learning experiences to the teachers, who—when they themselves experience the benefits of such a program—will be able to transfer it to their students.

One of the important achievements of the Eurasia Foundation in Vietnam has been to create a living community called the Peaceful Bamboo Family, which strives to embody in every aspect of its work and life the principles of Gross National Happiness. The Happy Schools teacher-training programs are conducted in our community so that the participants not only get a theoretical introduction to these notions but also can have a living experience of a community that embodies the values we teach. The Peaceful Bamboo Family created the first biodynamic garden in the country. When we bought the land ten years ago, it consisted of barren red dirt covered with weeds and thorny bushes. Today it is a beautiful, lush garden producing a large variety of fruit, vegetables, and herbs, proving that when soil is properly cared for, it can heal and regenerate in just a few years.

When we described the importance of a healthy diet in the last chapter, we saw that one of the tasks of agriculture is both to provide a healthy diet for humans and to heal the earth. In a country like Vietnam, which was bombed and poisoned for decades, healing the earth and soil through regenerative agricultural practices is a task of central importance. When participants join the Happy Schools program in our community, they can experience how gardening provides opportunities in all three areas: self-care (as it balances intellectual work with care for others), healthy and nourishing food for the community and beyond, and care for nature and the planet through biodynamic agriculture that consciously enriches soil with appropriate composting.

Another example is a practice that we call Sharing from the Heart, which I briefly described in chapter 4. Creating spaces where every member of the community is given the opportunity to share whatever is important to them, while others listen deeply and with empathy, creates a harmonious social environment. This practice has been taken up by several schools under the name of "quality class time"—the children and their teacher sit in a circle at the beginning of a lesson, and each child is invited to share their feelings or any experience that is currently important to them. This creates an atmosphere in which the child is perceived in their full humanity, instead of the traditional school environment, where the teacher generally just assesses academic performance.

In one school where I worked, I was told a moving story related to this practice: there was a little boy in the class who never did his homework, and although the teacher punished him and informed his parents, no progress was made. The situation continued to worsen for the boy until quality class time was introduced in the school. During one of these sharing sessions, the boy explained that he was very sad, because his parents were getting divorced, and there was a lot of shouting and fighting at home. When he came home from school each day, it was difficult for him to sit down quietly and do his homework. So not only was he was suffering at home, but also at school, where he was being punished for not doing his homework. Once the teacher understood his situation, she allowed him to stay in the classroom after school, so he could do his homework in peace and quiet. This example shows how a simple practice can bring significant change in the life and the well-being of a child, and by doing so, increase the well-being of the whole class, including the teacher. Without these moments of sharing, the teacher might have never learned why the boy was struggling, and his situation would have probably have gotten worse.

I would like to share another story about something that happened while implementing a similar program in Bhutan. A few years ago, I offered a GNH in Education workshop for over three hundred students and their teachers at a high school in Punakha, a small town located in a beautiful valley where two rivers meet. The town is well known for having the most spectacular *dzong* in the country. The *dzong* served as a stronghold against enemies in the past, and it now plays an important role as a combined administrative center and monastery. Almost every populated valley has a *dzong*, which usually is situated on a prominent site overlooking a stream or river. The *dzong*s serve as focal points of Bhutan's political, economic, religious, and social life. Their thick white walls, which slope inward in Tibetan style, shelter Buddhist lamas, government officials, and artisans. The Punakha High School is located above the fortress and enjoys an amazing view.

One of the exercises I led was a mindfulness meditation inspired by a poem of Thich Nhat Hanh:

> *Breathing in, I see myself as a flower. Breathing out, I feel fresh.*
> *Flower—fresh.*
> *Breathing in, I see myself as a mountain. Breathing out, I feel solid.*

Mountain—solid.

Breathing in, I see myself as still water. Breathing out, I reflect things as
they are. Water—reflecting.

Breathing in, I see myself as space. Breathing out, I feel free.
Space—free.

Sometime later, I returned to the school. As I walked in the main
courtyard where the students gathered every day for morning assembly, I saw two posters on the wall. Each had beautifully written poetic
comments on the meditation exercise that we had practiced during the
workshop. I asked the principal who had written these beautiful texts,
and he told me the following story:

> *In the middle of the school year, we had to admit a seventeen-year-*
> *old student, even though the class was already overcrowded; it was*
> *an emergency admission. The principal of his previous school had*
> *told me that this student had been severely misbehaving, and they*
> *thought that going to another school was a way to give him a last*
> *chance. We accepted him even though we weren't sure if he would*
> *be able to adapt to this new environment. And surely enough, after*
> *a short time, his misbehavior started all over again. He drank alco-*
> *hol, ran away from the hostel where he was staying, did not work*
> *properly in class, did not do his homework, and even used forbidden*
> *substances. Every other day, he was summoned by his class teacher,*
> *the vice principal, or members of the ethics board. We were at a loss*
> *as how to help him.*
>
> *Then, one day, during the morning assembly, I explained to the*
> *students the mindfulness exercise, and we practiced all it together.*
> *A few days later, when the student had once again done something*
> *wrong, and I had summoned him to my office. I suddenly had an*
> *idea. I asked him, "Do you remember the mindfulness practice we*
> *did the other day, and did you understand it?" He replied that he*
> *understood it and that he liked practicing it. So I asked him to prac-*
> *tice it regularly and to write on two posters the experiences he had*

while doing it. He agreed and a few days later he came with the two posters and asked where he could put them up. On these posters he had described how, by practicing this exercise, he had realized deep down that the stability of the mountain was already in him and that he only had to come back to himself to find it; that the freshness of the flower and the clarity of the lake were all part of his being, and that, most importantly, freedom was available at any time, even within the constraints of school discipline. It was not necessary to break the rules and push the boundaries to experience freedom.

When I read them, I was impressed. They were beautifully written and showed deep understanding, so I praised him and asked him to put them up in the courtyard and to sign his name— he was eager to hang the posters, but he felt shy about signing his name. The next morning, when all the students were together for the morning assembly, I spoke about how that student had been difficult, had not behaved well since he arrived in the school, and had been a great worry for his teachers. But I also read the posters he had written and said that I realized he had a wonderful potential and these beautiful seeds only needed to be watered to grow. After this event, the transformation was almost miraculous: his behavior changed completely, he stopped using drugs and alcohol, never again ran away from the hostel, and learned so well that he passed the yearly exam with good grades. His teachers and myself could hardly believe the transformation that had taken place.

Upon hearing this story, I was deeply moved that such a transformation was possible and could see that a number of factors had contributed to it: a caring principal creating a positive school environment, the mindfulness practice itself, the reflection process that started when he made up the posters, and the acknowledgment by the principal of the student's true potential in front of the whole school community. This event reinforced my belief that one should never despair about misbehaving teenagers. Given the proper attention, recognition, compassion, tools, and practices, most of them have the possibility to transform in the way this student was able to do.

Let us now have a more detailed look at the three components of the Happy Schools program:

1. Self-care

2. Care for others and society

3. Care for the environment and nature

Self-Care

Having spoken about mindfulness—the importance of slowing down and looking inward—let us now look at it in the educational context. The ability of students to pay attention in the classroom has become a major challenge. Several researchers describe our time as the "age of distraction," and there is no doubt that technological devices have changed human behavior and relationships dramatically. Most teachers experience first-hand the ever-growing challenge of keeping students focused over long periods of time. A recent survey of nearly 2,500 teachers found that 87 percent report that new technologies are creating an easily distracted generation with short concentration spans. In developed countries, attention deficit disorder has become an epidemic and represents a major challenge for schools. These are just some of the reasons why mindfulness and other methods of attention training have become necessary, and more and more schools around the world are introducing them as part of their daily practice.

A growing body of research demonstrates the benefits of regular mindfulness practice in the classroom.* Mindfulness and attention train-ing are practices that can help students of all ages tune their instruments of learning. This has an impact on their entire being—body, mind, heart, and brain—and has been proven to enhance students' relationships with

---

* "Research on Mindfulness," Mindful Schools, *https://www.mindfulschools.org /about-mindfulness/research-on-mindfulness.*

their peers and teachers. This means that the entire social climate of the school experience—so crucial to optimal learning—is also improved.

Awareness is a natural human faculty and is probably not appreciated within educational circles to the degree that thinking is appreciated, and while we spend a lot of time training children to think, the development of awareness is not systematically and intentionally trained. And yet this is an essential skill not only for developing critical thinking but also for cultivating emotional intelligence. Most time in the classroom is spent only on training the intellect, although artistic practices—music, painting, sculpture, and theater—are powerful and playful ways to develop emotional intelligence and social skills. Mindfulness training in schools can be taught as a kind of awareness education in which the muscle of mindfulness is awakened and strengthened through ongoing practice.

We have described in the first part of the book practical exercises such as mindful sitting and mindful breathing. Additional practices that can be appropriate for the classroom include mindful walking, deep relaxation, and mindful eating, which are easy and fun to do with children and adolescents.

Mindful Walking*

Why walk mindfully?

* To reconnect our mind and body to the present moment

* To enjoy slowing down and not rushing

* To cultivate awareness of the body through movement

* To become more aware of the links between emotion and movement

---

*Many of the mindfulness practices we use in the Happy Schools program are inspired by the Plum Village and have been adapted to the school context in the book *Happy Teachers Change the World*, by Thich Nhat Hanh and Katherine Weare (Berkeley: Parallax Press, 2017), *https://plumvillage.org/books/happy -teachers-change-the-world*.

∗ As an alternative to using a seated meditation to develop focus and calm; to relieve stress and anxiety and let go of repetitive thinking

∗ To experience the wonders of life, connecting more deeply with ourselves, with those who are working with us, and with the environment in which we walk

With mindful walking, we can experience being fully present as something we can do during any activity, anywhere and at any time—right in the midst of life. Moving practices like walking are sometimes more appropriate than sitting when our mind and body are busy or agitated.

When we notice that our mind has become lost in thinking, which happens naturally to everyone, we gently guide our attention back to our breath and our steps. As we practice slowing down and not rushing, we may notice that we have become used to rushing and getting lost in our thinking, planning, daydreaming, ruminating, talking, or listening to music while on the move. Mindful walking reminds us that it is enough just to walk.

When we are first learning to practice mindful walking, it's helpful, too, to focus on our feet and to walk more slowly. Walking mindfully, however, is not something we must do in an artificially slow way. Walking naturally, at a gentle pace, can help our bodies remain relaxed.

Walking should be enjoyable, not hard labor, with no need to change the breath—we are aware of just our steps and our breath.

If we are lucky enough to be outside in nature, we may like, from time to time, to stop, look around, and notice the beauty of life—the trees, the white clouds, the limitless sky. We can listen to the birds and feel the breeze on our face. Life is all around us, and we are alive.

In Vietnam, several schools that are part of the Happy Schools program have created a mindful walking path in their schoolyard or garden. They planted flowers and bushes next to the paths and used diverse materials on paths themselves—sand, pebbles, and grass—so that when walking barefoot, the children feel the different textures under their feet, which helps them to become more mindful of each step.

Deep Relaxation

Why practice deep relaxation?

* To increase our ability to reduce tension and relax body and mind

* To develop a sense of mind and body connection

* To increase our ability to be aware, to focus, and to pay attention to what is happening here and now—in the breath, body, and mind—by experiencing the body in relaxation

* To decrease our level of stress and anxiety

* To increase positive feelings, such as calmness, gratitude, acceptance, and happiness

Stress and tension are problems for many of us. Even young children are becoming increasingly affected by stress. Schools can be busy and unsettling places, offering little time to rest and recover. Deep relaxation offers us a concrete practice to reunite body and mind. By focusing our mind on our body, we give ourselves the opportunity for our body to release tensions, rest, heal, and be restored.

The Relaxation Process

Relaxation is a simple process. First we practice letting go of all thoughts, worries, and anxieties, bringing our attention to our breath and to the contact our body makes with the floor. Then we bring our attention to different parts of our body, focusing attention on each part, one at a time. As our awareness reaches each part,

* We breathe in and out, aware of that part of the body

* We become aware of any sensation in that part right now, giving it our full attention

* We invite that part of our body to relax, releasing any tension we find there

* We smile at that part of our bodies, sending it our love, tenderness, care, and gratitude for the work it does for us

* When the mind wanders, we simply note the wandering and bring our mind back to the part of the body we are focusing on or to our breathing

1. Getting settled

Invite the group to lie down on their backs. Allow time for the class to settle.

Gently invite students to get comfortable, with their legs stretched out, their arms by their sides, and their hands on their bellies.

Invite them to close their eyes if they wish.

2. Bell

Invite three sounds of the bell, with three in-breaths and three out-breaths between each bell, to begin the session.

3. The practice

Say to your students:

"Close your eyes, allow your arms to rest on either side of your body, and let your legs relax. Allow your whole body to start to relax and let go.

"As you breathe in and out, become aware of the floor beneath you and of the contact of your body with the floor, noticing all the places where you are in contact, such as heels, the back of your legs, back, and shoulders.

"With each breath, allow each part of your body to sink deeper and deeper into the floor, letting go of tensions, worries, thoughts, and ideas.

"Become aware of your belly rising and falling as you breathe in and out, rising, falling, rising, falling. You can place a hand there if you wish.

"As you breath consciously in and out, gently scan your whole body from the sole of your feet moving gently upward to the crown of your head, gradually letting go of all tensions.

"Come back to your in-breath and out-breath. Breathing in, breathing out. Your whole body feels like a water lily floating on the water. You have nowhere to go and nothing to do. You are as free as a cloud floating in the sky."

4. Music or singing (optional)

Play some relaxing music. If appropriate (e.g., with younger children), you could sing songs to allow time for students to rest in their bodies.

5. Getting ready to end

Say to your students:

"Bring your awareness back to your breathing, to your abdomen rising and falling."

6. The bell

Use a half sound to wake up the bell. Invite one side of the bell to signify the end of the session.

Mindful Eating

Why practice mindful eating?

* To become more mindful of the process of eating—slowing down, savoring and enjoying, and eating a sensible quantity of food chosen mindfully with thought and care

* To develop awareness of our own habit energies around food, eating, and consumption

* To develop a sense of gratitude through awareness of the connection between the food on our plate and the processes and people that brought it to us

Mindful eating can transform the everyday activity of eating—a basic human need that we normally do on autopilot—into a wonderful opportunity to bring mindfulness into our own lives, as well as the lives of our students. In this way, eating becomes a source of deep pleasure.

Unhealthy eating habits, such as overconsumption of junk food and sodas and irregular eating patterns and rhythms, are widespread among children and teenagers. Eating disorders represent a growing public health issue with young people, especially girls.

Mindful eating is a way to help young people become aware of the true needs of their bodies in terms of nourishment and healthy food.

Eating a fruit mindfully*

Prepare some fruit

Invite one sound of the bell to begin, giving everyone an opportunity to mindfully breathe in and out three times.

1. Introduce the practice

The first time they do this, students will assume they are getting the fruit to eat straight away, so explain the practice to them, so they don't feel foolish. First invite them to enjoy their breathing and to be aware of the body. Tell them that we will soon begin eating the fruit altogether.

Tell them that you will do the activity without talking so they can focus and that you will be guiding everyone through a series of reflections.

2. Be with the breath

Invite one sound of the bell to begin, giving everyone an opportunity to breathe in and out mindfully three times.

3. Hand out the fruit

Give a piece of fruit to each member of the class (or you can invite some students to hand them out).

Pick up your piece of fruit and invite each student to hold their piece of fruit gently in the palm of their hand.

---

*The "raisin meditation" used in the mindfulness-based stress reduction program by Jon Kabat-Zinn follows a similar process, *https://ggia.berkeley.edu/practice /raisin_meditation*.

4. Contemplate the food

Begin by reading aloud to the class a short verse like this one:

This fruit is a gift of the whole universe, the earth, the sky, the rain, and the sun.

We thank the people who have brought this fruit to us, especially the farmers and the people at the market.

Take a moment to imagine and visualize all the things that happened and all the people who helped to bring this fruit into your hand:

* Where it grew and how

* What caused it to grow and ripen (e.g., the earth, sun, rain, and so on)

* The various people: who grew it, tended it, picked it, packed it, transported it, sold it, delivered it, and so on

5. Look deeply

Look closely at this fruit as if you had never seen one before— and indeed, you have never seen this particular one. Notice the color, texture, shape, and how the light reflects on it. Roll it around in your hand to look at it thoroughly. Notice any differences between one side and the other.

6. Smell

Hold the fruit to your nose and smell the fragrance. Notice where exactly you sense it—nostrils, palate, throat? Closing your eyes can help focus on the scent.

7. Touch and peel

Gently peel the fruit and notice how this feels to the touch. Really look at the peel, the difference between the two sides— inside and outside—the color and the texture. Pay close attention to the aroma that's released as you peel it.

8. Place in the mouth and eat

Gently place a piece in your mouth, on your tongue. Try not to chew and swallow just yet.

Notice how your mouth responds—an increased salivation, for example, or an urge to chew.

Gently roll the segment around your mouth, noticing the texture and taste. Gently bite into the segment—you may be aware of the sudden burst of flavor. Notice where exactly in your mouth you experience it and your response.

Slowly and mindfully chew this segment.

Be aware of the impulse to swallow. Chew the segment well, resisting the urge to swallow for a little while to see how it feels.

When the segment is fully chewed, swallow.

Be aware of the whole feeling of swallowing in the back of your mouth, moving down your throat to your stomach.

9. After eating the first segment

Sit and breathe, experiencing the aftermath of the taste in the mouth and any sensations elsewhere in the body and mind.

10. End

Eat the rest of the fruit if you wish. Eat as mindfully as you wish.

Sit quietly, in touch with your breath, and reflect on the experience. If you enjoyed it, be thankful for all the conditions that made this fruit and the taste of it in your mouth possible.

All these mindfulness exercises have to be adapted to fit the age of the children, but the starting point is for the teachers to develop their own mindfulness practice, so they can be a credible example for the children.

From Self-Awareness to Self-Management

Mindfulness is the energy that enables us to recognize and accept our own emotions and experiences without overreacting to them. It can be moving to see how even young children, when taught mindfulness practice, are able to recognize and name their emotions without being disturbed by them.

Mindfulness is the foundation of all social and emotional learning, and the management of emotions comprises two components. One is transforming difficult emotions, and the other is intentionally cultivating positive attitudes.

In the context of the Happy Schools project, two additional dimensions need to be added: adapting the various practices to age groups and adapting to the local cultural and social context. In my experience, this adaptation process is best done by the teachers themselves, because they are locals and have first-hand knowledge of their social and cultural context. Secondly, they know their students and have in-depth experience of what works and what doesn't work with the specific age groups. Furthermore, giving teachers a ready-made curriculum that they simply have to implement reinforces a situation that is all too common in schools, namely, that decisions are taken by organizations such as education ministries and universities that are not in direct contact with the children. Many teachers suffer from the discrepancy between the official programs and the reality of their classroom. Our strategy, therefore, is to allow teachers to experience for themselves the value of self-care and care for others, as well as the benefits of the various mindfulness, social, and emotional practices. We encourage them to be creative and customize the way they implement these exercises, so that they are aligned with the needs and abilities of their children. The creation of peer groups among teachers, where they can share findings, resources, practices, and challenges, have also been found to be an integral part of maintaining a positive climate in schools.

There is no clear boundary between self-care and care for others. If we teach students to take good care of themselves, they will naturally develop the ability to take care of others.

Having implemented these exercises in Vietnamese pilot schools, we were pleased with the positive feedback we received from children, teachers, and parents.

We can see that self-care is the foundation on which care for others and care for the planet can be built. However, self-care alone is not enough to ensure a happy school. An important part of what children learn in school is through socialization, which is one of the limits of homeschooling: methods and content of learning may be appropriate, but socialization is lacking. One thing that children learn in school is how to be part of a larger community, that they are one among others, and that the quality of their relationships with their peers and their teachers determines, to a large extent, how they will be able to conduct their social life later on. Therefore, social skills and care for others are an essential part of the Happy Schools project.

Care for Others and Society

In the first part of the book, we learned the crucial importance of good relationships for happiness and well-being, that being integrated well into a community and having trust in the people around us are the basis of a healthy social life. Social skills are crucial to our own well-being and that of society, though they are not systematically and intentionally trained in school curriculums. The exercises that we described in the first part of the book provide practices that can help to develop good social skills.

The right social attitudes can be trained from early on, but it is primarily during adolescence that they become a central part of human life. We all remember how challenging the teenage years can be. Until that time, social connections are, by and large, a given—children play with their siblings, cousins, neighbors, and classmates. During adolescence, however, the inner emotional life of a young person becomes more autonomous. It is the time when we really discover friendship and love, and these experiences are not only enriching and deeply fulfilling but also often dramatic. Relationships become more of a personal choice, rather than being dictated by outer circumstances. The friendships of youth can have an enduring impact on one's life, and our first love is usually an unforgettable experience and can influence all our later relationships.

Young people are often sensitive and vulnerable in their emotional life, and approaching them with empathy, care, and compassion is of utmost importance. It is often difficult for them to explain in words the inner turmoil they're going through, but often they can express things through art that they would otherwise have difficulty sharing with others. For this reason, art and beauty should play a major role in the education of adolescents. At the same time, adolescence is a time when critical and independent thinking can be developed.

We described earlier that small children need to be confident that the world is a good and benevolent place; growing up, children need to discover the beauty of the world, and as teenagers, to gain confidence in their thinking to recognize what is true and what is false. So the ancient threefold virtues of goodness, beauty, and truth can be guiding stars for all our educational projects.

One cannot actually teach anyone how to build meaningful, long-lasting relationships, but one can provide the tools that will help to build them, and one can create safe spaces and opportunities for these relationships to be cultivated. When I look back at my own youth, I don't remember much of what I learned in school—although I am not dismissing the importance of all the skills that I acquired. What stands out in my memory are people: a teacher who understood me and strengthened my self-confidence, a friend with whom I could share my innermost feelings, the deep emotions arising from the discovery of the other gender—shyness, desire, longing, embarrassment, fulfillment, joy. When I look back at these years, which played such an important role in constructing my personality, there is little doubt that the human encounters played a central role. Once again, I am not under the illusion that any specific technique or practice can magically transform the difficult path of trial and error that we all have to go through in discovering human relationships, but there is also no doubt that with adequate training it is possible to lessen the suffering and disappointments that one often has to experience during this phase of life. This is why we believe that emotional intelligence and social skills should be a central part of any educational program. That which is practiced in these years could contribute to making society a more tolerant, peaceful, and understanding place. One example of such a practice is nonviolent communication.

Nonviolent Communication

NVC was developed by psychologist Marshall B. Rosenberg, based on the humanistic psychology exemplified by one of his teachers, the famous American psychologist Carl Roger. Rosenberg, summarizes NVC in these words:[*]

> *Nonviolent Communication (NVC) is a way of interacting with ourselves and others that's rooted in empathy and compassion. The ultimate goal of NVC is to foster authentic connections between people regardless of their differences. That focus on human connections makes NVC a powerful conflict resolution tool—once there is a genuine human connection, the original problem tends to solve itself. You can use NVC in almost any relationship or environment, including in families, schools, governments, businesses, and personal relationships. NVC can also help you reshape your inner dialogue to promote self-compassion, improving your relationship with yourself.*

---

[*] Marshall B. Rosenberg, "Nonviolent Communication," *https://www.shortform* *.com/summary/nonviolent-communication-summary-marshall-b-rosenberg?gclid=CjoKCQjw6J* *-SBhCrARIsAHOyMZj6RobMkVDl8iCoj3_7HLIcP7Xj-lwcM-W3uSma0hqk7jb57pcz8J0aAtH* *vEALw_wcB*. For more information: *https://www.cnvc.org/learn-nvc/what-is-nvc.*

With NVC, we learn to hear our own deeper needs and those of others. Through its emphasis on deep listening—to ourselves as well as others—NVC helps us discover the depth of our own compassion. This language reveals the awareness that all human beings are only trying to honor universal values and needs, every minute, every day. NVC can be seen as both a spiritual practice that helps us see our common humanity, using our power in a way that honors everyone's needs, and a concrete set of skills which help us create life-serving families and communities. The form is simple yet powerfully transformative.

This practice can help both teachers and students of all ages improve the quality of their relationships—both with themselves and with each other. The NVC process consists of four basic skills:

1. Observing a situation without evaluation.

2. Acknowledging the accompanying feelings.

3. Understanding how those feelings are a result of a met or unmet need.

4. Clearly requesting concrete actions and exploring how to honor all parties' needs in a flexible and creative manner, without demands.

These basic skills require mindfulness for their implementation. The following set of exercises is an introductory practice of nonviolent communication for school teachers. The speech templates are here for a pedagogical purpose, to support a new way to connect with self and others, and should be adapted to the culture and context of use.

Self-Empathy

Why practice self-empathy?

* To clarify what is happening inside oneself—
  self-understanding and self-connection

* To manage strong emotions

* To prepare oneself for difficult conversations

* To get clarity about inner choices and next steps

* To sustain a quality of relationship with oneself and an inner life that is enjoyable

Take time and space: When you are in pain, find someplace where you will not be disturbed, where you can complete the following steps, mentally or in writing, in peace.

Observation: Ask yourself: "What happened?" Replay in your head what happened until you find the most recent trigger event for your current experience. Describe this trigger event as if you had been a neutral observer of the event.

Interpretation: Ask yourself: "What am I telling myself about what happened? What meaning am I making of it?" Do not censor your language or try to be polite about what happened. Just let it flow. You can describe all that they have done to you, what they have created, what they've destroyed. You can express all your pain and anguish, fears and outrage, judgments, thoughts, analysis of the situation, and whatever else comes to mind.

Name feelings: What are the feelings behind all this? Make a list. List all of the feelings but do not use words that imply blame (such as bullied, ignored, cheated, betrayed, abandoned, victimized). Use only honest words that describe what is going on in your body now (sad, frightened, angry, worried, confused, anxious, resentful, overwhelmed, bitter, or jealous).

Name needs: Next, identify all the unmet needs you have that are behind those feelings (respect, appreciation, intimacy, recognition, cooperation, or support). "What's important to me right now? What do I care most about in this situation?" There might be different layers of needs.

Mourning: Allow yourself to mourn the fact that these needs are not presently being met. Be with yourself. Give yourself permission to feel the pain of not having these needs met. If you still feel the anger and resentment, go back to previous steps. Often, once we have completed the steps up to this point, a shift will take place, and suddenly we will not feel so angry. Instead, we will feel disheartened, sad, or hopeless. List the new feelings, and then list the needs behind those feelings. Allow yourself to mourn your loss again.

Requests: What do you want to ask yourself or someone else to do to begin to meet the needs you have right now? Make a specific and doable request to enable yourself to follow through with them. Specific requests answer most of these questions: What? When? Who? Where? How long? How often?

Creating a Caring Classroom Community

Many of the examples and exercises included so far are more suitable for secondary school students and adults. As has been discussed, adolescence is the most crucial time of life for the development of relationship skills, but the foundation can be laid early on. Therefore, let us now look at practices that are suitable for younger children.

In order to have a cooperative, caring classroom, we need to help children cultivate friendships, sharing, respectfulness, truthfulness, and caring. Part of this teaching aims to help children, over time, apply these attributes, establishing models who reflect these values and supporting families as the primary moral educators.

Friendship

Being part of a group is important to children. After they develop a sense of who they are, children struggle to understand who others are, first as family members, and then as members of friendship groups. As children change from focusing on themselves to focusing on others, they can be supported in making this important transition.

ACTIVITIES

Share examples

Ask children to share examples of what it means to be a friend. For example, being a friend means wanting to be close to someone and enjoying that person's company. Friends like each other and enjoy spending time together. Friends usually get to know each other very well. They learn each other's likes and dislikes; they can share their snacks or their toys.

Make friendship bracelets

Supply beads and yarn or string and have the children make a friendship bracelet to give to anyone they'd like. As the children work, talk about what their definitions of friendship are and how we show people that they are our friends.

Get to know each other

Encourage children to discuss how they are alike and how they are different, both physically and in the things they like to do. Talk about ways people can be different and still be friends.

Sharing

Children often have a difficult time seeing another's point of view. Sharing, in particular, is difficult, because they are not yet able to see the relationship between giving up something immediately and later getting something in return. They are also interested in helping each other.

ACTIVITIES

Ask children what they think

Talk about what it means to be fair and unfair. You might add that being fair means taking your turn, following rules, and treating everyone—including yourself—equally. Being fair means keeping your promises.

Share a snack

Bring in a snack for the children to divide up, so that everyone gets an equal amount. Ask them what they would do if new child joined the group or if some parents or other teachers decide to join them.

Play cooperatively

Help children sit at tables in groups of four. Have plenty of paper available and four colored markers of different colors on each table. Ask children to draw anything they'd like, the only rule being that they must use all four colors. As the children work, involve them in a discussion of sharing materials. After everyone is finished, ask them to share their thoughts about their drawings and the group dynamic that resulted from having to find a balance between their desire to use a certain color and the need for all of the children to use all four colors.

Respectfulness

During the school years, children gain a sense of who they are in relation to others. They become intensely aware of similarities and differences, often excluding those who are different in one way or another. Seeing themselves as different sometimes makes children feel less valued. But children are also intensely curious, and the growing competence that comes with learning helps them to be more inclusive of others.

ACTIVITIES

Share your thoughts

Explain that respecting someone means being careful not to hurt their feelings or damage their possessions. Tell a story about seeing a bird's nest in a bush, observing it to watch the parent birds coming to feed their chicks, but not disturbing it, because you don't want to scare the birds or hurt the chicks. Ask children to share other examples of ways people show respect.

Have a treasure hunt in nature

Make a list of things children might use their senses to notice outdoors. These might include seeing a feather, a hole in a tree, or a particularly colored flower; hearing a bird, a bee, or trees blowing in the wind; feeling the wetness of mud, a prickly plant, or tree bark; smelling pine or spruce needles, a flower, or the grass; watching the movements of an ant, a spider, or a leaf. Talk about ways we can show respect for all of these things in nature. Then take a walk to find them. Ask children for other suggestions as to how they can show respect for the environment, such as an outdoor clean-up walk.

Truthfulness

Children may bend reality to fit the way they think events should be or the way they wish things were. However, children are also beginning to develop a conscience, and they identify with the standards adults set for them. When their behavior varies from these expectations, children can begin to feel a little uncomfortable.

ACTIVITIES

Talk about truthfulness

Share this definition with children: When you tell the truth, you do not hide anything. You tell all the facts. Ask children to share what it means to them to tell the truth. Do they like this definition? Would anyone like to change it?

Make a list

Using chart paper, ask children to help you list situations where it was difficult to tell the truth. Start the discussion by sharing a few situations of your own.

Use illustrations

Invite children to draw a picture of someone telling the truth about something. Add their comments to the drawings. Later, ask children to share their drawings.

Caring

Although children are struggling to become more independent, they are still dependent in many ways. Relationships with adults, especially family members, are important. New and unfamiliar events remind them that they still need close relationships with the adults they thought they were growing away from. Seeing parents with younger siblings evokes pleasant memories of earlier experiences, and children struggle to realize that a special place for them continues to exist regardless of the changing environmental events.

ACTIVITIES

Have a "care share"

Ask children what they think it means to care about someone or something. Then share this definition: "If you are caring, you show this by being helpful and kind. When you care about another person, you are not rough but gentle. If you care about someone, you are interested in how that person feels, because it's important to you."

Show your care

Invite children to make a "Caring Card" for anyone they care about. Provide paper, magazines, collage materials, tape, and glue. Be available to take dictation so those children who choose to can express their feelings in words as well as pictures.

Take action

Talk about ways people show they care every day. Then make a list together of things your group can do, such as watering plants, feeding birds or fish, taking time to listen to a friend, and so on. Throughout the week, help children put these thoughts into action.

Conclusion

Referring to the UNESCO Happy Schools framework, most of the important conditions relate to the fields of self-care and care for others. Friendships and relationships in the school community rank as the most important factor among respondents in terms of what makes a happy school.

A warm and friendly learning environment ranks as the second most important factor for happy schools. The findings indicate that there is a need to place more emphasis on greetings and smiles and to introduce opener classrooms, colorful and meaningful displays, music, and creativity—thereby generating a more positive school atmosphere.*

Another important criterion for happy schools is the positive attitudes and attributes of teachers, including characteristics such as kindness, enthusiasm, and fairness. The role of the teachers is to serve as inspiring, creative, and happy role models for learners.

---

* "Happy Schools! A Framework for Learner Well-Being in the Asia-Pacific," UNESCO Bangkok, September 8, 2020, *https://bangkok.unesco.org/content /happy-schools-framework-learner-well-being-asia-pacific*.

Respondents also ranked positive and collaborative values and practices as being an important criterion in making schools happy. Such values and practices include love, compassion, acceptance, and respect.

Lastly, a secure environment—free from bullying—was another criterion ranked as important by respondents.

Let us recap the twelve factors identified as central to a Happy School community that are directly related to self-care and care for others:

1. Friendship and relationships in the school community.
2. Positive teacher attitudes and attributes.
3. Respect for diversity and differences.
4. Positive and collaborative values and practices.
5. Teacher working conditions and well-being.
6. Teacher skills and competencies.
7. Teamwork and collaborative spirit.
8. Learning as a team between students and teachers.
9. Mental well-being and stress management.
10. Warm and friendly learning environment.
11. Secure environment free from bullying.
12. Positive discipline.

Most teachers, parents, and students will, no doubt, agree that implementing these twelve factors in a school community would have a positive effect, both on the academic achievements of the students and on the well-being of everyone in the school—students, teachers, and staff. Nevertheless, without practical methods on how to bring about a happy school community, it will remain a wish list. Our objective is to provide practical examples and exercises that can be implemented within the classroom and that can support the teachers, as well as the students, in creating a happy school community.

Care for the Environment and the Planet

Education for Sustainable Development

UNESCO proposes two main objectives to achieve the goals of sustainable development:*

1. To reorient education and learning so that everyone has the opportunity to acquire the knowledge, skills, values, and attitudes that empower them to contribute to sustainable development.

2. To strengthen education and learning in all agendas, programs and activities that mold sustainable development.

But care for the environment cannot be separated from the two modes of care that we discussed earlier: care for oneself and care for others. These three modes of care support and strengthen each other when developed in the proper ways. If children receive mere moral imperatives to protect the environment—without experiencing what the transformation of the environment actually means for themselves, their families, and their societies in everyday life—there is little chance that they will change their day-to-day behavior.

What we need is to mobilize all three dimensions of learning:

* education of the head

* education of the heart

* education of the hand

Only if these three are developed in harmony can we expect to see the changes that will have a significant impact on sustainable development. The consumerist mindset cannot be stopped by simply

---

* "What Is Education for Sustainable Development?" UNESCO, *https://en.unesco .org/themes/education-sustainable-development/what-is-esd.*

forbidding children and young people the products they long for. Only if young people understand and experience the consequences of certain behaviors for themselves—and for their family, society, and the planet—can we hope to bring about lasting change.

Time in Nature and Gardening

As long as biology and sustainable development lessons remain in the classroom, their effects on children will be limited. Many city children have little exposure to the natural environment, and it is difficult to expect them to care for something they don't know. According to a survey conducted in the UK, 59 percent of children did not know that butter is made with milk, and 15 percent were unable to tell where eggs or milk come from.[*] Any program promoting environmental sustainability and ecological awareness needs to start by exposing children to direct experiences in nature. Activities in which children not only observe or enjoy nature but also cultivate a small garden on school grounds—or just potted herbs in the classroom—have positive effects.

When we bought the land for the Peaceful Bamboo Family some fifteen years ago, it was barren red dirt with only weed and brambles. After a few years of transforming the soil through biodynamic preparations,[†] and with a lot of hard and loving work, the land has completely transformed into a lush vegetable garden and orchard producing delicious and healthy products for the community and also for the public. The garden is used not only to produce food but also as a learning opportunity for our residents, as well as for thousands of schoolchildren who come to have a hands-on experience of organic gardening. Many children had never put their hands in the soil when they come for the first time, and they feel reluctant to touch the earth, having often

---

[*] *https://leaf.eco/about-leaf/meet-the-team59%*

[†] "What Is Biodynamics?" Biodynamic Association, *https://www.biodynamics.com /what-is-biodynamics.*

heard from their parent, "Don't touch that; it's dirty." But very soon, planting seeds, pulling weeds, or tending vegetables is a source of great joy, and they can spend a long time fully immersed in these activities. Many classes have taken up growing little vegetable and flower beds in their school, and if there is no available space, at least growing aromatic herbs in containers on the windowsill. Some parents have told us that their children also encouraged the family to grow plants at home.

Over the last few years, the Peaceful Bamboo Family has welcomed thousands of primary school children for day-long experiential learning workshops in our organic garden. They learn how to take care of a garden—planting, watering, cleaning, and nurturing, as well as preparing compost or feeding animals. This kind of experience is the foundation of environmental awareness.

Deep Ecology and the Work That Reconnects

The universe is a communion of subjects,
not a collection of objects.

—THOMAS BERRY

This third area of care, care for the environment—learning to protect our fragile environment and live in harmony with nature—is a key aspect of happiness in the Happy School project. To truly learn this, children need a felt sense of connection with the natural world. One way to invite students to connect with nature is through the practices and lessons of the Work That Reconnects (WTR) framework, which comes from the Deep Ecology philosophical tradition.

The term Deep Ecology was coined by Norwegian mountaineer and philosopher Arne Naess in the 1970s. Ecology is simply the scientific study of nature. Deep Ecology is an environmental philosophy and a social movement based in the belief that humans must radically change their relationship to nature from one that values nature solely for its usefulness to human beings to one that recognizes that nature has an inherent value. Deep Ecology's core principle is the belief that the living environment as a whole should be respected and regarded as having certain basic moral and legal rights to live and flourish, independent of its instrumental benefits for human use.

In Bhutan, the traditional shamanic pre-Buddhist culture is still very much alive; most people consider lakes, mountains, or forests not as inert material formations, but as the manifestation of spiritual entities. Therefore, it is much easier in such a cultural context to create the heart connection with the ecosystem that inspires ecological behavior.

The Work That Reconnects is an educational framework developed by Joanna Macy that comes from the Deep Ecology tradition.* It argues that the harm that humans have caused to nature—including climate change, the mass extinction of species, soil degradation, and ocean acidification—is due not only to our behaviors and systems but also our false assumption that nature is something separate from ourselves and something that we can exploit for our own gain. Humanity needs to reconnect with nature if we are to be responsible members in what Macy calls the Web of Life. What follows from this reconnection is a desire to protect our fragile environment and live in harmony with nature.

Facilitating the Work That Reconnects

The curriculum is open source and available in Macy's book *Coming Back to Life: The Updated Guide to the Work That Reconnects* (written with coauthor Molly Young Brown). The WTR framework offers a variety of activities and lessons that facilitators can choose from to customize the experience for their intended audience. It can also complement other curricula, such as Deep Ecology practices. Moreover, although the framework was originally developed for adults, *Coming Back to Life* has a chapter on adapting WTR for children and teens.

---

*Joanna Macy and Molly Young Brown, *Coming Back to Life: The Updated Guide to the Work That Reconnects* (Gabriola Island, BC: New Society Publishers, 2014).

The outline for WTR workshops and classes is described in the book as "the spiral." The spiral maps a journey for the four successive stages of WTR.

Coming from Gratitude

Honoring our Pain for the World

Seeing with New Eyes

Going Forth

The spiral begins with Coming from Gratitude because, as Macy writes, it "quiets the mind and brings us back to source, stimulating our empathy and confidence." The practices in this stage help the students get to know each other, ground themselves physically, celebrate life, and recognize their gifts and talents.

In the second stage, Honoring our Pain for the World, students are invited to identify what worries and angers them and what makes them feel hopeless and sad. The intent is that their compassion will be strengthened through the realization that their pain is not only a personal subjective experience, but a shared and legitimate worry for the well-being of our planet.

The stage Seeing with New Eyes offers practices that clarify our relatedness to other beings in the Web of Life. Finally, Going Forth frees them to enjoy the harvest of the lessons and synthesizes them into intentions and practices they can do in their daily lives. The process also includes concrete steps they can take.

The Work That Reconnects: Practices

The Human Camera

The Human Camera is a practice for stage one, Coming from Gratitude. It can be used even with very young children (though they should be paired with an adult or older child). One person is the photographer and the other is the camera. The photographers guide their cameras (who keep their eyes closed), searching for beautiful and interesting things to take photos of. When they find something, they point their camera at it and "takes the photo" by tapping the camera's shoulder. The camera opens their eyes for just three to five seconds and gazes at the beautiful or interesting scene in front of them—committing the scene to memory—then closes their eyes again, so the photographer can find something else to photograph. Try creative shots: different angles, close-ups, or panorama shots. In this practice, the participants should talk as little as possible. Give photographers about ten minutes to take at least three photos. Then the pair switches roles.

When everyone is finished, have each child draw a favorite photo they took as the camera on an index card and share the photos in a group. For older children or teens, have them debrief in these small groups. Some debrief questions might be: What did you notice? Which role did you like better, the human camera or the photographer? What will you remember the most?

Open Sentences on Gratitude

Open Sentences is a practice for spontaneous expression that can be used in any of the four stages of the WTR spiral—the following is how it is used for stage one, Coming from Gratitude. Open Sentences helps people listen as well as speak their thoughts and feelings frankly. Students, divided into pairs, sit face-to-face and refrain from speaking until the practice begins. One is partner A, the other partner B. The facilitator has a card with a list of a number of "open" (unfinished) sentences, like "Some things I love about being alive on earth are . . ." and when the students are ready, the facilitator reads the first open sentence out loud. Partner A repeats it and then completes the sentence in their own words, addressing partner B, and keeps talking spontaneously on that subject for a couple minutes. The facilitator rings a small bell to indicate that time is up, and the speakers stop speaking. The facilitator waits for a few seconds, so the partners can rest and reflect on the exercise, and then reads out the next open sentence. The partners can switch roles after each open sentence or at the end of the series. The listening partner—and this is to be emphasized—keeps absolutely silent and listens as attentively and supportively as possible to their partner. Allow about thirty minutes for the whole practice.

You may want to invent your own open sentences or use these favorites of ours. The last one is always read last:

* Some things I love about being alive on earth are . . .

* A place that was magical to me as a child was . . .

* A person who helped me believe in myself is or was . . .

* Some things I enjoy doing and making are . . .

* Some things I appreciate about myself are . . .

Open Sentences on Honoring Our Pain

The process is the same, but the open sentences are different:

* Recently I felt a strong connection to life and felt really glad to be alive. What made me experience this was . . .

* Recently I saw something that made me feel very troubled about the world. What I saw was . . .

* One way I take care of the world is . . .

The Web of Life

Participants stand in a circle without speaking. The facilitator gives a ball of yarn to one of them, who wraps the end of the yarn loosely around their wrist and then tosses it to someone else in the circle, who also wraps the yarn around their wrist and tosses the yarn. The participants toss the ball of yarn randomly, without any particular pattern, to people anywhere in the circle. When they've run out of yarn, it forms a web connecting everyone in the circle. Once the web is complete, the leader can make observations like the following:

> *All of existence is an interconnected web, and we are part of it. Notice how strong it is when we are all holding our strand. Notice how what happens in one place affects the whole web. Notice what happens to the web if one strand is hurt or weakened.*
>
> *Some people only care about people who are like them or places that are near them. This web shows why we should care about both people who are like us and also people who are different from us. It is why we need to care about the places on Earth near us and far from us. We need all kinds of people and kinds of life for the web to be strong. Our destiny is interconnected with the destiny of all people and all forms of life on our planet.*

Practice with a Group

The Starfish Story

This is a practice for stage four, Going Forth. It's a fun activity for groups of children. To prepare, first cut out several starfish-shaped pieces of cardboard, one for each participant. Pass out the starfish, then tell the starfish story as follows (it best to tell the story rather than read it). When you've finished, allow some time for the group members to talk about its meaning for them.

Once upon a time, there was a wise man who used to go to the ocean to do his writing. He had a habit of walking on the beach before he began his work. One day, as he was walking along the shore, he looked down the beach and saw a person moving in an unusual way—bending down and then reaching up in an arc.

Was it a dancer? He walked faster to catch up. As he got closer, he saw that the person was a boy. And he was not dancing at all. The boy was reaching down, picking up small objects, and throwing them into the ocean. The man came closer still and called out, "Good morning! May I ask what you're doing?"

The boy paused, looked up, and said, "Throwing starfish into the ocean."

"Why are you throwing starfish into the ocean?" asked the wise man, somewhat startled.

To this the boy replied, "The sun is up, and the tide is going out. If I don't throw them in, they'll die."

Upon hearing this, the wise man said, "But do you not realize that there are miles and miles of beach and starfish all along every mile? You can't possibly make a difference."

At this, the boy bent down, picked up yet another starfish and threw it in the ocean. As it splashed into the water, he said, "It made a difference for that one."

After telling the story, designate an area that represents the beach and another that is the ocean. Have each child draw a picture of a starfish on their starfish-shaped piece of cardboard and, on the back of it, write one thing they already do or will do to protect the environment. When everyone is ready, the first child says a few words about what they wrote on the starfish and then throws it back in the ocean. And all together, everyone says, "We made the difference for that one." Then the next child speaks and throws their starfish, and everyone responds, and so forth, until each child has spoken. For instance a child might say:

"I will eat less packaged food to reduce plastic waste."

"I will make sure I always turn off the light when I leave my room."

"I will not let the water run longer than necessary when I take a shower."

My own grandchildren insist on taking the train rather than the airplane when travelling with their parents within Europe.

Open Sentences on Going Forth

The open sentences practice can also be used for stage four, Going Forth. It is a good practice to use before the main events of/in a workshop to get people in the right frame of mind. Responses can be written and shared with the whole group.

Something I learned today about the web of life is . . .

Something I can do every day to help the web of life is . . .

Something I could do with other people to protect and preserve the environment is . . .

We are facing an unprecedented ecological crisis. The Intergovernmental Panel on Climate Change (IPCC) published its latest report in February 2022, and there is strong scientific evidences clearly showing the urgency for a radical change in human behavior if we want to avoid major ecological disruptions that will also have devastating social, economic, and political consequences.[*] We all know this theoretically, and yet we are not able to adapt our conduct accordingly. This situation shows that intellectual knowledge alone is not enough to modify behavior; we need to be touched emotionally and feel the relevance of a situation to our own life to be motivated to act. This is precisely what the Works That Reconnects enables—it helps us create a heart relationship with the ecological reality. This profound connection has to be cultivated from childhood to be deeply ingrained in the person. We can hope that if this kind of program is systematically included in the overall school curricula, it can contribute to educating students who will truly feel responsible for the earth and all living beings.

Design for Change

When I lived in Bhutan, one of my tasks was to contribute to implementing Gross National Happiness in the education system. In this context, I met with a wonderful educator, Mrs. Deki Choden, who is the founder and director of ELC primary and high school. I was introduced for the first time to Design for Change (DFC)[†] in her school, and I was deeply impressed by what her students had achieved through the DFC process. I would like to share one of the projects that ELC implemented, called Saying No to Packaged Food.[†] It is a four-step process that can be applied even with primary school children.

---

[*] "Climate Change 2022: Mitigation of Climate Change," IPCC, *https://www.ipcc .ch/report/sixth-assessment-report-working-group-3*.

[†] Design for Change, *https://www.dfcworld.org/SITE*.

[‡] "ELC Says No to Packaged Food_new.flv," dfcbhutan1, video, 3:28, *https://www .youtube.com/watch?v=fR_v0bs2S98*.

Saying No to Packaged Food

Step one is called Feel. It's about identifying a problem that bothers the children. At the ELC school, the students shared in small groups and recognized that the issue that disturbed them the most was the growing amount of plastic trash on the campus, in the city, and everywhere. They made an outing to a nearby landfill to have a first-hand experience of the worsening situation of waste in Thimphu, the capital of Bhutan, where the school is located. This step is called Feel because it is not enough to have a theoretical knowledge of a problem; it is necessary to connect it with an emotional experience to be motivated to bring about change.

Step two is called Imagine. Once the problem was identified, the students brainstormed to conceive how they could practically contribute to solving the challenge of plastic waste. They came up with the idea "Say no to package food!" Most of the children normally brought snacks to school wrapped in plastic, and they calculated that if the 360 students of their school stopped bringing plastic waste six days a week, it would reduce the problem by about 112,680 pieces of trash a year.

Step three is called Do. This step is about implementing the intention that has been imagined. So the students pledged that their school would contribute zero waste to the landfill. Food waste would be composted, paper recycled, and any plastic waste would be transformed into items that could be sold at the school fair, such as pencil holders or stuffing for cushions.

The last step is Share. This step is about communicating about the project in order to scale it up. The children presented their idea to a conference of school principals, visited other schools, and were invited to appear on national television. High officials from the royal government of Bhutan visited them to hear and see first-hand what had been achieved.

It became a national movement with many schools across the country joining into the "Saying No to Packaged Food" initiative. They estimated that if 170,000 school children of Bhutan joined the project, it would reduce the plastic waste by 53 million pieces in a year! The DFC process has been used in many countries, and hundreds of innovative projects have been launched. But most importantly, it empowers the children and helps them realize that they don't have to wait until they are adults or in an important position to make a difference and contribute to making our world a better place.

The United Nations website states that "climate change is now affecting every country on every continent. It is disrupting national economies and affecting lives, costing people, communities and countries dearly today and even more tomorrow."* Children are aware of the ecological challenges we're facing and appreciate the opportunity to share their feelings about it in ways that are safe and supportive. The Happy School project aims to prevent the next generations from becoming numb, detached, and overwhelmed with despair for the future. The various elements of the module care for the environment and the planet in the Happy School curriculum—organic gardening, the Work That Reconnects, Design for Change—encourage students to care for the natural world and contribute meaningfully to sustainable development in Vietnam and in the world.

> *Today's interconnected global challenges demand responses that are rooted in the spirit of our collective humanity. I believe that the risks and opportunities we face call for a paradigm shift that can only be embedded in our societies through education and learning. The role of education as a catalyst for building a better and more sustainable future for all has gained increasing recognition, leading to the declaration of the United Nations Decade of Education for Sustainable Development.*
>
> —Irina Bokova, director general of UNESCO

---

* "Climate Action," United Nations, *https://www.un.org/sustainabledevelopment /climate-action.*

As Irina Bokova rightly points out, we need a paradigm shift that can only be achieved by redefining the goals and methods of education. The Happy Schools program and curriculum is based on the assumption that the three modes of care are deeply interconnected: self-care, care for others and society, and care for the environment and the planet.

Happy Schools in Vietnam

The pilot project "Happy Schools" began in 2018 in Hue, Central Vietnam, with nine public schools: three primary, three lower-secondary, and three upper-secondary schools. So far, we have trained 181 teachers, and directly impacted 4100 students. The project has three mains components: teacher training and development, classroom implementation, and overall changes within the education system.

We collected much feedback from teachers, students, school administrators, and parents. The responses we received exceeded our expectations: 100 percent of the teachers would recommend the training to their peers. Most teachers reported not only changes in the perception of their role but also improvements in their personal life, including in their way of parenting. The changes in their way of teaching included less lecturing, more acting as role models, using interactive methods, and having better relationships with their students.

The COVID-19 crisis slowed down the implementation process in the schools, but at the same time, while many young people were facing difficulties—including depression, isolation, eating disorders, and other emotional problems due to the stressful situation—those who had been part of Happy Schools were better equipped to face these challenges.

Examples of Testimony from Teachers and School Administrators

What differentiates Happy Schools from other educational trainings is the quality of the practice. All the necessary conditions are met: well-grounded facilitators, a mindful surrounding, and a quality of deep listening. All that enables us to deep dive into the practice. Practicing is the only way to apply what we've learnt into real life.

The biggest change for me is a new perception about happiness, and it changes me not only as a teacher, but also as a parent, especially in my relationship with my teenage daughter. I care more about her feelings and emotions, also her relationships with teachers and friends. I learn to accept when she doesn't get good results at school, and I help her to learn from her difficulties and to find a better way to study after that "failure."

Happy Schools is not something separate from the overall curriculum. It is already there, in each lesson, each poem we teach. Happy Schools helps me bring the depth to the existing content, to my literature lesson plan. Now, when I teach "Letter from the Native American Leader" and other texts that are highlighting environmental challenges, my students and I enquire together and reflect on the limits of the current ego-centered approach.

When the students are happy at school, their parents are also more at peace. I think this happiness is the result of my consistent attempt to integrate social emotion learning into our teaching.

As a school administrator, I learned a much more persuasive and inspiring way to work with my coworkers and to resolve conflicts; we also identified the core values upon which our team is built. I can feel such a family-like atmosphere in our school.

Teachers solve classroom challenges more effectively. They also share, in a much calmer and more compassionate manner, about the "difficult kids" in the inclusive classes, or about challenging situations when they have to deal with demanding parents. Our teacher council is united and we feel connected. We feel deeply responsible toward our students, so that the parents and the local government are extremely appreciative of our work and trust us more.

When we practice empathy and deep listening it improves the quality of communication and feedback among students, teacher-student, teacher-parent and generally in the school community.

I'm thankful that my son joined the Happy Club. One day, he came home with a handmade card and told me "Mom, I love you. Thank you!" At that moment, I was surprised and didn't know how to react. We never had such a communication in my family. I was taken aback and then clumsily asked him, "Why did you say that? Did you do anything wrong?" When I reacted like that, I saw he was disappointed and hurt. Later, his teacher explained to me that it was a practice of gratitude that they had learned in the Happy Club. I felt embarrassed about my reaction and was then able to have a wonderful conversation with my son. I think he is teaching me how to express and receive gratitude.

Some of the Projects That Came from the Program

* Students studied the food chain after experiencing the biodynamic garden in the Peaceful Bamboo Family and observing the interdependence of different natural elements.

* When delivering lessons, many teachers start to hold space for the students to experience and reflect the content by themselves.

* Students wrote literature essays giving a voice to natural elements and beings that are suffering from climate change.

* There have been initiatives to reinvent the traditional learning space both physically and psychologically to foster a safe and supportive learning environment.

* Some schools have implemented outdoor classrooms, where the students and their teacher sit in a circle and see each other's faces without any obstacle.

* A teacher collected what students wanted to say to their parents and put the messages on the wall for a parent meeting. The parents were deeply touched to read kind and grateful messages from their children.

* Mindfulness and emotional check-ins have become a daily ritual to start a learning session or a meeting in the school.

* Many teachers have used conflict-resolution tools such as caring circles, watering flowers, and deep listening.

* In every class meeting, half of the time allotted is for Happy Schools practice and nurturing class relationships.

* Across all school levels, there are student clubs that apply Happy Schools practices. In these clubs, students become ambassadors of happiness and advocate for change.

* Alive and Green is a student club run exclusively by students; they work together to take responsible actions for the environment and practice happiness skills as a way to improve mindful and joyful collaboration.

* Another school has the I, You & the Environment Club, which serves as a lab for students and teachers to cocreate lessons combining care for nature and happiness skills.

* There has been a surge of awareness among the school administrators to gradually change their policies in a way that supports the culture of care and eco-friendly behaviors.

* One school transformed an unused stretch of land in the school's courtyard into a "Happy Path," a beautiful garden where the students can practice gardening and mindful walking. This project was born out of the collaboration of the whole community: school managers, teachers, students, parents, and volunteers from Hue University. Parents contributed in different ways: finance, building materials, or working at the construction site.

* There has been more active involvement from teachers, parents, and students to promote well-being in school; acting for the community's happiness has become a responsibility shared by everyone.

* The schools have found different ways to improve the teacher's well-being with several initiatives such as regular teacher sharing circles, mindful practices, and emotional check-ins at the beginning of meetings and workshops to share the practices among colleagues.

* Parents are more involved in the school community. They work with the teachers to facilitate and help teachers to spread the message to other parents.

* There are regular meetings with parents to involve them in the school experience of their kids. In the meeting, parents shared about the deep transformation they observed in their children. One mother said, "I realized that I have to transform myself to become a better mother." All parents want their children to be happy. and they are grateful if they can get support for it.

Acknowledgements by Authorities

Thua Thien Hue's Department of Education and Training recognizes the impact of Happy Schools toward the improvement in the quality of relationships in school context, and they have the intention to apply the framework on a larger scale after three years of piloting.
—The head of the education department of Hue province

I greatly appreciate the educational approaches which the school is implementing. Developing the school according to the Happy Schools framework is an appropriate approach.
—The chairman of the People Committee in Hue Province
(equivalent to a state governor)

There are many benefits from the Happy Schools program for different skills that the students can learn, including better communication with each other, and skills to help them reduce stress and perform better in their studies. We wish to apply Happy Schools to other schools in the province. What makes me so keen on scaling up Happy Schools is because I see how it is changing the quality of relationships within our school communities.

—The head of the primary schools department

Next Steps

After this successful first pilot phase, we are scaling up the project by implementing it in Hanoi, the capital of Vietnam, where the National Ministry of Education will be able to assess the impact of the program directly.

In order to be able to reach out to more teachers and schools all across the country, we are currently developing an online version of the Happy Schools curriculum that will be open source, so that there will be no financial obstacle for poorer regions and schools.

Furthermore, we have adapted the program to meet the needs of the European context, and we are piloting it in several schools in Switzerland. The project in Switzerland is developed in cooperation with the Adolescent Health Department of the University Hospital in Lausanne, Vaud. A team of researchers will be measuring the impact on the mental and physical health of the students.

We also plan an international scientific symposium where international experts will share the latest scientific findings related to the impact of mindfulness and social and emotional learning and related practices for children and adolescents.

12

GNH IN THE WORKPLACE

We have discussed in previous chapters how the current economic system is not only a source of social inequality and ecological disruption but also generates suffering at a personal level. In addition, we saw how the idea of *Homo economicus* portrays humans as narrowly self-interested agents always trying to maximize their benefits as consumers and their profits as producers. A heartless, egoistical being, *Homo economicus* pursues material benefits without any consideration for values, ethics, or human relations such as love and friendship. Furthermore, this implicit assumption amounts to a self-fulfilling prophecy, as it creates an economic system that results in massive institutional failure, creating results that nobody wants.

If we internalize *Homo economicus* and identify with this distortive view of what it is to be human, we disconnect from our true nature, fueled by the illusion that material consumption can fulfil our deeper aspiration for meaning, identity, and self-actualization. As long as we derive our identity and purpose from a narrow, materialistic approach that equates happiness with material ownership and consumption, we remain alienated from our highest potential. This creates a fundamental dissatisfaction, an existential unease that no amount of money and wealth can heal. As Erich Fromm wrote, "Greed is a bottomless pit that exhausts the person in an endless effort to satisfy the need, without ever reaching satisfaction."*

---

*Erich Fromm, *Escape from Freedom* (New York: Farrar and Rinehart, 1941).

When we discussed happiness in part one of this book, we saw that being connected with our true self is one of the important components for a meaningful life. Yet in today's workplace, a majority of employees complain about stress. Workers feel far removed from being able to be their authentic selves at work. In a study from 2016, the German magazine *Der Spiegel* reported that 86 percent of German workers complain about job-related stress.[*] The main causes were time constraints, a bad workplace atmosphere, emotional stress, and working overtime, resulting in psychological and physical symptoms such as depression, sadness, irritability, tension in the neck, back pain, headaches, and so on. To bring about a happier society, therefore, improving working conditions plays an important role.

The feeling of having a meaningful job that makes a positive contribution to society is also an important factor for the well-being of both employees and the organization. In recent years I had the opportunity to work with a number of companies that decided to improve conditions for their workers by focusing on happiness and well-being.

I believe that changing the way businesses work, along with changing the way children are educated, are the two strongest leverage points to transform society. In chapter six, "From Gross Domestic Product to Gross National Happiness," we discovered some of the problems of the current economic system. In order to introduce the practice of GNH in business, let us look at some of the current contradictions within the business world. In his book *Change Everything: Creating an Economy for the Common Good*, Christian Felber identified some of the key challenges:[†]

* Contradiction in values: In our personal and social lives, we strive to live in accordance with human values—trust, honesty, respect, empathy, cooperation, and sharing. The free-market

---

[*] "So Gestresst Sind Deutsche Angestellte," *Der Spiegel* (June 5, 2016), *https://www.spiegel.de/karriere/stress-bei-der-arbeit-jeder-zweite-hat-rueckenschmerzen-a-1095569.html*.

[†] Christian Felber, *Change Everything: Creating an Economy for the Common Good* (London: Zed Books, 2019).

economy is based on the rule of the systematic pursuit of profit and ruthless competition, thus promoting egoism, greed, envy, and irresponsibility.

* Neoliberal economy is an ideology, not a science: The fundamental assumption of the free-market economy is that competition is the most efficient method we know, but this fundamental assumption of economics doesn't rely on any evidence-based research. Furthermore, the other untested assumption, which dates back to Adam Smith, is that the invisible hand of the market will mysteriously turn the sum of all egoistic behavior into the common good. Again, this hypothesis is not backed by evidence-based research. Common sense, as well as observations of current economic challenges, clearly shows that means and results are usually of the same nature, meaning that the sum of individual egoistic behaviors leads to an egoist society where greed and over-consumption have become the norm.

* Mistaking means and goals: The current system is based on defining profit as the ultimate goal of all economic activities. Therefore, everything else—people, nature, capital—is simply seen as a means of attaining the goal of maximizing profit. But when we reflect on the true purpose of economic activities, we realize that it is to fulfil legitimate human needs. Profit is merely a necessary by-product of economic activity.

* The need for a paradigm shift: Consider the concept of development in the organic world. If we plant an acorn and nurture it, the acorn becomes an oak tree that bears fruit—acorns. Development is the manifestation of its own nature, of its own being, by growing and unfolding. That is natural development. But in the way development in the economic world has been defined, especially in the twentieth century, it is not an organic process of becoming according to one's own nature. It has been, by and large, enforced from outside by an ideology that reduces development to its economic components. While economic development is doubtless important, the economy itself is not an end; rather, it is a means, the end of which is the satisfaction of human needs. The goal of all economies, therefore, should be to produce goods and services that enhance the well-being of all people.

In the light of what we have just described, we see that implementing Gross National Happiness in the field of business means, on the one hand, taking care of the well-being of the employees and other company stakeholders and, on the other, redefining the vision and the mission of the company from the point of view of a new economic paradigm. As more entrepreneurs and business people become aware of the contribution that they can make toward a better society—examples include sustainable brands, ethical banking, and impact investment, just to name a few—it could become one of the strongest factors of social and ecological transformation.

The Main Components of a GNH Project for an Organization

We have seen that the GNH approach combines two fundamental elements: a holistic way of measuring the development of a nation, an organization, a school, or even an individual, and the development of happiness skills. Together, these two dimensions create the outer structural framework and the inner mindfulness-based conditions of happiness and well-being. Therefore, when implementing a GNH project in an organization, it is important to develop both aspects in a balanced way.

If we were to focus solely on the structural aspects, the change would not be deep and sustainable, because systems are the manifestations of the way people think feel, act, and relate to one another and to the world. They are the products of a certain mindset, of assumptions, and of the narrative that gives meaning to what we do. If the mindset does not change, the structural renovation alone will not bring about true transformation.

Conversely, if we focus only on the inner dimensions and on individual transformation, without addressing the structural issues, we might overburden the people who are held responsible for problems that may be systemic.

For instance, if we want to lessen stress in the workplace, a good way to start is to have the employees practice mindfulness. But we should not forget that the causes of stress might be related to objective situations that need to be addressed, such as toxic management practices, gender bias, ethnic prejudices, or unfair working conditions. Putting the responsibility on the individual alone without addressing these issues would be not only unfair but even counterproductive, as it might delay the necessary change.

Furthermore, mindfulness is not only a technique to focus one's attention, it also has an ethical dimension that should always be included in the process. To give an extreme example, if a sniper practices concentration, his shooting will be more accurate, and he will have a higher chance to hit his target. But was the killing justified in the first place?

To use a more common example, if a stock trader practices mindfulness, they might make more profit because they will be more focused and have faster reactions. But the question remains if the kind of operation they are conducting is ethically justified or if they create more social inequality.

When the fifth king of Bhutan spoke about GNH, he said, "To me, GNH is simply development with values."* The value aspect or ethical dimension should always be included in any GNH-inspired project.

After having implemented GNH project in a number of organizations and companies, I have tried to summarize the main components

---

*GNH Centre, Bhutan, *https://www.gnhcentrebhutan.org*.

that should be taken into consideration for a successful outcome. These elements have all been successfully implemented in the Happy Biti's project that we have conducted in Vietnam for the past four years.*

Vision, Mission, Values, Behavior

Revisiting the vision and mission of an organization in light of GNH is an important starting point, because it conveys the very purpose of the institution. It creates the narrative that gives meaning to everything that is done, and it is the basis of the organizational culture. It also gives the foundation to formulate values that are the ethical guidelines for the people working in the company. These values should be translated into practical behaviors that can be observed and assessed. In this way, we can ensure a coherent flow from a more generic and somewhat abstract level to very concrete dimensions that guide everyday activities.

Identifying and Training GNH Ambassadors

In all organizations, there is an explicit hierarchy of titles and responsibilities, but also an implicit hierarchy that is based on the reputation, charisma, and popularity of certain people. It is important to identify who the influencers are in each context, those who will likely be the early adopters of the innovation and whose voice and opinion carry weight with their colleagues. This usually includes people who have a certain formal position and power but also other members of the community whose influence is important, although less institutional. The success of the project will often depend on identifying the right target audience. We usually create mixed groups that are representative of the variety of functions, departments, hierarchical levels, demographics. In Biti's, for instance, the GNH ambassadors are groups of thirty-five people who participate in three workshops over a year. These workshops focus on the "three reconnections": living in harmony with self,

---

*See the interview of Biti's CEO page 248–51

with others, and with nature. We practice mindfulness, social and emotional competencies, and Deep Ecology and other related activities. The process is similar to the one described in the Happy Schools program, but is applied to a business or an NGO, depending on the context.

Most of the exercises that we have described in the previous chapters can also be used in this context, such as mindful sitting, mindful walking, mindful eating, and especially the social and emotional practices such as nonviolent communication, deep listening, and beginning anew.

When I was the head of learning and development at the International Committee of the Red Cross, I used to offer a silent mindful meal once a week in my office, and whoever wanted to join was free to do so. Another practice that has been systematically adopted in several companies that have implemented GNH projects is to begin every meeting with a moment of mindfulness and to then have a round of emotional check-ins before diving into the agenda. Even though it might feel a bit strange in the beginning, when people are new to the practice, in all these companies it has become a small ritual that everyone enjoys, because it creates a welcome moment of calm in busy schedules.

The GNH ambassadors have several roles: they communicate and spread the GNH message, they are role models to showcase a different way to interact, and they typically are the ones introducing the moments of silence before meetings and facilitating check-in practices; they gradually become trainers and act as multipliers.

Developing a Mindful Management Culture

We have created a twelve-month "resonant leader and manager" course based on Mindful Leadership and Emotional Intelligence applied to management. During the pandemic, when the senior executives from Biti's were more available, we took the opportunity to meet twice a month to present the various skills, to have a forum to share among peers, and to take questions that arose from the practical situations they were facing due to the COVID-19 crisis. It was an occasion to see if these methods would help them in challenging times. It was crucial to focus on the well-being of the employees, as everyone was stressed and anxious. It was comforting to observe that most of the executives were able to navigate the troubled waters of the pandemic with an impressive level of confidence and commitment.

Defining the Right Indicators

The Center for Bhutan Studies and GNH Research has done an impressive work in redefining the GNH indicators that were created for a nation so that they can be applied to a business.* It was an initiative proposed by the then prime minister of Bhutan, HE Mr. Tshering Tobgay.

We used these indicators as a starting point, but we also realized that there was a need to adapt and contextualize them to each specific country, industry, and organization. we saw that if the stakeholders are not actively involved in the definition of the indicators and variables, they don't feel responsible for the implementation of the results. What we measure is what we are aware of, and for change to be possible, it is necessary to redirect the collective awareness of the organization. By creating an open social space where people can share what is important to them and what they feel is relevant to the company, we create a buy-in that would not be possible to achieve if the measurement were imposed and predefined by a group of experts. The challenge is to find the right balance between enough commonality that allows for comparison between companies and enough contextualization, so that the survey is relevant to this specific entity. In Biti's, the first survey was constructed on indicators defined by the Happy Biti's team on the basis

---

*GNH Certification, *https://www.bhutanstudies.org.bt/tag/gnh-of-business.*

of the *GNH of Business* manual, and now that they have a baseline, the management is fine tuning it so that it is more relevant to the company and its culture.

Once the survey has been conducted and the results are shared, it is important to define priorities, decide on corrective actions, and communicate about it so that people perceive that the GNH program is not just a marketing trend but that the leadership is serious about trying to enhance the well-being of both internal and external stakeholders.

Implementing Gross National Happiness in a Company

The first large-scale implementation of Gross National Happiness in business I experienced was when the GNH Center Bhutan was approached by Harald Link, the chief executive officer and owner of the B.Grimm Group of Thailand, who asked us to support his company in implementing GNH values. Now a multi-business corporation, B.Grimm is the oldest infrastructure developer in Thailand. It was established in Bangkok in 1878, when Bernhard Grimm, a German pharmacist, and his Austrian partner, Erwin Mueller, founded the Siam Dispensary. The business prospered and was soon made the official pharmacist of the Thai royal family. In 1903, Adolph Link was hired to manage and expand the business. Link was an ambitious young man, and over following decades, he (and later his sons) expanded it greatly. By the 1960s, there were divisions in widely varying fields, from health care equipment to telecommunications and mechanical engineering. In the late 1980s, Adolph Link's grandson, Harald Link, took over the business and expanded it further, with branches in such fields as real estate and power generation. Today the B.Grimm Group has revenue in the billions, and they employ over two thousand people.

So when Harald Link asked us to help him implement GNH in his company, I was somewhat overwhelmed, having never worked before with a business of that size before. We started by presenting the GNH framework and tools to the company's management and partners to try to perceive whether it was a serious intention or simply some greenwashing or publicity stunt. After a number of in-depth discussions with the senior management, we realized that it was a serious endeavor based on a belief in the moral responsibility of the business toward society and the planet. Therefore, with a memorandum of understanding signed between the GNH Center Bhutan and B. Grimm, we agreed to collaborate on the project and began the process of discovering how to implement GNH on such a large scale and in such a complex business context.

Vision and Mission

As we described in the introduction of this chapter, one of the key problems with businesses is that, more often than not, they have lost a sense of their true mission—serving the well-being of society by responding to legitimate human needs in terms of producing goods and services. So the first step with B.Grimm was to look into the vision and mission of the company to see if it was aligned with Gross National Happiness values. In the case of implementing GNH at a national level in Bhutan, the starting point had been to enshrine happiness in the constitution. Likewise, it was important to clarify what the vision of the leadership was concerning the ultimate goal of B.Grimm, beyond its financial success. The outcome of this reflection was a reformulation of the corporate philosophy, which is now, "Doing business with compassion for the development of civilisation in harmony with nature."

By "developing civilization" they mean creating the proper conditions for the well-being and happiness of people. So when we look at this vision, we recognize the three dimensions that that make up the foundation of true happiness: *compassion* as an inner quality, *development* as a manifestation of care for society, and *harmony with nature* as an expression of care for the planet. B.Grimm further explains its corporate philosophy in the following way by quoting the Dalai Lama:

"If you want others to be happy, practice compassion. If you want to be happy, practice compassion." The company website goes on to say that "everyone wants to be happy. . . . Most want to do what they love. If people know what it is, most want to do what inspires them. . . . Most like to be close to their friends. Most want to be valued and contribute to a higher good. At B.Grimm we believe that if we do business with compassion for the development of civilisation in harmony with nature, we can bring happiness to everyone."*

In order to "do business with compassion," B.Grimm incorporates four Buddhist values: loving kindness, compassion, joy, and equanimity—or *metta, karuna, mudita,* and *uppekha* in Pali (see diagram). B.Grimm's description of their corporate philosophy continues:

> For people in a society to be truly happy, satisfying their needs has to come with equitable socio-economic development within the limits of what nature can provide, integrated with good governance and all the while allowing people to maintain their cultural identity and practices. In the Gross National Happiness philosophy of Bhutan these factors are called the four pillars of balanced development. If they are not carefully considered, other people will suffer and true abiding happiness cannot exist.
>
> B. Grimm has always been following these same four pillars with its many social programs alongside our business activities to develop and promote religion, education, environment, sports, music and arts.

In summary, we see that the first outcome of the GNH program at B.Grimm was the ability to formulate clearly a business purpose that is much broader than simply maximizing profit. Although the B.Grimm Group continues to be economically successful, there is an understanding that this need not be incompatible with being a force

---

* "Corporate Philosophy," B.Grimm Group, *https://bgrimmgroup.com/purpose -vision-values.*

for the happiness and well-being of both employees and the broader public. Indeed, it was of utmost importance to clarify that the GNH approach was not in contradiction to a profitable business, but on the contrary, it could have a beneficial impact on *both* sides. For instance, setting up a meaningful corporate philosophy contributes to the sense of purpose, commitment, and engagement of the employees, making them feel that their job is not merely a way to earn a living but also a way to make a positive contribution through one's work.

It also fosters recruitment of young talent. We know that in today's business environment, recruiting talented and engaged young professionals is crucial for the success of a company, and those companies that offer a more meaningful job opportunity will be favored by the younger generation, many of whom are looking a purposeful life, not just a job.

In addition, companies that emphasize the well-being of their employees experience lower employee turnover, something extremely desirable, since a high turnover rate involves high levels of resources, competencies, and experience being wasted. Employee engagement is a constant challenge for organizations, and a lot of training and team-building activities are used to try to enhance it. In the end, however, it is the meaningfulness of the work and the sense that the company truly cares for its people that are the most important factors for retaining engaged and loyal employees.

It is understandable that a company such as B.Grimm, which not only has a comprehensive and meaningful corporate philosophy but also acts in accordance with these values, attracts the motivated and talented workers and is able to keep them. This is how B.Grimm describes its commitment toward its employees:

> *We believe in doing business with compassion. We provide a positive-cultural working environment with development programs to build up your strength helping you to advance [in] your career of choice. Moreover, we help employees balance their family life with work and stand by them both in good and in difficult times. Help, guidance, financial aid, and scholarships serve to return the loyalty and trust that*

our staff puts in us. We also invite families to join our various outings and social activities and to engage in community support. This way we can lift the spirit of our people at work and support their relationship with their loved ones.

. . .

At B.Grimm we hold the principle that social responsibility starts with your own people. To begin with, every employee has equal opportunities, regardless of nationality, religion, gender, color, age, sexual orientation, or disability. In fact, we welcome diversity in the workplace as it enriches our company and inspires new perspectives.

To provide a working environment that supports the people [we support them] in following their religious practices and in balancing their work and family life. We also offer development and engagement programs of choice.

. . .

In addition, we are in constant dialogue with our employees and notice time and again that our staff takes great pride in B.Grimm's social engagement. Therefore we make sure to provide our employees with plenty of opportunities to join our social activities, and therewith the chance to extend their care and service beyond their work. *

It is encouraging to see that a company such as B.Grimm is able to thrive by doing good, proving that business activities and positive values that enhance the happiness and well-being of both internal and external stakeholders are not mutually exclusive.

Measuring What Matters

At national level, the GNH survey enables the government to be aware of the multidimensional development of the country, and this, in return, enables the right allocation of resources and priorities.

---

* "People," B.Grimm Group, *https://bgrimmgroup.com/people.*

Likewise, companies also measure their progress, but most of the time, the only indicator that is taken into consideration is the financial one: the bottom line, the return on investment, and the shareholder values thus created.

While there is now a trend to go beyond the limited financial indicators and consider the triple bottom line—financial results as well as the ecological and social impacts of a company—GNH goes further: its Nine Domains include the triple bottom line as well as offer a more differentiated analysis of the impact of the company on its employees, stakeholders, society at large, and the environment. Most of the time, key performance indicators (KPIs) are narrow in their outlook, so one of the important aspects of implementing GNH in an organization is to develop the right set of indicators that will allow the company to track its progress in a more holistic way.

When the GNH Center works with a company, we don't come with a ready-made set of indicators that are simply implemented. Rather, we cocreate—together with management and the employees—indicators that truly reflect the values and commitments of the specific organization. This process is based on a general proposal that has been developed by the Center for Bhutan Studies in its research paper, "GNH Certification," which encompasses the Nine Domains and a series of indicators.* The process of cocreating the indicators is in itself a transformative learning process, because it encourages all the stakeholders to reflect on what they consider to be important, both for them personally and for the company as a whole. Implementing a GNH survey, therefore, is not simply a mechanical, statistical process; it is an opportunity for the system to perceive itself by reflecting on what is truly important, what truly matters. Otto Scharmer describes the core competency of leadership as "the ability to redirect collective attention." What we measure is what we are attentive to; therefore, the

---

*Karma Wangdi, Tshoki Zangmo, and Jigme Phunstho, "GNH Certification," *Center for Bhutan Studies*, April 6, 2018, *http://www.bhutanstudies.org.bt/gnh-certification*.

key challenge is to define clearly what our core intentions are and to make sure that we align our attention—what we measure—with our intentions.

In my experience, the Nine Domains seem to be quite universally applicable, although not all domains will have the same weight in each context. But in order to assess the domains, we need to define indicators and questions, and these can vary quite a lot from one context to another. A corporate philosophy, the vision and the mission statement, are always formulated in general terms, whereas the process of defining indicators is a way to embody and actualize these general concepts into actionable objectives and action plans. Let us now look at the Nine Domains as adapted to a business context.

Applying the Framework of the Nine Domains to a Company or Corporation

The following presentation is a summery based on the research conducted by Karma Wangdi, Tshoki Zangmo, and Jigme Phunstho from the Centre for Bhutan Studies. I want to acknowledge the quality of their work and honestly admit that without their publication, it would have been very difficult for us to conduct the GNH survey in organizations.

The indicators of the assessment tool are grouped under the same Nine Domains of Gross National Happiness that we have already discussed in general terms. Here it is about applying the same indicators for a company:

1. Psychological Well-Being

2. Health

3. Time Use

4. Education

5. Community Vitality

6. Cultural Diversity and Resilience

7. Good Governance

8. Ecological Diversity and Resilience

9. Living Standards

The Nine Domains were adapted from the GNH index framework, which enables us to develop concrete assessment indicators. As mentioned, we only use these indicators as an example and encourage each company to create its own indicators that are pertinent to its type of organization and industry. They also provide a necessary precondition and a starting point for integrating GNH in organizational practices. To emphasize the importance on the well-being of both workers and communities, it is important to assess both how a company focuses on employee and stakeholder happiness and the organizational commitment towards society and environment.

First, we focus on the employees' well-being, and as we continue the process, we gradually include the happiness of all the stakeholders, such as customers, providers, and partners. The second component captures how a commitment to GNH guides a business in integrating responsible behavior by contributing to the areas of culture, environment, and community building.

Psychological Well-Being in the Workplace

The construct captures both the cognitive and affective assessment of a worker toward their work and the workplace. It includes the following indicators:

1. Job Satisfaction

2. Workplace Trust

3. Job Security

4. Discrimination

5. Harassment

6. Positive Emotion

7. Negative Emotion

1. Job Satisfaction

A happy worker is a vital resource for any kind of business. Workers generally want to feel respected and trusted. They want to work in a safe environment with good opportunities to advance and develop their skills and knowledge. When a company creates such enabling environments, workers tend to be satisfied and, thereby, help build a strong, stable, and sustainable business. The indicator is based on two questions. First, workers are asked how satisfied they are with their job. Second, we examine how satisfied they are with their organization as a workplace.

2. Workplace Trust

Professional success is based on relationships founded on trust. Daily business decisions are based on conscious or unconscious trust. The level of trust that workers and managers have in each other regulates teamwork, and good teamwork encourages trust. Hence, workplace trust is a key indicator of an existing healthy relationship between employees and managers. It has been further linked to positive workplace attributes such as empowerment, autonomy, cooperation, and supervisory support.

3. Job Security

Businesses should not overlook the importance of offering workers long-term job security, as it is one of the most significant factors in workers' preference lists. Job security is as essential as employees' salary and health care benefits. Job security has also become a key element in influencing employees' decision to join and stay with the organization.

4. Discrimination

Discrimination here refers to a differential (inferior) treatment experienced by workers due to their background, such as gender, race, and age. Such discrimination reduces workers' self-esteem and access to opportunities. It brings psychological, emotional, and physical harm to workers. Business leaders will have to encourage a work culture where workers have equal opportunities, and formulate programs and procedures to counteract and combat discriminatory practices.

5. Harassment

Workplaces can be hostile environments with persistent, abusive, intimidating, malicious, or insulting behaviors. Harassment denotes any act of threat or violence or other disruptive behaviors experienced in the workplace. This indicator evaluates the experience of harassment suffered by workers across three related events: sexual harassment, physical abuse, and verbal abuse. A study reported that the number one cause of stress is a toxic workplace culture (i.e., harassment), followed by the number two cause, lack of communication.[*]

6. Positive Emotion

Emotions are either induced by one's personal life or by an organization's policy or procedures. Either way, studies indicate that emotions felt in organizations have direct consequences in outcomes of their work roles. Workers who express positive emotions are seen to have a positive impact. They are said to be more creative and efficient while experiencing such emotions.

Compassion, contentment, generosity, gratitude, and joy have been identified as constructing the positive emotion indicator. Such emotions aim to foster a community of support and positivity. Workplace compassion may imply feelings that purposely help others or attend to the needs of others.

---

[*] Megan Thompson, "The Top 10 Causes of Stress at Work," WeThrive (April 15, 2021), *https://wethrive.net/mental-health-at-work/the-top-10-causes-of-stress-at-work*.

7. Negative Emotion

Just as positive emotions have a positive impact on workers, negative emotions tend to produce negative impacts on workers too. The negative emotion indicator is constructed using five negative emotions: anger, sadness, frustration, anxiety, and disappointment. Anger refers to responses toward workplace situations when a worker feels wronged due to a multitude of factors. Anger could be directed toward colleagues, supervisors, clients, or managers. Likewise, sadness redounds in feelings of melancholy or misery at work. Frustration runs closely with anger but may not cause a worker to react in a more physical manner. Prolonged frustration might lead to bursts of anger at a later stage. Workplace anxiety is a learned response to stress and may appear in forms of fear, such as fear of working in groups or fear of being judged.

Health in the Workplace

Work is an important determinant of worker health, which can result in both positive and negative health effects. Studies show that workers' health and productivity are closely associated. The domain of health focuses on the internal experiences and environmental factors that influence health in the workplace, and reviews both physical and mental conditions of workers. It is composed of indicators such as occupational stress, nature of work, common spaces for various non-work purposes, safety, injury, illness, and disability. In developed countries, most of these items are regulated by governmental rules and laws, but multinational companies often have factories in developing countries and that do not follow the regulations that would apply in their own country. Therefore, these indicators should be assessed in all the venues belonging to the organization.

1. Occupational Stress

2. Health Risk Exposure

3. Safety Equipment

4. Illness and Injury Incidence Rate

5. Disability Incidence Rate

6. Fatal Injury Incidence Rate

7. Return to Work Policy or Procedure

1. Occupational Stress

Occupational stress is a physical and emotional response due to unexpected or conflicting demands in a workplace. A study reported that 79 percent of workers in the UK experience stress at work.* Occupational stress is an experience of prolonged tension that makes workers develop many mental health issues, such as anxiety and depression. The stress indicator here entails harmful reactions such as losing concentration or sleep and becoming anxious or restless due to excessive pressures or job demands. Common causes of stress include consistent increase in workloads, continuous overtime work, a mismatch between skills and expectations, and a hostile work environment.

2. Health Risk Exposure

Depending on the nature and size of a business, workers may be exposed to a range of harmful substances. The health risk exposure indicator examines the work environment and safe working conditions.

3. Safety Equipment

The safety equipment indicator includes the examination of the existence and usage of personal protective equipment.

4. Illness and Injury Incidence Rate

This indicator is collected from the administrative body of the business, which is asked to report on the number of non-fatal incidences that led to physical or mental harm. The incidences are recorded for

---

* "The 2020 UK Workplace Stress Survey," Perkbox, *https://www.perkbox.com/uk /resources/library/2020-workplace-stress-survey.*

the previous year. The information on injury or illness is used to express the number of illness and injury in relation to the number of persons employed.

5. Disability Incidence Rate

As the name suggests, the indicator signifies non-fatal episodes at work involving considerable harm leading to the long-term disability of the workers concerned. Long-term disability here refers to any illness or injury suffered for at least six months.

6. Fatal Injury Incidence Rate

In addition to the disability incidence rate, it is important to consider the rate of fatal illness or injury.

7. Return-to-Work Policy or Procedure

If workers remain connected to the workplace, it may contribute to their overall healing process, so a return-to-work policy, procedure, or plan refers to reintegrating injured and disabled workers into the workplace. The plan may include providing adequate adjustments to work conditions to facilitate a smooth transition.

Time Use in the Workplace

Technology has made it difficult to separate work from our personal lives. Employers' increasing use of to make workers accessible round the clock reduces workers' ability to balance the spheres of work and private life. The time-use domain attempts to assess workers' experiences in meeting the needs of both work and non-work areas of life and aims to reduce the conflict between work and non-work activities. The domain comprises six indicators:

1. Working Hours
2. Work Pressure
3. Flexi-Time

4. Work-Life Balance

5. Adequate Breaks

6. Sleeping Hours

1. Working Hours

Today's work culture requires workers to spend longer hours at the workplace. This increase in work hours has led to work-related conflicts. Studies have reported that long working hours often increase the risks of occupational illnesses and injuries. Therefore, businesses will have to integrate worktime regulations to protect workers from such health hazards.

2. Work Pressure

Workers may need a certain amount of pressure to complete their tasks. When the work demand exceeds workers' ability due to inadequate time, resources and skill, it will add to work-related stress.

3. Flexi-Time

A flexi-time indicator denotes working arrangements that allow a certain degree of flexibility in the time and days of work. Flexible working arrangements may have a positive impact on workers' engagement and motivation. One of the Swiss companies we are working with has introduced trust-based work time. Employees don't have to report the number of working hours they spend in their office, as long as they meet the objectives that they have to attain. During the pandemic, when most of the workforce was working from home and little supervision of time spent working was possible, this company fared better than most, because its employees were already used to self-organizing their working time.

4. Work-Life Balance

Workers who can balance work and non-work tend to have greater satisfaction with life by experiencing lower levels of stress. The demand on workers' time and energy can significantly affect social and family lives.

5. Adequate Breaks

The availability of breaks for lunch and tea or coffee is essential for workers. Businesses should encourage workers to take regular breaks and create an environment that steers them away from overworking.

6. Sleeping Hours

Good-quality sleep, and enough of it, is important for our health. Sleep affects our ability to sustain attention, performance, and interpersonal relationships. A sleep duration of seven to eight hours is recommended, as it lowers the risks related to diabetes, obesity, and blood pressure, and it reduces the risk of workplace accidents.

Education in the Workplace

Business establishments should provide workers with programs to update and acquire skills. The training domain incorporates human resource indicators, like workplace skill development and training programs. It includes indicators that attempt to capture opportunities offered by employers for their professional and personal development.

1. Paid Long-Term Study

2. Paid Short-Term Study

3. Training

4. Performance Appraisal System

5. Worker Engagement

1. Paid Long-Term Study

This indicator examines administrative records on the number of workers who have taken paid long-term leave to study. Since such scholarships cannot be applied to all workers, assessment will be carried out in terms of the proportion of workers who have had such opportunities in the past five years.

2. Paid Short-Term Study

As with long-term study, information on short-term study is gathered from administrative data. Short-term implies those studies that are less than six months in duration. The indicator is expressed as a proportion of workers sent for short-term studies in the past five years.

3. Training

This indicator reflects the number of workers who attended training to enhance their skills and talents. This training pertains to skill development through instruction and practice provided to improve work performance. Such training programs involve specializing in employment-related skills or acquiring new skills. Training also includes those sent for personal development, focusing on the growth and overall advancement of workers.

4. Performance Appraisal System

Performance appraisal is a vital component of human resource management. It allows businesses to provide positive feedback, as well as identify areas for improvement. The indicator attempts to evaluate the presence of performance appraisal systems in business establishments. It also assesses workers' perceptions of fairness, accuracy, and biases with the performance ratings.

5. Worker Engagement

Worker engagement refers to the level of freedom and appreciation given by their employers. Workers may experience these aspects while communicating with coworkers, supervisors, or clients.

Community Vitality and the Workplace

Any business is bound to have an impact on its local community. As soon as a business is set up, it will bring economic benefits, but it could also cause considerable social, environmental, and cultural upheaval.

For example, disruption can be caused by the uneven distribution of the benefits created by the business, which can transform existing social norms. For example, the effect of the tourism industry in many developing countries can create a divide between those who have access to foreigners—and therefore earn hard currencies—and those who have no such access. In terms of Gross National Happiness, businesses must fulfil their social obligations, and in domain of community vitality, therefore, businesses must engage actively in community building. The domain comprises four indicators, as shown below:

1. Corporate Volunteerism

2. Corporate Donation

3. Local Business

4. Social Venture Design

1. Corporate Volunteerism

Volunteering is a great way of paying a community back. This indicator gauges businesses to make a difference in the lives of local residents through volunteering activities and community initiatives. Volunteers drawn from the business sector can also share skills and expertise that would otherwise remain out of reach for people in the local community.

In terms of community vitality, volunteering may involve the development of basic infrastructure, antipoverty measures, or supporting communities in times of natural disasters. In terms of the local environment, volunteer programs may include reforestation, water conservation, waste reduction, and energy conservation. Such interactions do much to reinforce relationships with the local community.

Biti's, the shoe company in Vietnam that has implemented GNH in recent years, set a wonderful example of both corporate voluntarism and corporate donation during the COVID-19 crisis. Although their own revenue had drastically diminished, they distributed free meals to tens of thousands of people who had lost their income and donated equipment to hospitals.

2. Corporate Donation

This indicator refers to the amount a business donates in cash or in kind toward a range of activities or events. These may involve promoting or conserving culture, the local environment, or the community itself. Community philanthropy has great potential to influence a business's values, as social changes are witnessed directly.

3. Local Business

This indicator refers to the creation of products with locally available raw materials and the skills involved in that process. The indicator also gauges whether a business has caused any damage to community infrastructures. These may include power and communication infrastructures, houses, water sources, sewage systems, and roads.

4. Social Venture Design

With the increase in demand for businesses to make profits by serving social purposes, the line between government and business roles in community development seems to be fading. We incorporate the social venture design indicator to encourage businesses to create positive impacts in societies. Vision and mission statements, goals, operations, products, and services are studied to evaluate whether the business has integrated social impact and other vital components into the business model.

Cultural Diversity and Resilience in the Workplace

Culture incorporates both tangible things, in the form of objects, and intangible aspects, such as values and practices. Businesses, as a part of society, have a role in ensuring that culture is encouraged, recognized, respected, and supported. In general, most business executives/leaders are not aware of the benefits of supporting cultural programs and, as a consequence, are not involved in initiating cultural programs. But we have seen in the case of B.Grimm how cultural engagement plays a central role in their social engagement. Furthermore, the organizational culture is also an important factor of a successful company.

1. Culture Design
2. Cultural Property
3. Cultural Participation

1. Culture Design

This indicator gauges whether the core operation of a business is directly involved in endorsing or fostering the promotion and development of tangible and/or intangible aspects of cultural tradition or innovation.

B. Grimm is intensively involved in supporting education and also artistic activities in Thailand, and the sponsorship they provide helps preserve traditional culture.

2. Cultural Property

Some businesses may cause the displacement or destruction of cultural property in communities. We evaluate the number of incidences of cultural property damage or deterioration during the establishment of a business or in the course of its operations.

3. Cultural Participation

Businesses will have to take part in promoting and encouraging cultural participation. This may include supporting cultural events by negotiating working hours with employees so they are able to participate in those cultural events. This indicator evaluates workers' access to such opportunities. This dimension is very important in Bhutan, where religious festivals play an important role in maintaining the traditional culture, as well as the community vitality.

Good Governance in the Workplace

Some businesses may seek profit unethically by exploiting workers or resorting to corrupt practices. Under the domain of good governance, executive leadership and government will have to develop policies and procedures to hold the business accountable to the highest legal, ethical, and operational standards. The domain emphasizes that businesses conduct their operations with ethics, integrity, and transparency. It comprises eight indicators:

1. Regulation
2. Board Effectiveness
3. Public Shareholding
4. Whistleblowing Channel
5. Turnover Rate
6. Compliance
7. Customer/Client satisfaction
8. Common Space

1. Regulation

Effective written policies and procedures are required for a business entity to address workplace-related issues. Documents and guidelines explaining such rules and regulations reflect a business's compliance commitment and help educate workers on their rights. Such standards will have to be easily accessible and distributed to workers.

2. Board Effectiveness

The board of directors is one of the most suitable mechanisms to improve governance in businesses. The indicator here gauges board effectiveness, gender composition, and independence. For gender composition, the numbers of male and female directors are compared. For independence, we assess directors' relationships and interests.

3. Public Shareholding

This indicator gauges whether a business has invited the public to subscribe to the company shares through an initial public offering (IPO), and assesses the percentage of shareholdings by the public. The indicator is applicable to registered companies and so can be ignored while evaluating non-registered enterprises.

4. Whistleblowing Channel

The whistleblowing channel allows workers to report any bad behaviors such as corruption, harassment, or fraud that they have observed or experienced in a business establishment, without fear of retaliation. Effective policies on whistleblowing may improve the ethical climate by raising the workers' confidence and protection.

5. Turnover Rate

Turnover is often portrayed as a major issue in business operation, as it has a direct impact on the morale and productivity of remaining workers. Workers often leave their jobs due to dissatisfaction in the workplace.

6. Compliance

An increasing number of fraudulent practices have been reported by businesses. For Gross National Happiness to be integrated, businesses need to develop a culture of transparency and accountability within their operations. These include corruption, money laundering, illegal financing of political parties, anti-competitive practices, tax evasion, violation of environmental rules, the publication of misleading advertisements, discrimination, abuse and harassment of workers, worker injury, child labor, and forced labor. These regulations are meant to ensure that businesses are being run with integrity and transparency.

7. Customer/Client Satisfaction

Customer satisfaction is crucial for the success of a business. A business will have to develop strategic programs to promote customer satisfaction, such as monitoring and tracking satisfaction, understanding customer expectations, and providing effective measures to increase satisfaction. The indicator measures/gauges a business's initiatives on procedures to assess customer/client satisfaction levels and the frequency of conducting customer satisfaction surveys.

8. Common Space

Businesses will have to provide workers with comfortable spaces to encourage inspiration, creativity, innovation, and reflection, since workers spend a great deal of their time at work. A common space indicator consists of four variables: access to common spaces for interacting with coworkers, having meals together, carrying out spiritual or wellness activities, and green space that provides contact with nature. The spiritual space or the wellness room is often overlooked in offices, despite its association with workers' happiness. Providing such spaces encourages workers to practice mindfulness and other contemplative exercises to reduce occupational stress and increase happiness.

Ecological Diversity and Resilience in the Workplace

Businesses are major contributors to ecological problems such as pollution, water contamination, loss of biodiversity, and changes in water systems that the livelihood and health of those in the local community. In this domain businesses are encouraged to develop systematic ecofriendly operations as part of their daily conduct.

Businesses will have to understand that environmental benefits are long-term and intergenerational, and they must not be reduced to a mere monetary value. Ecological indicators have long been used to detect impacts and conditions of nature. This domain comprises indicators that highlight environmentally conscious activities for increasing well-being and happiness in communities. Due to the ecological crises and the challenges of climate change, this dimension will become increasingly important, and any serious GNH project will focus strongly on the ecological impact of the company.

1. Renewable Energy

2. Energy

3. Emissions

4. Solid Waste

5. Hazardous Waste

6. Liquid Waste

7. Eco-Design

1. Renewable Energy

An effective energy strategy can help businesses become competitive, enable them to be sustainable, and help them position themselves as socially responsible to stakeholders. This indicator has been included to encourage and support business models whose operations and practices are based on and around the use of renewable energy.

2. Energy

Reducing energy consumption is not only beneficial to the environment but also saves money. Businesses may start reducing consumption by improving energy efficiency. Through the energy indicator, we evaluate a business's efforts in monitoring energy use and assess initiatives to reduce energy consumption. Some common initiatives include reducing energy waste and optimizing energy use by using energy efficient appliances, sensors, or timers.

3. Emissions

Businesses will have to stop greenhouse gas emissions into the atmosphere. These emissions are the leading cause for climate change, resulting in disastrous consequences. Businesses have opportunities to reduce emissions at every level of their operational procedures. The emission indicator guages the business establishment's efforts across three aspects: endorsing goals for reducing emissions, monitoring initiatives, and adopting measures to reduce pollutants.

4. Solid Waste

Industries produce a large amount of hazardous waste with a varying degree of toxicity. Indiscriminate waste disposal methods may lead to land contamination and water pollution. The solid waste indicator measures generation, treatment, disposal, management, and reduction techniques of waste.

5. Hazardous Waste

If not managed properly, hazardous waste poses great harm to the environment and our health. Hence, businesses must adopt strict protocols for managing hazardous waste from its production through its treatment or disposal. We evaluate whether businesses follow systematic and adequate procedures to manage and reduce the production of hazardous waste.

6. Liquid Waste

This indicator is focused on procedures and practices to reduce the production of liquid waste. Liquid waste generated from industries is often untreated or only partially treated and is often directly discharged into local watercourses, contaminating the water. This presents a threat to human health and the environment with both immediate and long-term consequences. Businesses are assessed to see if adequate procedures are adopted to manage liquid waste.

7. Eco-Design

This indicator gauges whether a business is producing ecofriendly products or services to reduce environmental impacts. For instance, a company would rate high in social venture design (see Community Vitality, above) if it provides energy sourced from wind, sun, or water, which would reduce the use of fossil fuels. Likewise, a business specializing in wind energy, water source management, and rainwater harvesting would also contribute to environmental conservation, as would a business establishment that recycles plastic bottles. This indicator helps us to understand the larger consequences of business ideas or models on the environment.

As mentioned earlier, the indicators here are examples to show how companies may measure their overall performance based on the Nine Domains of Gross National Happiness. An important task in the implementation process is to co-design indicators that are relevant for a specific industry while maintaining the integrity of the framework. The Eurasia Learning Institute for Happiness and Well-Being (ELIHW) is currently developing a certification process for organizations that want to comply with the GNH framework.

Living Standards in the Workplace

Clearly, businesses make investments in order to make financial returns. However, the extent to which the financial return is shared among workers, shareholders, or community members is often debatable. The domain of living standards includes the material comfort of the workers, and we encourage profit sharing by introducing plans that reward workers with the fruits of their labor, fostering a sense of ownership of the business. The living standards domain comprises various profit-sharing strategies such as pay, benefits, and others, as shown below.

1. Adequate Pay

2. Retirement Benefits

3. Insurance

4. Adequate Leave

5. Fringe Benefits

6. Pay Gap

1. Adequate Pay

For this indicator, we require businesses to disclose the pay structure of its employees. We examine the total income of workers, including pay, bonuses, and allowances. Income is found to be associated with employee motivation and behavior in the workplace.

2. Retirement Benefits

This indicator gauges workers' access to retirement benefits. Retirement benefits include contributions made by the business establishment toward pensions and provident funds. Retirement benefits play a role in the overall job satisfaction of workers.

3. Insurance

The insurance indicator gauges whether businesses provide any form of insurance coverage for its workers. An adequate insurance coverage for employees can help them pay for medical care and sustain a living in the event of occupational injury or illness leading to permanent disability.

4. Adequate Leave

This indicator gauges paid leave given to workers, including leave granted for medical reasons, bereavement, maternity, paternity, public holidays, and casual leave. Casual leave refers to leave sought for a short duration because of sickness or a personal emergency.

5. Fringe Benefits

Providing fringe benefits to workers is vital for establishing a support system within an organization. This is an important component of worker compensation that also acts as a supplement to pay. This benefit comprises housing, transportation, meal subsidies, and childcare.

6. Pay Gap

Aggregate income inequality has risen steadily over the years, and there is an increasing concern about pay inequality within businesses. Income inequality affects employee morale and productivity and is negatively related to firm value. The pay gap indicator is the ratio of highest to lowest yearly earnings among full-time, year-round workers.

Aligning Systems and Decision-Making Tools

When we discussed the Gross National Happiness framework at national level, we saw that, alongside the GNH index,* the GNH Commission used a screening tool based on twenty-two indicators to assess the foreseeable impacts of government projects and laws on the overall well-being of the population. Similarly, the GNH index that we have described can be used not only to assess the current situation of an organization but also for important decision making by executives and managers. In so doing, decision makers create the habit of assessing the consequences of their actions in a holistic way, rather than, for example, just looking at financial returns. This contributes to changing the corporate culture so that day-to-day decisions and actions are truly aligned with the vision, mission, and values.

Furthermore, it is necessary to gradually align the various systems of the organization so that they reflect the GNH framework. When we worked with B.Grimm, for example, the starting point was the human resource department, because it is relatively flexible, and by adapting it to the new values, there is little risk of disruption to the overall functioning of the business. HR processes are at the heart of the corporate culture.

* Recruitment: Whom do we hire and based on what criteria? Are we limiting our assessment to technical competencies, or are we assessing the whole personality of the candidate—their emotional and social skills, their ability to work in a team, to remain efficient in stressful situations, and to embody ethical values that are aligned with the corporate values? Do we assess their motivation and long-term aspirations?

---

*The GNH index is the tool used to make the GNH survey, the nine domains, thirty-three indicators, and over 150 variables.

When I was the head of learning and development at the Red Cross, our recruitment process was rigorous, as we were sending people to war zones. We had to make sure they had the strength of character and humanitarian values that would allow them to embody the ethos of the Red Cross in extremely challenging contexts. Our recruitment process had three phases: the first selection was based on the candidate's curriculum vitae, letter of application, formal qualifications, and previous experiences, from which the best were selected for a detailed face-to-face interview. Those who had passed this first phase were then invited for a day-long assessment process, during which we assumed professional competencies were of the highest standard. Groups of eight candidates spent the whole day in simulation games and trials that reproduced real-life situations that they might encounter in the field. During that time, a group of four professionals observed the candidates' behavior, reactions, communication skills, and decision-making abilities. It was rare that more than four out of the eight would move up to the final selection process, which was a month-long induction course during which the candidates would role-play the kind of situations they might experience in a war zone. Only at the end of this lengthy process would candidates be recruited and sent to the field.

Obviously, working in a company does not require the same extreme vetting process necessary when sending young professionals to war zones. Nevertheless, I share this example in order to show that if we want to assess applicants' competencies in a holistic way, and not solely on the basis of diplomas and technical expertise, we need to design recruitment processes that allow for the reception of these much broader capabilities, knowing that the recruitment process is crucial for the future development of the organization.

* Appraisal: Most organizations have a formal yearly or biyearly appraisal system that is often coupled with bonuses and promotions. Again, it is useful to enquire what is assessed during a performance appraisal. Is it limited to technical performance or financial results? Or does it include relationship skills,

teamwork, engagement, and the alignment between personal values and behavior and corporate values and culture? The recent Me-Too movement has shown how, in many organizations, people in leadership positions may display completely immoral behaviors and never be held accountable for them because their position protects them from serious scrutiny. Obviously, in a GNH-oriented organization, there need to be processes and feedback loops that allow the identification of unacceptable behavior early on, making sure that disciplinary action is taken immediately.

* Talent management and promotion: The people we promote in our organization are the living embodiment of the values we want to uphold. Therefore, an organization that promotes managers and executives who might be extremely talented in a specific field, but who also have deep ethical flaws and display behaviors that degrade the people over whom they have authority, thereby manifests the reality of its corporate culture independently from whatever values are otherwise displayed.

* Compensation: The salary scale of an organization is a strong marker of the corporate culture. Keeping the salary differential between basic income and the highest salaries within a reasonable limit is also part of the message that the company is sending out.

These few examples illustrate the kind of human resources system transformation that a Gross National Happiness project can bring about.

Further down the line, a GNH project might go as far as mapping an entire supply chain to make sure that every step of the process aligns with GNH values. This might seem difficult to reach, but I would like to share an example of a company that has already implemented such a process. In 2013 Eileen Fisher, the founder and owner of the New York–based Eileen Fisher fashion company, joined a GNH program— The Global Well-Being Lab: Innovating beyond GDP. This experience inspired her to create her "Vision 2020" statement that declares, "Our vision is for an industry where human rights and sustainability are not the effect of a particular initiative, but the cause of a business well run. Where social and environmental injustices are not unfortunate outcomes, but reasons to do things differently."* This led to the mapping the full supply chain in a program called From Farm to Factory, taking into consideration all the different phases of the production process:

* Fibers: We pledge to use the most sustainable fibers we can lay our hands on. All our cotton and linen will be organic by 2020. . . . We'll use wool from sheep that are responsibly raised—on land that is managed with deep concern for the environment . . . .

* Color: We've been working . . . to shift our global dyehouses toward responsible chemical, water, and energy usage. . . .

* Resources: We're committing to . . . leaving less fabric waste on the cutting room floor. Using less water, emitting less carbon, . . . investing in alternative energy and cutting our reliance on air shipping. By 2020, our US retail and office spaces won't just be climate neutral. They'll be climate positive.

* People: We've trained workers at our key suppliers . . . to voice their rights. . . . We've invested in alternative supply chains that pay fair wages.

* Mapping: It's no small feat to map a supply chain, but it's a matter of integrity. We need to verify how every last fiber is grown and every last garment is dyed. We need to know that every factory, spinner and mill is following strict labor standards. . . .

---

* "Sustainable Fashion . . . Eileen Fisher's Journey of Social Consciousness . . . from Human Rights to Environment and Reuse" Peter Fisk (October 28, 2018), *https://www.peterfisk.com/2018/10/sustainable-fashion-eileen-fisher-has-become-a-leader-in-clothing-with-a-conscience.*

* Reuse: At the end of the day, we make stuff. Where it ends up is our responsibility. We start by designing our clothes to last, so they'll stay in your closet longer. And when you're done with them, we take them back to resell. To date, over one million garments have been collected and sorted. As for the pieces we can't sell? They are tomorrow's raw material, to be reborn as new textiles or refashioned as new clothes. . . .*

This is an impressive example that shows how the commitment of a responsible business leader can transform in an industry that is known to be one of the most polluting. At the same time, Eileen Fisher is the example of a brand that manages to be socially and ecologically responsible, while remaining financially successful.

A Shift in Consciousness

In chapter three, on the inner conditions of happiness, we saw how the starting point of any true social innovation begins with a shift in mindset and a process of inner transformation. The same holds true when implementing a Gross National Happiness project in a business context. In my experience, all the successful projects began with the buy-in of the leadership at the highest level. For this reason, family-owned businesses are easier to transform, if the owners are honestly committed to bringing about change. First, they are not dependent on shareholders, and second, family businesses tend to think in terms of legacy and impact for future generations. Third, many of these businesses have a family tradition that includes certain values that were instilled by the founders. This is, obviously, not always the case, but three of the companies I have worked with fall under this category: B.Grimm (although now the power of division has gone public, while the overall direction has been maintained), Eileen Fisher, and Biti's.

---

*Ibid.

The Happy Biti's Project

Biti's is the largest shoe company in Vietnam. It started as a small workshop with twenty workers in 1982. From that modest beginning—mostly producing flip flops—Biti's has grown into a nationwide business producing twenty-five million pairs of shoes (of different categories and styles) every year. It now has fifteen hundred stores countrywide and employs around ten thousand workers.

Cindy Vuu, the current chief executive officer and the daughter of the founder, is the first Vietnamese business leader to implement a Gross National Happiness program in a company. We interviewed her to understand the perspective, motivation, and vision of a CEO and co-owner of a major company.

THV: Could you please introduce yourself and explain your position in your company.

CV: My name is Cindy, and currently I am the CEO of Biti's, a family-owned business, of which I am the second generation. My parents are the founders of the company.

During my school years, I always used to spend time in the factories to understand the kind of work I would be doing with the company. After graduation, I worked as an export manager. At the time I met a lot of colleagues who had long-standing experience in the shoe-manufacturing business. I remember they always used to say, "The shoe industry is full of hardship! I don't want my children to work in the shoe industry." This led me always to aspire to transform our industry. I always asked myself, *How can we produce shoes in a happy way, without the hardship?* This is when I first got the idea for Happy Biti's. The leading question was: *How can we produce shoes in a happy way?*

Later on, I created my own brand to experiment the spirit of a startup company, and to experience what it is like to work in a startup. In 2010 I implemented Enterprise Resource Planning, a program to help to manage IT in the company, and in 2016–17, I moved to the marketing department. Here we implemented a very successful marketing campaign called Biti's Hunter, which is a very popular brand among young people.

THV: Could you tell us about the history and current situation of your company, including its vision, mission, strategy, and factual elements?

CV: Our company is the biggest shoe brand in Vietnam. We have been in the industry for thirty-seven years, so people in Vietnam consider Biti's as the heritage brand, the shoe brand that helped re-establish the country after the war and helped the economic development of the country. Our mission is to produce good products for the Vietnamese consumer.

Our slogan and mission since we started the company has been "Cherish Vietnamese Feet," and almost every Vietnamese person owns a pair of Biti's shoes. In fact, we are often considered to be one of the best-known childhood brands; when we first started, parents bought our products for their children, and now as these children have grown up, they are buying our shoes for their children. Our company covers different kinds of products—sandals, flip flops, and shoes, from infant sizes to adult—therefore, we cover a wide range of complexity in the company.

We currently have almost ten thousand employees, four factories, and seven branches around the country. One of the biggest differences between our company and others is that we cover the end-to-end process: we source the material and we produce and sell the shoes.

One of the missions going forward is that we want to create a happy productive working environment in which all of us learn, live, and work together as a happy community. I feel very inspired by this mission.

THV: What was your motivation when you decided to embark on the Happy Biti's project?

CV: I have been working in the company for forty years, and sometimes the work is happy, and sometimes it is not happy. When I started to practice mindfulness and to develop my own happiness skills, I saw how this really helped my life so that I feel very fulfilled. I want to help my colleagues to reach a happy state just as I have. It is really important to me that my colleagues enjoy and find meaning in their work, that they find opportunities to grow through their work and that they can be happy. The Happy Biti's Project allows for a different way to look at life and work to emerge. It is so important to me to bring this awareness to my colleagues, so they can be successful in their work but also have a happy life.

THV: What has been done so far?

CV: So far we have organized three retreats. The first was for the executive team, in order to introduce the Happy Biti's Project and happiness skills and align at the top level. The second retreat was for thirty-five ambassadors, so that they can be the Happy Biti's ambassadors inside the company. During this retreat, the focus was on developing happiness skills and connection with self. We also had a compassionate communication training session, in order to help people communicate better in the team. I found the workshop of compassionate communication effective because, with ten thousand people working together, we can reduce the number of conflicts between that many people. In the company at the moment, for example, whenever a conflict arises, we hold a session to identify the needs of each person and find a way to resolve the conflict together, creatively. Most importantly, we try to do things in an authentic way—some relationships are better than others, and there are sometimes conflicts that are more difficult to resolve, but we try to be authentic in whatever we do.

A team from Biti's also spent three days visiting and experiencing Tinh Truc Gia (the Peaceful Bamboo Family) in Hue, which is a living community for people living with disabilities and which embodies the values of GNH. This was a powerful experience, because it allowed the team to really see that everything they learn through the Happy Biti's Project, such as mindfulness and happiness skills, is not just a concept, but overarching values that are capable of being experienced and embodied.

THV: What are the next steps that you envision?

CV: Right now we are in the process of bringing awareness about happiness in life and work, so the next step is to work together with Eurasia Learning Institute to formulate a GNH framework to measure the happiness and the success of the company. I always think about three dimensions: profit, people, and planet. We are in business, but we want to make sure that the end result will focus on these three pillars, so that we have a sustainable business in which people are happy and grow together, doing our best not to harm but to preserve the environment.

THV: What are your highest hopes for this project?

CV: My highest hope is for all my colleagues to be happy at work, with all of them finding meaning in their work. I hope that, as a flourishing community, we can spread happiness out to the surrounding community, so that at the end we can change Vietnamese society.

When I wrote the first draft of this book, I interviewed Cindy Vuu, the CEO of Biti's. At the time, we had just signed a memorandum of understanding to support the implementation of GNH in her company. The project was called Happy Biti's. Now, four years later, a lot has happened in the company, and during the last two years, the business has been deeply impacted by the COVID-19 crisis and the several lockdowns that were enforced in Vietnam.

I continued to follow the development of the project from Switzerland, where I stayed during the pandemic. Recently, I was able to come back to Vietnam after more than two years, and I was impressed to witness first hand all that has been implemented through the Happy Biti's project.

Biti's reformulated its vision, mission, and core values in the light of the Happiness Project:

Vision: To become the Asian brand that embraces happiness paths of all.

Mission: To cultivate a happy and effective community of working and learning together.

*Community = Customers, Staff, Partners, Society

Core values: Happiness and serving.

Integrity, Teamwork, and Continuous improvement.

The latest achievement is the full GNH survey conducted with a sample of over six hundred participants representative of the workforce in terms of gender, age, and position. Although the survey has been done at a difficult time, as the company is just beginning to recover from the crisis, the results are positive and seem to confirm that the GNH project has had a real impact on the well-being of all the stakeholders.

The two domains that had the highest score were psychological well-being and organizational culture, both with a positive result of 84 percent. The two weakest domains were time use and living standards, although even these two domains did not have very low scores, with a positive response of (respectively) 67 percent and 69 percent.

I took the opportunity to interview Cindy Vuu four years after the earlier interview to hear directly from her what she had experienced since then and what were the main lessons learned:

THV: We had an interview four years ago, could you share what has happened with Happy Biti's during the past four years.

CV: Each year, we have trained thirty-five happiness ambassadors in happiness skills. Their mission is to embody, communicate, and become trainers. So far, we have trained three batches. At the company level, we address happiness and well-being based on the nine domains of GNH. The whole project is based on the concept of "Happy Me, Happy Biti's," The idea is that each happy employee will enhance the happiness of the organization. We really focused a lot on the "Happy Me" part and on the role of the company to create the conditions to make it possible. We cocreate this together with our colleagues.

THV: You mentioned you had, every year, about thirty-five GNH ambassadors. Could you explain what the three retreats that the GNH ambassadors went through were about? Did you observe any change in the people who went through the retreats and how are these changes implemented also in their work in the company?

CV: The first retreat is focused on connecting with self. We practice mindfulness and emotional intelligence learning to be aware of difficult emotions and also cultivating positive emotions, acknowledging the good things in our life. We also need to be aware of our weakness and strengths and aware of the direction that our lives should take. We have a clearer picture about ourselves that increases our self-awareness.

The second retreat is [about] connecting with others through compassionate communication, deep listening, and empathy, which is very important, because people can identify their emotions and their needs. Basically, the conflict rarely happens at the level of the needs, but we struggle about the way we want to fulfill these needs. If two people have the clear understanding about their needs, they can find ways to help fulfill these needs together in ways that are mutually beneficial.

The third retreat is [about] connecting to nature, because nature is a part really nurturing and healing for us. We strengthen our awareness of our interdependence with all life-forms, and develop projects to reduce our ecological footprint and contribute to a more sustainable future as individuals and as a company.

With those three retreats, people learn concrete ways to enhance the happiness level in themselves and collectively. I think the most important factor of all is mindfulness. We slow down, we observe what's working, what's not working.

After the retreats, our intention is to practice and to put into action and implement in our daily [lives] what we have learned. For example, we start all our meeting with two minutes of mindfulness to bring the people back to the here and now, so they can be fully present for the meeting. Then we have an emotional check-in with everyone so that we become aware of the energy level that they currently have and that we know how everyone feels, so we can offer support when necessary. Another activity that is very beneficial is a weekly hour to practice mindfulness together and other happiness skills. We create a space for people to share the difficulties they encountered during the week and embrace that space together as a learning space.

We really try to focus on the practice, because in the retreat, we may learn from the head and then we touch our heart, but actually in our daily work, we really put it in practice. Also, in our company, before starting the work in the morning, we practice mindful qi gong movements, and these common exercises are beneficial for the health and also create a sense of community.

Over the years, these practices have become part of our company culture and most of our employees enjoy it a lot. Almost everyone knows how to practice mindfulness, emotional check-in, and mindful movements.

I heard from many of my colleagues that they would like to introduce it in their families as well. So, in a next step, we will explore how to include the families as well.

THV: You also had management training—"Resonant Leadership"*—for about a year for the senior executives. Can you say a few words about that?

CV: I think the role of the manager inside the company is also to be a role model, and the course really helps us to create a space to understand how to be a resonant leader. We learn different skills—for example, we practice mentoring and coaching, how to help the team member to perform at their best. Self-awareness is also very important too, because as manager, if, for instance, we act or speak out of anger, we can create a negative environment for our team. We learn a lot of skills, but most importantly we create a space for the senior executives to deepen their understanding of the social-emotional learning, and we give them tools that can help them to manage their teams and their responsibilities in a better way.

THV: Like all the companies, you went through two very difficult years because of the pandemic and lockdowns and so on. Can you say a few words how your company has managed to navigate through this difficult time? And if you feel that [the] Happy Biti's project was helpful or not, and what actions did?

CV: We were in lockdown for four months. And our revenue dropped between 15 percent and 30 percent, because all the stores closed. At that time, I faced a very big challenge, because I did not know how I would support our ten thousand workers financially—for them to sustain their life. That was my fear, because I felt so much responsibility toward our workforce. But during that time, we able to create a team to respond to the COVID-19 crisis, and our team

---

*Resonant leadership is an idea coined by Daniel Goleman. Resonant leaders work on emotional intelligence to direct their feelings to help a group meet its goals. Resonance is the ability to synchronize with one another; thus, resonant leadership can adjust the needs of a team of people.

met every day to see what the initiatives we could take to solve the problems.

Every day, we would assess the problems and we reflected on how we were going to solve it together. Because most of my team had learned happiness skills, we really felt aligned as a team. Because of our deep connection, we did not have any conflicts during this challenging time. And that gave me a lot of courage and support, because if on top of the difficulties, we would have conflicts in the management team, it would have created additional hardships and we could have felt very demotivated. But together we really embraced and transformed the situation, and there were many positive initiatives that came out of those meetings. I think the general concern for the happiness and well-being of all the people motivated us, and we found ways to guaranty sufficient allowances for every worker to meet their needs and those of their family.

We were able to discuss the financial situation in a completely transparent way, and this allowed us to find ways to solve this problem together. This gave us a strong stability and confidence that we could support all our workers and that on the long run, the company would still be sustainable.

Beyond that, we also looked at ways to support the larger community, so we organized food import from the countryside, both for our own workers and for people who had lost their jobs. We were able to distribute over fifty-five thousand free meals to people who had fell into destitution. We also bought and gave mechanical ventilators to help hospitals treat COVID patients.

All these initiatives were inspired by looking at the nine domains of GNH and reflecting how we could support both our own staff and the larger community through various projects. This brought a lot of joy and sense of purpose to our team, because even though we were facing difficulties, we were still able to contribute in a meaningful way to society.

We also used the available time to offer many courses and practical trainings so that people did not feel their time was wasted, but on the contrary, it was an opportunity to learn and develop further.

THV: I know that you did your first full GNH survey. Can you say a few words about that?

CV: I felt so happy when I looked at the result. Of course, this is the first time we do it, so we still need to have a lot of improvement. But it helped us to set objectives to be achieved by 2025. But quite a few domains already showed good results. The weakest results were time use and living standards, so we will do our best to improve that.

We are a shoe manufacturer, and our work is very labor-intensive. It's very difficult to increase the salaries, and we have to work long hours. So these are the two things we need to address. We will have to be very creative to find ways to improve these two domains. When you look at the mental health [domain], the score is very high. On culture diversity, the score very high. We must have done something right in the past, especially the Happy Biti's really boosts up the mental health level of our employees. That's is the very good thing.

THV: So what are the next steps that you envision?

CV: We want to scale up the project to the whole company. We also want to address the mission, the vision, and core values of our company, because they come out of the Happy Biti's project.

Basically, for the vision, we want to embrace the happiness path of all. Because we are shoe company, and we are envisioned through our shoe products, we can show the people happiness path for all, not just for human beings, but for the nature as well. And we try our best to cultivate this community of working and learning together in happiness and in effectiveness. We want to achieve that our whole company and its operations are based on the concept of happiness and of serving others. Now, we think how to implement that more and more in our daily operations, because that is where we're going to keep the practice and align everything we do with what we believe in.

From Happy Individuals to a Happy Organization

When we help a company in its shift to become a Gross National Happiness organization, it is important to remind ourselves that systems and structures are always a manifestation of the way people think, feel, act, and relate to one another and to the world. Therefore, to be sustainable, structural changes need to go hand in hand with a shift in consciousness. If we manage to strike the right balance between structural changes and inner transformation, we create a virtuous circle in which the conducive environment supports the transformation of consciousness, and the new mindset allows for the different systems to be truly efficient.

An example of such a virtuous circle is illustrated by the Biti's story. On one hand, we trained happiness ambassadors who infused mindfulness as well as social and emotional learning in the company. At the same time, the senior management improved its management style to be aligned with these values and attitudes. Finally, the company conducted a GNH survey to identify the areas that needed to be improved to create a conducive environment that fosters happiness for all. These various actions reinforce each other mutually and create an ecosystem that guarantee that the Happy Biti's project can be sustainable.

The challenge is to be able to gradually transform the long-standing habits that determine behaviors and relationships within an organization. Therefore, when we work with businesses or other organizations, our priority is to create transformative learning events that support a new narrative that is aligned with the vision and the mission of the company. When we worked with B.Grimm, we developed programs at three different levels. First, we trained GNH ambassadors—people within the organization that we identified as having good communication skills, a large network, and whom other staff members readily listened to, regardless of their formal title and position. These people were known to be innovators, early adapters who displayed an appetite for change and new ideas. Their task was to spread the message of GNH both through formal channels of communications—such as newsletters, websites, and specific information events—and through informal channels, such as conversations, routine staff meetings, and similar events. Second, we trained GNH trainers, who practiced happiness skills in an intense way and acquired a good knowledge of the GNH framework principles, indicators, and methodologies. This group included people from human resources but went far beyond this limited constituency to include engineers, salespersons, and other professionals that were known to have good competencies in training others and passing on skills and knowledge. Third, we had specific workshops for the senior management. These workshops were much shorter and quite intense residential retreats, as we knew that it was crucial to have the buy-in of the senior executives and management if the project was to be successful.

Therefore, today, whenever we get a request from an organization or a business, we always want to make sure that the motivation is a serious and honest one, and not simply a cynical public-relations exercise. In the business world, especially, the shift from a purely profit- and competition-oriented view of the economy toward a new economic paradigm—one based on care, collaboration, altruism, and compassion—is a challenging one. When I first started developing GNH projects for companies, I had doubts about whether it was possible, in the current mainstream economy, to offer such radical transformations. Looking back, my takeaway is that in any organization, we first need to focus on the human beings. Deep down, we all have similar aspirations, and if we can access this fundamental human desire for happiness and show that it is possible to reconcile our deepest aspirations with our daily work, it is a message that most will want to embrace.

Many senior business people have told me, "We know that the current system cannot continue in the same way; we know we need to change, but we don't know how to bring about the necessary transformation." And so, when a clear framework and methodology such as GNH is offered, it is surprising to see how many people are willing to at least give it a try. For this change to come about, however, it is not enough for people to have understood a theory or some concepts, no matter how appealing they might be. It is necessary also to have direct experience of the inner transformation that happiness practices can bring about. Because levels of stress and suffering at work are very high in many corporations, I often found a surprising openness and willingness to embrace new practices among business people. I frequently heard moving reports from participants after just three or five days in a workshop. They told me how the simple practices of mindfulness, deep listening, or nonviolent communication had changed their lives—not only in the workplace, but also in their families.

Once I led a workshop for business people in China, and one of the participants was the CEO of a lighting company. At the end of the workshop, he wanted to share his experience and told us that his wife and children lived in Shanghai, a thousand or so kilometers (over six hundred miles) from his workplace, because he felt that the quality of life and the schools were better in Shanghai. He dedicated all his time to working in order to earn enough money to ensure the financial security of his family. But this lifestyle came at a great cost: he was under extreme stress, and this stress was having a negative impact on the working climate within his factory. He only saw his family a few times a year, and when he went to Shanghai to be with them, he was so exhausted that he could not really spend quality time with them. During the workshop, he realized that although he had earned a lot of money and was now quite wealthy, his own happiness and wellbeing, as well as that of his family, had not improved; on the contrary, they had significantly decreased. He also realized that the way he was behaving with his staff—because of his own dissatisfaction—was not contributing to improving the engagement of the employees. It was moving to hear this senior manager sharing his stories with tears in his eyes, pledging to strive for a better balance in his life by putting the well-being of himself, his family, and his employees at the center of his attention.

This is just one of many examples of defining moments that people experience when going through a GNH in business project. What begins as an institutional or management initiative often turns out to be a life-changing experience that encourages people to reconsider their priorities and to reorganize their personal and professional lives in such a way that it is more aligned with their deepest aspirations and values.

One question that is often asked is whether such a shift in mindset can be compatible with running a successful business. So far, my observation has been that it is absolutely compatible, and examples such as B.Grimm, Eileen Fisher, and Biti's are there to show that running a socially and ecologically responsible business based on the values of compassion, altruism, and solidarity can go together with being financially successful and sustainable.

AFTERWORD

FOR A BETTER FUTURE TO BE POSSIBLE

When the winds of change blow, some people
build walls and others build windmills.

—CHINESE PROVERB

The starting point of this book was the recognition that humankind is going through significant changes. These crises can be seen not only as challenges, but also as great opportunities. Most of the predictions concerning the future are based on a linear understanding of development, projecting the parameters of the past into the future, mostly taking into consideration the material dimensions of life. As long as we consider the future only in light of the past and think of development as a mechanical process, the prospect is bleak. From an ecological, social, or economic point of view, this kind of discourse contributes to a feeling of despair or cynicism that is not helpful when trying to find new solutions. Most institutions and systems as we know them have been created to respond to yesterday's problems, and these responses are not relevant for the current situation or for the rapidly evolving context in which we live.

Culture is fundamentally a narrative, a story that we tell ourselves and others to make sense of the world in which we live. By "narrative" or "story" I don't mean a simple tale that has no relationship to reality; I mean it as the way we interpret existence, using the pictures, words, symbols, concepts, knowledge, and theories at our disposal to create a coherent explanation that is meaningful and workable. In the course of history, the cultural narratives humans have told have changed, and some people think that this is proof that these stories didn't have any intrinsic reality. I don't share this belief. Our ever-evolving cultural narratives are an expression of the evolution of consciousness, in the same way that the experience of a child is replaced by different experiences when they become an adolescent and then an adult. That's not to say that that our childhood experience was wrong; it had its value at the time and gradually evolved as we gained a new understanding of ourselves and the world.

Likewise, the stories that humanity has used to make sense of experience—from the ancient gods of Hindu, Egyptian, or Greek mythologies to the story of creation in the Bible or in the Koran, or from the descriptions of the universe by Greek philosophers and scientists to the most recent scientific discoveries—can be seen as complementary accounts in our efforts to grasp a reality that is far more vast and complex than human thoughts and words can encompass. This doesn't mean that these various myths or theories were absurd or superstitious, but that they offered at a given time our best possible attempt to understand and name the world in which we live. I am convinced that there are universal truths hidden in the ancient myths, sacred books, artworks, and scientific theories.

The problem that we face today is a twofold one. The first factor is that our fascination with scientific discoveries has reduced our understanding of the world to its material dimension. This focus has caused us, by and large, to lose sight of the psychological, emotional, ethical, and spiritual dimensions of human life, without which we cannot grasp our full humanity. The second factor is that the current narrative of neoliberal economy does not hold the solutions for today's and tomorrow's challenges. That narrative may have once been an appropriate response to our problems, but like the narrative that the sun revolves around the earth, it no longer serves us as a true explanation of the world we live in.

Therefore, the first great task ahead of us is to cocreate a new narrative, a new understanding of what it means to be human, on this earth, today, with our responsibility toward the planet and toward all life forms. An in-depth transformation of our educational, economic, social, and political systems will only come about as we gradually develop this new narrative that gives meaning, hope, and direction to our common efforts.

In ancient times, it was the task of a select few—prophets, pharaohs, kings, wise men, priests, scientists, and philosophers—to create and communicate the fundamental myths and stories that gave meaning and order to society. In our time, this situation has changed—no messiah, no great prophet, no charismatic leader will appear and reveal the new story that we need. It has to be a process of collective intelligence, harnessed through dialogue and creative processes. It is one of the greatest tasks in our time to create open spaces of trust, freedom, and creativity where people come together to cocreate the stories we need. This does not mean rejecting all the wisdom, knowledge, and experience that has accumulated over thousands of years of our existence; on the contrary, it is necessary to explore both the wisdom of the great traditions, as well as the latest scientific research findings to allow a more holistic and comprehensive understanding to arise.

There are several examples of these efforts that are already under way. One of them is the Mind & Life Institute (with whom I have had the opportunity to work and whose research informed the first educational project that I implemented—A Call To Care—in Bhutan and Vietnam). Through dialogues between His Holiness the Dalai Lama and other prominent spiritual masters with some of the best scientists of our time, the Mind & Life Institute has helped bring about a different way of exploring human nature: "The mission of the Mind & Life Institute is to alleviate suffering and promote flourishing by integrating science with contemplative practice and wisdom traditions."

Likewise, institutions like Schumacher College (founded by the ecological pioneer Satish Kumar) and the Presencing Institute (founded by Dr. Otto Scharmer) combine science with a holistic perspective to address the challenges of our time.

The need for a more holistic approach to meeting the challenges of our time is gradually gaining recognition, even in the most prominent scientific arenas, although a lot still has to be done before it is the guiding principle of education, business, and politics. GNH is a powerful example of formulating a new perspective that combines deep human values with a systematic reflection on and exploration of a new economic and development paradigm informed by scientific knowledge and research.

Another area of great importance is to lay the groundwork for a contemporary secular ethics that can help guide our further development. In the past, morality was based on religious beliefs that the social order imposed on individuals. In our time, we need to go beyond preestablished rules and dogmas and awaken an ethical process that enables us to find the right answers in each specific situation. Our time calls for ethical creativity and imagination. More and more we are faced with dilemmas that are completely new, such as how to regulate artificial intelligence, biotechnology, genetic manipulation, and big data. The dogmas and commandments of yesterday will not help us find answers to these complex issues.

An interesting example of the effort to create new ethical processes are the Fourteen Mindfulness Trainings created by Thich Nhat Hanh.[*] They are not called rules, commandments, or precepts, but mindfulness trainings—their very name shows that the requirement is for each one of us, as well as for all of us collectively, to strengthen our awareness, to become more mindful, so we will become aware of the consequences of our actions. In this case, the moral compass is relatively simple; it is based on the question of what brings happiness to self and others and what brings suffering to self and others. Yet the way to answer these simple questions is complex, and the Fourteen Mindfulness Trainings invite us to explore fourteen different areas that are both inside of us— the way we think, feel, and make decisions—and outside of us—the

---

[*]Fourteen Mindfulness Trainings, Plum Village, *https://plumvillage.org/mindfulness-practice/the-14-mindfulness-trainings*.

way we act and the consequences of our actions on others and on the planet.

Strategies for a Better Tomorrow

Cocreating the new narrative with an underlying ethical foundation is, I believe, the first fundamental task of our efforts to create a better future. But this is only the first step. It will provide a foundation and framework, but it will only become a reality if we put it into action. Two types of actions are therefore required, providing proof that our vision of what the future can actually be implemented. On one hand we need to create "seeds of the future," small-scale pilot projects to try out and experiment with new ways of living and working together. Furthermore, we have to have the courage to go into mainstream organizations to bring transformation from within. An example is the Happy Schools project, where we work within the existing public schools system in Vietnam.

Many people will look at programs like GNH and think it is an unworkable, utopian dream. So we must create pilot projects that demonstrate that our new visions for the future can actually be implemented in the real world. It is necessary for people to have direct experience of schools, communities, businesses, cities, or even a whole country putting into practice the ideas we are pursuing. Many already exist: the Peaceful Bamboo Family is one such pilot project, and the B.Grimm Group is another—and there is, of course, the country of Bhutan. And there are other communities, eco-villages, and other similar initiatives around the world that demonstrate that it is possible to live a healthy and happy life in harmony with nature. At town and city level, the transition-town movement exemplifies the possibility for larger communities to transform in a sustainable way. In the field of education, alternative schools such as the Green School in Bali, the Steiner/Waldorf movement (which has hundreds of schools worldwide) and the Early Learning Centre in Bhutan are living examples of education rethought and reimagined so that the needs of and their development are situated front and center in a way that is also in harmony with others and with the planet. When it comes to economies, many ecological and sustainable startups are trying to explore the new economic paradigm. One interesting example is the Business Alliance for Local Living Economies (Balle), which represents tens of thousands of small entrepreneurs and communities developing living economies for the benefit of all.

The second task is to transform the system from within. This is a monumental undertaking, because most of the world's population lives and works in the current systems. If we want to alleviate the suffering of the many, we must have the courage to "enter into the skin of the dragon." This is why, in the field of education, we have made the choice not to create separate schools that fully embody all the attributes of a Happy School, but rather to work within the existing national school system in Vietnam to incorporate some of the missing dimensions—such as care for self, others, and the planet—within the current curriculum.

Transforming the system from within becomes more complicated as the institution becomes bigger—corporations and cities, rather than schools, for example. I had the opportunity to advise the mayors of Munich, Stuttgart, and Vienna about creating new districts. Even though the proposed changes were limited in scope, I felt that contributing to refocusing the attention of local authorities on the well-being of their citizens was nevertheless a worthwhile effort. In the field of business, working with large corporations such as B.Grimm or Biti's also has had its limitations in terms of the depth of transformation that is possible. But whatever improvement can be brought is better than the status quo; the changes they have made have had an impact on many thousands of workers, their families, and all the other stakeholders who work with these companies.

Of course, our efforts have not always been successful. My meeting with the CEO of the Swiss pharmaceutical company Hoffman is one example; I left without convincing them that the transformation of the corporation was possible and beneficial. Then there was the time I spoke to hundreds of employees and managers of the German car manufacturer Audi. Here again, I don't think that they took any action to change their business model after this first contact. I must admit that the timing may have been difficult, as I happened to give my talk in the very week when their CEO was arrested for having manipulated the CO_2 emissions of their diesel cars. It could have been an opportunity to rethink the way they do business, but it is impossible to know what seeds might have been planted in hearts and minds. When causes, conditions, and time are ripe, the seed will sprout, and one day flowers will bloom. Surprisingly, as I write these lines, five years later, I just received a message from of the senior managers of Audi, who writes that my talk had deeply impacted her. She asked for advice on how to go forward. Sometimes, seeds take a longer time to sprout.

When I am invited by large corporations to discuss GNH, I always ask myself if it makes sense to devote time and energy in contexts where the chances of a real transformation are relatively minor. Nevertheless, I feel a moral responsibility to try my best and share the ideas and values that I believe to be important for our future. One never knows what the consequences might be. There might be only one person in the audience who is really touched, but that one spark might have an impact that I cannot oversee. Many years ago Philip Kapleau, one of the pioneers of Zen Buddhism in America, was invited to speak in a university, but as the day grew near, he saw that only a handful of people had signed up to attend his talk. He asked himself if it was worthwhile to speak to such a small audience, but in the end, he decided to go anyway, and one of those few participants that day was Jon Kabat-Zinn, who later developed the mindfulness-based stress reduction (MBSR) program, which has since gained worldwide traction. Jon Kabat-Zinn has said that this encounter with Philip Kapleau was one of the decisive moments that led him to develop MBSR.

Likewise, Thich Nhat Hanh accepted invitations to speak at Google, Salesforce, the World Economic Forum in Davos, and the

British Parliament. Although such large institutions might not make drastic changes to the way they do business, introducing them to these ideas can contribute to a shift in consciousness, and we cannot always perceive directly what consequences it will ultimately have. At Google, a mindfulness and social and emotional learning program called Search Inside Yourself was developed. At Salesforce, which is the world leader in customer relationship management, meditation rooms and regular mindfulness practices for employees were created. And the British Parliament set up a cross-party parliamentary group called the Mindfulness Initiative: Mindful Nation UK, which has launched initiatives for schools, workplaces, criminal justice, policing, the military, and more. At the World Economic Forum, mindfulness workshops have become a regular offering and are some of the most attended events.

In conclusion, I believe that working simultaneously on the three dimensions—creating the new narrative, planting seeds of the future in pilot projects, and transforming existing organizations and structures from within—is crucial to the bringing about of change. These three aspects create an interdependent ecosystem that strengthen each other. Since I left my position as program director at the Gross National Happiness Centre in Bhutan in 2018, my goal has been to promote this threefold transformation wherever possible, with my colleagues from the Eurasia Learning Institute for Happiness and Well-being.* What encourages me in this effort is the perception that more and more people, especially among younger generations, have a tremendous enthusiasm for contributing to the changes we so urgently need.

One of the most striking examples is the story of Felix Finkbeiner. In 2007, when he was nine years old, he gave a class presentation on global warming in which he argued that children should plant one million trees in each country around the world. Finkbeiner and his classmates planted a tree on March 28, 2007, and he founded Plant-for-the-Planet, an organization to raise awareness of climate change and plants trees

---

*Eurasia Learning Institute for Happiness and Well-being, *http://elihw.org*.

around the world. After three years, the organization planted its millionth tree. When Finkbeiner was ten years old, he spoke before the European Parliament, and at thirteen, before the UN General Assembly. Today, Plant-for-the-Planet has 130 employees and 70,000 members around the world. The organization has hosted over twelve hundred workshops for young people (between the ages of ten and fourteen), during which participants learn about global warming and the importance of trees, practice public speaking, and make plans on how they want to contribute to tackling the environmental crisis we're facing.

Another example is Swedish activist Greta Thunberg. On August 20, 2018, Thunberg, then fifteen years old, decided not to attend school one Friday; instead she spent the day protesting outside the Swedish parliament. She demanded that the Swedish government reduce Sweden's carbon emissions in accordance with the Paris Agreement. After that first day of protest, she began sitting outside parliament every Friday, holding up a sign that said "School strike for climate." Thunberg has since gained worldwide attention and has inspired school students around the globe to take part in similar strikes. She has become one of the most prominent youth activists in the world. As of March 2022, students—over fourteen million—have held strikes in over 7,500 cities around the world.

Finkbeiner and Thunberg are just two examples. There are many more young people all over the world who might not be as well-known but are just as engaged. These young people convince me—and should convince all of us—that there is hope for our future. At the same time, as an elder, as a father and grandfather, and as someone who is deeply moved by the beauty and generosity of our fragile planet, I ask myself how we can make sure that future generations will have a chance to enjoy the same abundance and grace. This book is intended to be a humble contribution toward the better future that we all want.

ACKNOWLEDGMENTS

A book is always a collective venture. When I reread this manuscript, I realized that I hadn't invented anything new and that most of my writing has consisted of shaping and relating ideas, concepts, references, practices, and methods that are the result of the work of many people.

First and foremost, I must express my deep gratitude to His Majesty Jigme Singye Wangchuck, the fourth king of Bhutan and "father of Gross National Happiness."

I also owe a lot to HE Jigmi Y. Thinley, who was prime minister of Bhutan when I arrived at the GNH center and was the chairman of our board. He was instrumental in helping GNH gain international notoriety. It was then HRH Princess Ashi Kesang Chodren Wangchuck who led the center with grace and benevolence.

I would also like to thank the entire BNB Center team and, in particular, Dr. Saamdu Chetri, the executive director, and Dr. Julia Kim, with whom I set up all the first GNH programs.

There is also the entire Eurasia and ELI team in Vietnam, Switzerland, and Germany, who are too numerous for me to mention, but without whom all the GNH implementation projects in the education in universities and in companies would not exist.

How not to mention my wife, Lisi—we have just celebrated our fiftieth year of marriage—as well as our wonderful family, who are the source of our happiness and stability.

In conclusion, I bow with respect in memory of Venerable Thich Nhat Hanh, who guided me with wisdom and compassion for so many years and without whom I could not have done and written what is related in this book.

SELECTED READING

Bregman, Rutger. *Humankind: A Hopeful History*, trans. Elizabeth Manton and Erica Moore. New York: Little, Brown, 2020.

Delors, Jacques. *Learning: The Treasure Within Report to UNESCO of the International Commission on Education for the Twenty-First Century*. https://unesdoc.unesco.org/ark:/48223/pf0000109590.

Felber, Christian. *Change Everything: Creating an Economy for the Common Good*. London: Zed Books, 2019.

Frankl, Viktor E. *Man's Search for Meaning*. Translated by Ilse Lasch. Boston: Beacon Press, 1992.

Fromm, Erich. *Escape from Freedom*. New York: Farrar and Rinehart, 1941.

Goleman, Daniel. *Emotional Intelligence: Why It Can Matter More than IQ*. New York: Bantam, 1995.

Goleman, Daniel, Richard Botatzis, and Annie McKee. *Primal Leadership: Unleashing the Power of Emotional Intelligence*. Boston: Harvard Business Review Press, 2013.

Goleman, Daniel, and Richard J. Davidson. *Altered Traits: Science Reveals How Meditation Changes Your Mind, Brain and Body*. New York: Avery, 2017.

Habermas, Jürgen. *The Theory of Communicative Action*. 2 vols. Translated by Thomas McCarthy. Boston, Beacon Press, 1981.

Largo, Remo H. *The Right Life: Human Individuality and Its Role in Our Development, Health, and Happiness*. New York: Penguin, 2019.

Li, Qing. *Forest Bathing: How Trees Can Help You Find Health and Happiness*. New York: Viking, 2018.

Macy, Johanna, and Molly Young Brown. *Coming Back to Life: The Updated Guide to the Work That Reconnects*. Gabriola Island, BC: New Society, 2014.

Nhat Hanh, Thich. *The Blooming of a Lotus: Guided Meditation for Achieving the Miracle of Mindfulness*. Rev. ed. Translated by Annabel Laity. Boston, Beacon Press, 2009.

———. *Love Letter to Planet Earth*. Berkeley: Parallax, 2013.

———. *The Miracle of Mindfulness: An Introduction to the Practice of Meditation*. Translated by Mobi Ho. Boston, Beacon Press, 1975.

Nhat Hanh, Thich, and Katherine Weare. *Happy Teachers Change the World: A Guide for Cultivating Mindfulness in Education*. Berkeley: Parallax, 2017.

Powdyel, Thakur S. *My Green School: An Outline*. N.p., 2018.

Scharmer, C. Otto. *The Essentials of Theory U: Core Principles and Applications*. Oakland, CA: Berrett-Koehler, 2018.

Stevens, Larry Charles, and Christopher Chad Woodruff, eds. *The Neuroscience of Empathy, Compassion, and Self-Compassion*. London: Academic Press, 2018.

ABOUT THO HA VINH

THO HA VINH was born in 1951, the son of a Vietnamese father and a French mother. He was the program director of the Gross National Happiness Center (GNH) of the country of Bhutan from 2012 to 2018. Earlier, serving as the head of training, learning, and development at the International Committee of the Red Cross, he trained humanitarian professionals to work in war zones and Afghanistan, Pakistan, Palestine, and Darfur. He holds a PhD in psychology and education from the University of Geneva in Switzerland and is an ordained lay Buddhist teacher (Dharmacharya) in the Plum Village tradition of Zen Master Thich Nhat Hanh.

PARALLAX PRESS, a nonprofit publisher founded by Zen Master Thich Nhat Hanh, publishes books and media on the art of mindful living and Engaged Buddhism. We are committed to offering teachings that help transform suffering and injustice. Our aspiration is to contribute to collective insight and awakening, bringing about a more joyful, healthy, and compassionate society.

View our entire library at **parallax.org**.